RESURRECTION PE

SARUM THEOLOGICAL LECTURES

RESURRECTION PEOPLE

Studies in the Resurrection Narratives of the Gospels

David Catchpole

DARTON · LONGMAN + TODD

First published in 2000 by
Darton, Longman and Todd Ltd
1 Spencer Court
140–142 Wandsworth High Street
London SW18 4JJ

ISBN 0–232–52376–2

A catalogue record for this book is available from the British Library.

Designed by Sandie Boccacci
Phototypeset in 11¼/14pt Bembo
by Intype London Ltd
Printed and bound in Great Britain by
Redwood Books, Trowbridge, Wiltshire

For Ann

CONTENTS

PREFACE

The material in this book consists of a substantially expanded version of the Sarum Theological Lectures 2000. For the honour of being invited to deliver those lectures I would like to express gratitude to my colleagues at Sarum College. The Dean and Chapter of Salisbury Cathedral generously provided the truly inspiring setting for the lectures: their hospitable welcome was greatly appreciated.

My warm personal thanks, as well as those of Sarum College, are owed to the St Luke's College Foundation for financial support for the lectures. Having spent fourteen fulfilling years as the St Luke's Foundation Professor of Theological Studies at the University of Exeter, an appointment which would not have been possible without the support of the Trustees of the Foundation, I am all the more grateful.

The Barbara Levy Literary Agency and the publishers J.M. Dent kindly gave me permission to quote the text of the poems 'Everyone Sang' by Siegfried Sassoon, and 'Nuclear' by R.S. Thomas, respectively. To them I express my thanks, as well as to two other presses, Sheffield Academic Press and the Edwin Mellen Press, who generously allowed me to use and to develop further some ideas set out originally in two previously published articles: 'The Beloved Disciple and Nathanael', in *Understanding, Studying and Reading. New Testament Essays in Honour of John Ashton*, edited by C. Rowland and C.H.T. Fletcher-Louis, JSNT Supplement Series 153 (Sheffield: Sheffield Academic Press,

1998), pp. 69–92; 'The Role of the Historical Jesus in Jewish-Christian Dialogue', in *The Future of Jewish-Christian Dialogue*, edited by Dan Cohn-Sherbok, Toronto Studies in Theology 80 (Lampeter: Edwin Mellen, 1999), pp. 183–216.

Katie Worrall and Helen Porter, Commissioning Editor and Managing Editor respectively at Darton, Longman and Todd, gave help and advice throughout the production process. I am glad of this opportunity to express my appreciation to them and their colleagues at the company.

Several friends gave generously and thoughtfully of their time, expertise and advice as the material for this book was taking shape, most notably Professor Graham Stanton, Professor Christopher Tuckett, and my former colleague Dr David Horrell, a partner for several years in the delight and the privilege of trying to open up the study of the New Testament both to undergraduates and to students on 'Theology Quest and Questions' at the University of Exeter. Naturally I must, as is conventional, exonerate them from responsibility for such errors and misunderstandings as doubtless abound in these chapters.

In a very special way I would like to express heartfelt thanks to Ann, my wife, who brought cool and detached judgement to bear on the material while at the same time constantly encouraging me. She knows what I owe to her, and it is to her that I dedicate this book.

Certain standard conventions are followed in the text of this book. The term 'MarkR' stands for Marcan redaction, and similarly MattR, LukeR and JohnR. The term 'diff.', as in 'Luke 24:9 diff. Mark 16:8', refers to the difference between one version and another. The majority source-critical position among New Testament specialists is the presupposition throughout this work, that is, that Matthew and Luke used Mark and a second written source, Q. Arguments are mounted in chapter 4 for the additional conclusion that the relationship between the Gospel of John and the Synoptic Gospels is one of direct literary dependence.

For those readers who may be beginning the process of scientific study of the Gospels, it may be a help if I mention that most invaluable of tools, *Gospel Parallels*, fifth edition (London: Nelson, 1992), edited by B.H. Throckmorton Jr. The process can be set in motion by working with the 'triple tradition' (where Matthew, Mark and Luke all provide parallel versions), underlining precisely and pedantically the words in Matthew and Luke which derive from Mark, and then moving on to the 'double tradition' (where Matthew and Luke correspond), and underlining in Matthew and Luke all words that they have in common. It will then be possible to see at a glance where editorial (redactional) changes have been made. That opens up the field of redaction criticism, which is one of the methods employed in this book.

The scriptural quotations used in this book are taken from the New Revised Standard Version of the Bible, Anglicized edition, copyright © 1989, 1995, Division of Christian Education of the National Council of the Churches of Christ in the USA. On occasions, however, I have incorporated my own rendering of the Greek.

Chapter One

FALTERING CHRISTIANS, FAILED CHRIST: THE PERSPECTIVE OF MARK

INTRODUCTION

One evening in the middle of April 1919 Siegfried Sassoon was feeling, as he put it, 'dull-minded and depressed, for no assignable reason. It was a sultry spring night, and after sitting lethargically for about three hours after dinner, I came to the conclusion that there was nothing for it but to take my useless brain to bed.' On his way to bed he paused, and 'as though from nowhere' a few words floated into his head:

> Everyone suddenly burst out singing;
> And I was filled with such delight
> As prisoned birds must find in freedom,
> Winging wildly across the white
> Orchards and dark-green fields; on – on – and out of sight.
>
> Everyone's voice was suddenly lifted;
> And beauty came like the setting sun:
> My heart was shaken with tears; and horror
> Drifted away . . . O, but Everyone
> Was a bird; and the song was wordless, the singing will
>   never be done.

For Sassoon that was 'an expression of release, and signified a thankfulness for liberation from the war years which came to the surface with the advent of spring' (Sassoon 1945: 140–1). And for members of the Christian community, is it not in similar vein an expression of what one might call the Easter spirit? If feelings are of the essence of human existence – and they are – and if Easter is at the very least about the feeling of liberation and transition from winter to spring, then to enter into the world of Sassoon's poem is to enter into the world of resurrection people.

The darkness, the horror, the wanton writing off of human life that was the Great War need no present amplification. But an exploration of the darkness, the horror, and the loss of good human life with which Mark's story of Jesus ends *is* needed if we are to enter into the world of that Gospel, and to read its ending as a Sassoon-like celebration of the extravagant divine reversal which was signalled one morning at the tomb of Jesus of Nazareth.

But let us set the scene for the story of Jesus as told by Mark. As a literary piece, the Gospel could have ended quite impressively with Mark 15:39: 'Now when the centurion, who stood facing him, saw that in this way he breathed his last, he said, "Truly this man was God's Son!" ' What could be more resonant than a final concession by the commander of the murderous execution squad, the representative of the opponents of Jesus, that what Jesus had said and what Marcan Christians believed about him was in spite of everything right and true? In a Gospel peppered with christological one-liners 'Truly this man was God's Son!' is not only typical but also in need of no sequel or supplement. In a Gospel introduced by an affirmation of Jesus' divine Sonship (1:1), what could be more appropriate than that it should end with an admission of that same divine Sonship? A compelling *inclusio* indeed! Following this line of thought, we recall that Mark left his readers without any narrative of appearances of the risen Jesus, but instead chose to invest in memories of what Jesus had said in advance about resurrection. Had he left his readers without a narrative of what happened at the tomb, but chosen instead to rely on what Jesus had said in advance, they could not have complained. And nor could we!

That should make us all the more impressed that Mark did not do what, within his own frame of reference, he certainly could have done. And not only so, his way of bringing the story to what we might call a second conclusion is signalled with some care. (i) A hitherto unmentioned group of women appear in the wings, passively watching the crucifixion sequence of events, and then again passively watching the burial, before finally taking centre stage as active players in the drama at the tomb. They are the human thread binding the 'crucified . . . buried . . . raised' sequence into a three-in-one unity. Within that unity, however, it becomes clear that Mark wants to encourage a special intensity of concentration upon the third story in the sequence. Those who were attached at the end of the first and second episodes, and who have watched . . . doing nothing . . . and watched again . . . doing nothing . . . now swing into action. (ii) The second story connects up with the first via the person of the centurion, but in and of itself that story has no Christian theological content. It is no more than preparatory – thoroughly preparatory, in that it is careful about the when, where, and how of the burial, but still preparatory. (iii) The alert and discerning reader can detect literary tensions within the third story, a fact that suggests that Mark has been creatively at work upon it. Here his Christian theological convictions come to the surface. This is where he exploited the potential of a story which he had inherited. This is where we may discern why he did not end his Gospel with the reluctant admission of the leading executioner, 'Truly this man was God's Son!' And we, for our part, may hope through the discovery and separation of tradition and redaction to enter his mind, and thus to follow through the story of Jesus to its climax and completion.

There are four points in the Marcan story of the visit of the women to the tomb where amplification of a pre-Marcan version of the story looks likely.

First, the women's intention to anoint Jesus' dead body – in itself a little odd after the lapse of so much time – gives their visit an innocent purpose. It is not a necessary part of the story, as Matthew's omission of this detail in Matthew 28:1, 'they went to see the tomb', confirms. Although we cannot be certain, this detail in Mark 16:1 may well not be pre-Marcan. If so, verse 1 is reduced to a time-note and a list of the women's names: the former is overtaken by the second sabbath reference in verse 2, and the latter which must surely be traditional (though probably expanded in typical Marcan style by the addition of the reference to the sun's having risen, cf. Mark 1:32) could easily have been part of the original introduction of the story. And, incidentally, a traditional list of the names of the women is likely to have been in the longest of the three forms, that of Mark 15:40, with the other two shorter versions being selections, rather than the other way around.

Second, the conversation of the women is part of a dislocated sequence: first, as a preliminary to the women's reaching the tomb, it requires that the words 'they go to' (ἔρχονται ἐπί) in verse 2b should cover their setting out for, and their movement towards, the tomb – but ἔρχομαι ἐπί elsewhere in the New Testament invariably describes actual arrival at an end-point or destination (for example, Mark 11:13). Second, the comment in verse 4b, 'for it was extremely large', explains the women's concern expressed in verse 3 and not the sight of the stone already rolled away in verse 4a. Since an arrival at the tomb in verse 2 leads naturally and smoothly into the view of the openness of the tomb in verse 4a, and since the openness of the tomb according to verse 4a naturally permits entry to the tomb in verse 5, we are bound to enquire whether there are any good reasons why verses 3, 4b might be a secondary addition. Indeed there are! The question, 'Who . . .?' prepares effectively for the disclosure of a divine intervention – the reader knows that 'it had already been rolled back' is a divine passive – and the comment about the size of the stone (even though it was rollable by one man, 15:46) serves to emphasise the magnitude of the problem and therefore the impressiveness of the solution. In just the same way the evangelist had expanded upon the total and complete failure of all human effort to control the uncontrollable Legion (5:3–5) – and then the transcendent Jesus had appeared on the scene and achieved the seemingly impossible (5:8).

Third, the message given to the women in verse 7, 'But go, tell his disciples and Peter that he is going ahead of you to Galilee; there you will see him, just as he told you', is widely accepted as an insertion by the evangelist. (i) The connection with verse 6 by means of 'but' is weak, and the young man's announcement is formally complete at the end of that verse. Indeed the narrative progresses very naturally from verse 6 to verse 8. (ii) The reminder, 'just as he told you', points back to Mark 14:28, which is itself manifestly an intrusion in its own setting. There Jesus announces that all the disciples will be deserters, in line with Zechariah 13:7 (v. 27). Peter protests that he is an exception to that gloomy generalisation (v. 29). Jesus insists with some formality and the precision of a triple time-note – 'this day, this very night, before the cock crows twice' – that the desertion will happen and take the form of a triple denial (v. 30). Peter persists and renews his protest, backed by all the rest, that it will not happen (v. 31). Into that straightforward and smoothly sequential exchange there is inserted verse 28, 'But after I am raised up I will go before you to Galilee.' That saying is very obviously an intrusion, and it encourages the same inference in respect of Mark 16:7: the latter alludes to it, and also adopts the same pattern as 14:27, 29–31 in speaking of 'the disciples and Peter' – that is, the disciples in general and Peter in particular, notwithstanding his attempt to distance himself from the rest.

Fourth, 'and they said nothing to anyone, for they were afraid' (v. 8b) should be assigned to MarkR. (i) The issue of communication to others was raised only by the MarkR verse 7, and is hardly necessary in view of verse 8a, 'So they went out and fled from the tomb, for fear and trembling had seized them'. This provides an entirely satisfactory ending: nothing more needs to follow. (ii) With verse 8b involved, there is an excess of references to an already extended fear/amazement complex, cf. 'they were alarmed . . . Do not be alarmed . . . fear and trembling seized them' (vv. 5b, 6a, 8a). (iii) Silence and fear are notable Marcan commonplaces: silence repeatedly, and fear not infrequently (cf. 4:41; 5:15, 33, 36; 6:50; 9:32; 10:32).

This leaves the following pre-Marcan story, with MarkR additions italicised:

> [1]*When the sabbath was over*, Mary Magdalene, and Mary the mother of James [the younger and of Joses], and Salome *bought spices, so that they might go and anoint him*. [2]And very early on the first day of the week, *when the sun had risen*, they went to the tomb. [3]*And they were saying to one another, 'Who will roll away the stone for us from the entrance to the tomb?'* [4a]When they looked up they saw that the stone had been rolled away; [4b]*for it was very great*. [5]As they entered the tomb they saw a young man, dressed in a white robe, sitting on the right side; and they were alarmed. [6]But he said to them, 'Do not be alarmed; you are looking for Jesus of Nazareth, who was crucified. He has been raised; he is not here. Look, there is the place where they laid him. [7]*But go, tell his disciples and Peter that he is going ahead of you to Galilee; there you will see him, just as he told you.'* [8a]So they went out and fled from the tomb, for fear and trembling had seized them; [8b]*and they said nothing to anyone, for they were afraid.*

The beginning of this pre-Marcan story is not entirely distinct,

Resurrection People

but its form is complete and self-contained. Its combination of six elements provides the key to its interpretation and classification: the so-called young man (νεανίσκος), his position on the right-hand side, the whiteness of his clothing, the initial reaction of alarm that he causes even without speaking, his announcement of a divine action in raising Jesus, and the final reaction of fear and trembling. Such a combination strongly suggests an angelic epiphany story. Thus, the three, unmistakably transcendent, persons who visited Abraham are described variously by Josephus as young men (νεανίσκοι) and angels (Josephus, *Antiquities* 1:200). The parents of Samson are met by someone variously described as an angel of the Lord/God or a man of God, whose appearance is impressive, whose effect is fear, and whose task is the delivery of a divine message (Judges 13:3–23). Raphael, the angelic travelling companion of Tobiah, the son of Tobit, presents himself as a young man (νεανίσκος) in Tobit 5:5–9, and when finally identifying himself to father and son generates reactions of shaking and fear (Tobit 12:16). Heliodorus, the agent of King Seleucus, was confronted and attacked by 'two young men [νεανίαι] . . . remarkably strong, gloriously beautiful and splendidly dressed', a confrontation which produced darkness and terror, and was labelled 'a divine intervention'; subsequently, they appeared again, 'dressed in the same clothing', and having spoken this time rather more mercifully 'they vanished' (2 Maccabees 3:22–34). The world of these stories is the world of the pre-Marcan story. It is a world into which the story-teller is content to move: s/he wants to stress the exercise of a power which is nothing other than divine in the opening of the tomb; s/he wants to affirm that God – no less – is involved with this otherwise ambiguous empty tomb; s/he wants to underscore the numinous awe felt by the women as they rush away from the place of resurrection (Dwyer 1996: 185–95).

It is worth pausing to consider the implications of this pre-Marcan story for 'Mary Magdalene, and Mary the mother of

James the younger and Joses, and Salome'. (i) We need to resist the tentative suggestion of an equation between the second Mary and Mary the mother of Jesus (thus, van Iersel 1998: 486–7). This is exceedingly unlikely, notwithstanding the naming of the first two of Jesus' brothers as James and Joses in Mark 6:3: had the mother of Jesus been involved she would surely have displaced Mary Magdalene as first in the list, not to mention having her relationship with Jesus himself highlighted. And although, of course, the evangelist might have been wrong, he certainly did not have such an equation in mind when writing 15:40, for, as we shall see, he elsewhere distinguishes sharply between family members (including Jesus' mother) and those who followed in Galilee. (ii) The tradition gives great honour and respect to this group of otherwise unknown women: to be recipients of an epiphany is normally to be singled out for special affirmation and validation, and to be a trio of recipients and then reporters of such an experience is to be acknowledged as convincing witnesses.

At the core of the pre-Marcan story is, of course, the heavenly announcement: 'Jesus of Nazareth, who was crucified, has been raised; he is not here.' The juxtaposition 'he was crucified . . . he has been raised' is surprisingly infrequent in the Gospels and Acts. Two 'Lucan' speeches by Peter in Acts (cf. 2:24, 32, 36; 4:10) show that at that later stage it was a juxtaposition which expressed the core of Christian preaching, and doubtless at the earlier pre-Marcan stage things were no different. That gospel upon which faith rested, and which had brought people into the Christian community, was the word of an angel, no less!

Intrinsic also to the heavenly announcement is the parallelism, 'he has been raised; he is not here'. That means that the pre-Marcan tradition understood resurrection as incorporating in some way the physical body, that is, as a return to life, a re-storation, and a just vindication of a faithful martyr. Not for the originator of this tradition the cosy and primarily intellectual understanding (Segal 1998: 102) of after-life in terms of the soul's immortality, or even the exaltation of a dead person to the heavenly sphere. For him or her it was as for the narrator of honoured martyrdoms of times gone by: from Eleazar the elderly scribe to seven young and law-abiding brothers together with their devoted mother, strong in the conviction that 'the Creator of the world, who shaped the beginning of humankind and devised the origin of all things, will in his mercy give life and breath back to you again . . .' (2 Maccabees 7:23).

And now from pre-Mark to Mark! Our next concern must be to explore the meaning conveyed by the richly significant angelic epiphany story once it had been redacted and attached to the story of the crucifixion.

MARK AND THE ABANDONMENT OF THE MESSIAH

An exploration of the Marcan story of the crucifixion (15:21–39), climaxed as it is so powerfully in the centurion's concession that 'Truly this man was God's Son!', unfortunately cannot proceed via a disentangling of tradition and redaction: on that there is nothing remotely like a consensus, and any construction runs the risk of collapsing under its own weight. But a rather more form-critical analysis of the shape of the finished product, and a comparison with other similar stories, does offer the prospect of progress.

First, the narrative divides the day of the crucifixion into three-hourly intervals, much like the customary Jewish division of the night (cf. Luke 12:38). But this is more than a convenient subdivision of time. Things happen at the change-over from one period to the next: crucifixion at 9 a.m. (v. 25), the onset of darkness over the whole of Palestine at 12 noon (v. 33), the lifting of the darkness and the death cry of Jesus at 3 p.m. (vv. 34, 37). This schematising of events is doubtless intended to accentuate the darkness and what happens at the time of the third specified hour, that is, Jesus' agonised cry of abandonment.

Second, that cry of abandonment, 'My God, my God, why have you forsaken me?' has been in a sense anticipated by Mark's quotation of Zechariah 13:7 in his 14:28: 'I will strike the shepherd . . .'. This death of the Messiah has been brought about, hard though this may be to believe, by God himself. Within the crucifixion narrative the point is made with almost unbearable force by a quartet of quotations from Psalm 22. It is of the greatest moment that these allusions are in the reverse order of their occurrence in the psalm – a 'backwards reading of Psalm 22' (Robbins 1992: 1164, 1175–81). The six hours of crucifixion began with the dividing of clothing, in line with Psalm 22:18; they continued with mockery and the shaking of heads, and repeatedly the call for 'salvation', in line with Psalm 22:7–8; they moved on to the final insults levelled at Jesus by his companions in death, echoing Psalm 22:6; and they ended with that tortured cry, drawn directly from Psalm 22:1. This means that the dying Jesus does not die in the faith, confidence and trust towards which the singer works his way in the final verses of the psalm. Not at all: in Jesus' end is the psalmist's beginning. Of confidence in God there is none, of hope there is no glimmer.

This story should be contrasted with the stories of other Jewish martyrs. Of the famous seven brothers, commemorated in 2 Maccabees 7, the first died in an atmosphere of encouragement, 'The Lord God is watching over us and in truth has compassion on us . . .' (vv. 5–6); the second denounced his killers, adding that 'the King of the universe will raise us up to an everlasting renewal of life' (v. 9); in similar vein the third, ' . . . from Heaven . . . I hope to get [bodily parts] back again' (v. 11), and the fourth, 'One cannot but . . . cherish the hope God gives of being raised again by him' (v. 14); although the sixth brother would introduce the notion of deaths demanded by God in consequence of the nation's sins (v. 18), the context had been provided by the fifth brother, 'Do not think that God has abandoned his people' (v. 16). The use of essentially the same verb – only the compound prefix varies (καταλείπω/

ἐγκαταλείπω) – in 2 Maccabees 7:16 and Psalm 22:1/Mark 15:34 serves to throw into terrible relief the stark contrast between the two scenes. The martyr Jesus becomes almost an anti-martyr figure: martyrs pray and trust and hope and place on record their convictions with their last breath, whereas Jesus prays, yes, but without faith, without hope, without an answer to the ultimate question. He holds on to God with desperate intensity – 'My God, my God . . .' – but has God held on to him? In his view, he has not.

Third, God's abandonment of his Messiah is made all the more poignant, indeed all the more unbearable, by its being conditioned by what happened immediately before. Framed by references to the two terrorists who were crucified with him (Robbins 1992:1168) and who made their hostile verbal contribution to his suffering (vv. 27, 32b), the narrative details the antagonistic taunts of 'those who passed by' (v. 29) and 'the chief priests, along with the scribes' (v. 31). The taunts are grounded in the proceedings before the Sanhedrin (Mark 14:55–64), in which context a careful distinction was drawn between an allegation by some unspecified persons, a discrepant allegation which did not prove legally sustainable (14:56–9), and a separate acknowledgement wrung from Jesus by the high priest (14:61b–4). In moving from the high priest's house to Golgotha the narrator revives the recollection of these two issues, but while preserving the separate identity of the two taunting groups he also assimilates them ('*in the same way* the chief priests', v. 31a) and introduces into each taunt the new idea of salvation ('save yourself . . .', 'he saved others, himself he cannot save', vv. 30a, 31b) and descent from the cross (vv. 30b, 32). For all that the reader is aware of the assimilation, s/he remains conscious that the allegation about the temple was false and a distortion of what had truly been said in private in Mark 13:2. But the question of his being 'the Messiah, the King of Israel' (v. 32) is different: that claim has indeed been voiced, it is indeed being tested, and according to 'the thoughts of humankind' (8:33), it cannot be sustained if Jesus dies. And that is exactly what he does – he dies.

At this precise point the narrative comes alongside and depends directly upon the two-scene drama constructed by the writer of the Wisdom of Solomon, who in turn uses a scheme which is at home in wisdom tales of the persecution and subsequent exaltation of pious Israelites (Nickelsburg 1972: 58–62). The drama begins in Wisdom 2 with a consultation among the persecutors. Of the object of their hostility, the righteous servant of God, they say:

> [13]'He professes to have knowledge of God, and calls himself the child/servant of the Lord . . . [16b]he calls the last end of the righteous happy, and boasts that God is his father. [17]Let us see if his words are true, and let us test what will happen at the end of his life; [18]for if the righteous man is God's child, he will help him, and will deliver him from the hand of his adversaries. . . . [20]Let us condemn him to a shameful death, for, according to what he says, he will be protected.'

This prepares for a confrontation between two quite distinct ideologies. According to the first of them, death is taken to be the end, nothing less than the dissolution of the spirit (Wisdom 2:1–3), nothing short of disaster and destruction (Wisdom 3:2, 3), literally the point of no return (Wisdom 2:1, 5). Any claimed relationship with God has therefore to be demonstrated this side of death (Wisdom 2:18, 20). In a Jewish environment this ideology would be typical of the Sadducees. According to the second ideology, things work differently: death is taken to be only an appearance – i.e. the body genuinely dies, but the 'real person' continues – so death is the prelude to a higher life in the presence of God and on a par with the angels (Wisdom 5:5). Any claimed relationship with God can survive death, and be confirmed in spite of death. The conflict between the two ideologies will be resolved when the persecuting 'death-is-the-end' group 'see' the exalted ones whom they have persecuted,

Resurrection People

and with 'dreadful fear . . . amazement' have wrung from them the critical admission: 'Why have they been numbered among the sons of God, and why is their lot among the holy ones?' (Wisdom 5:5)

Jesus, like the righteous servant of God, also dies – 'a victim with whom people play for entertainment – to see what happens – and whom God allows to die' (Robbins 1992: 1170). In that death his opponents cannot but locate the exposure of his claims, and specifically the messianic claim, as fraudulent (Nickelsburg 1980: 173). They believe that they have submitted this miracle worker to the test, 'Let us see if his words are true . . .', and he has signally failed that test. He has not saved himself: worse still, God has not saved him.

For the reader of Mark's narrative there are, however, two important markers put down as a result of the adaptation of the Wisdom scheme.

First, while Mark 15:25–32 is deliberately fashioned as a counterpart of the narrative of the Sanhedrin proceedings, there is in the taunt scene no recall of Mark 14:62, ' . . . and "you will see the Son of Man seated at the right hand of the Power", and "coming with the clouds of heaven." ' Why should this be? Surely because the 'seeing' in question is, like the 'seeing' of Wisdom 5:2, the vision of judgement being exercised by the one whose claims have been rejected. The high priest and his colleagues will, in Mark's view, be judged by the one they presently presume to judge (cf. Wisdom 4:16: Nickelsburg 1972: 61). That is the context in which they will have to acknowledge his messiahship. Risen and exalted, he will set the record straight for ever.

Second, there is in the taunt scene no recall of Mark 14:61b, 'the Son of the Blessed One'. In place of 'the Messiah, the Son of the Blessed One' we have 'the Messiah, the King of Israel', thus ironically reinforcing the place of Jesus in Jewish history, the identification of Jesus with the Jewish tradition (cf. the only other Marcan reference to Israel in 12:29), and the prospective rule of Jesus over the Jewish community. The matter of Jesus' status is made, as it were, 'in house', bearing in mind that 'Israel' (and therefore the term 'the King of Israel') is an 'inside name' used in communication within the Jewish community, whereas 'Jews'-language (and therefore the term 'the King of the Jews') is used in communications with or by persons outside that community (Tomson 1986: 140, 279–80). But as far as divine Sonship is concerned, it is left to the Roman centurion to make that acknowledgement, to attest the truth, albeit unwittingly (Nickelsburg 1980: 175). It is not, as in the Wisdom scheme a postmortem acknowledgement, but one provoked by the manner of Jesus' death or, more precisely in view of the hiatus caused by verse 38 in the flow from verse 37 to verse 39, by what happened in the moment of Jesus' dying: 'the curtain of the temple was torn in two, from top to bottom' (v. 38) – a divine sign, hitherto refused (cf. 8:11–12), of the authenticity of the dying one, and a further pointer to the judgement which is to come (cf. Mark 13:2; Josephus, *Jewish War* 6:288).

In sum, then, Mark draws upon a pattern of thought which sees the dying Jesus as a martyr. A martyr, and indeed more than a martyr, for his sense of abandonment by God means that the dark night of his soul is as unrelieved and oppressive as the three hours of darkness with which his life concludes. The same pattern of thought, as exhibited in the book of Wisdom, concludes with divine confirmation of the martyr's authenticity and of the validity of every one of his claims. That means that *somehow* human rejection of the victim of human injustice will be divinely reversed – and seen to have been reversed. Mark 15 cannot possibly be the end of the story.

The decision to adopt and adapt the pre-Marcan tradition of the women's discovery of the empty tomb therefore presumes an extra sign-type disclosure of divine intervention – one whose necessity needs to be explored. *Was* it necessary? Yes, if the uniqueness of Jesus' status, and the specialness of his death, were to be asserted. The righteous person in Wisdom is a typical figure – see how he represents the poor, the widowed, and the elderly (Wisdom 2:10) – but Jesus is more than typical. The confessing martyrs in the Jewish hall of fame died to resolve the problem of Israel's having sinned against God, and to achieve reconciliation (2 Maccabees 7:18, 32–3), but none of them was Son of God or King of Israel. So while Mark incorporates a scheme which is at home wherever injustice and persecution prevail, that scheme had apparently to be transcended for new and distinctive christological reasons.

FROM THE MARCAN CHRIST TO THE MARCAN CHRISTIANS

The passage of Jesus of Nazareth, their Messiah, through death to resurrection was certainly the focus of the faith of the Marcan Christians. But it was more than that: it was something for them to share. His experience was a model for theirs, theirs a mirror of his. They therefore had what might be called a vested interest in his resurrection. The evidence of their predicament needs to be reviewed briefly.

The most important evidence is provided by Mark 13, the farewell discourse, a component part of the story of Jesus where particularly close contact is made with the situation of the implied readership. That is always the way with final speeches: they present as future directions what is in fact determined by present needs. Mark 13 is no exception, and yet – here is something of a surprise – the implied audience of Jesus is in Palestine, which is almost certainly not where Mark's readers are situated. This brings us to the really rather compelling evidence that within Mark 13 as it stands there is an extended quotation of a leaflet, recoverable in verses 7–8, 14–20, 24–7, and dating from the time of the crisis when that most modest and self-deprecating of Roman emperors, Gaius Caligula, threatened to have a statue erected in the Temple – a statue of himself (Theissen

1992: 125–65)! Controversial though this proposal may be (Collins 1992: 77–81), it still seems to me the best available hypothesis. It accounts for some obvious discrepancies: (i) between divine destruction and human desecration of the Temple (vv. 2, 14); (ii) between a plural audience and a series of individual readers of a text which is neither the book of Daniel nor the Gospel of Mark itself (vv. 5, 14, 23, 37); (iii) between addressees located in Jerusalem and those who, like Mark himself, are far removed from that scene (v. 14); and (iv) between an author who makes no use whatever of Christian ideas and the Christian evangelist. It also allows text material to emerge which lays down a carefully staged apocalyptic timetable and is heavily impregnated by Danielic references. The situation to which this leaflet speaks threatens, so it appears, to reopen the wounds of the traumatic Jewish experience at the hands of Antiochus Epiphanes, and to reopen the pages of the book of Daniel which had been composed as a tract for those terrible times.

What is important is that Mark must have felt at the time he was writing that the leaflet was of renewed relevance. We know that the situation in the late 60s was rather similar to that in the late 30s in respect of wars and rumours of wars, nations rising against nations, and kingdoms against kingdoms, as well as earthquakes and famines (Hengel 1985: 21–3). We know from Tacitus that the fear of an edict similar to that issued by Gaius Caligula haunted the Jewish community even after the relief of his assassination in early 41 CE and during the reigns of several of his successors (*Annals* 12.54.1, cf. Theissen 1992: 150). The world of the Marcan Christians must have seemed uncannily and certainly uncongenially similar to that of the Palestinian Jews, with whom the Palestinian Jewish Christians had doubtless identified thirty years earlier. If they sensed that once again the Temple might be endangered by the exertion of Roman authority, it is not at all surprising that the earlier leaflet should be updated, recycled and Christianised. And such recycling is never clearer than in verses 9–13:

⁹'As for yourselves, beware; for they will *hand you over* to councils; and you will be beaten in synagogues; and you will stand before governors and kings because of me, for a testimony to them. ¹⁰And the good news must first be proclaimed to all nations. ¹¹When they bring you to trial and *hand you over*, do not worry beforehand about what you are to say; but say whatever is given you at that time, for it is not you who speak, but the Holy Spirit. ¹²Brother will *hand over* brother, and a father his child, and children will rise against parents; ¹³and you will be hated by all because of my name. But the one who endures to the end will be saved.'

This rather roughly fashioned section enables us to look through a window, as it were, into the circumstances of the Marcan Christians. The recurrent theme is the involvement of Christians in formal proceedings before the various authorities, Jewish and gentile, the key connecting thread being the verb 'to hand over' (παραδίδωμι). Only once is that verb given an explicit subject. On that occasion the key connecting thread appears, perhaps most tragically and poignantly of all, in connection with dysfunctional families. The antagonism faced by Christians within their own families crosses the generation gaps – 'brother against brother . . . father against child . . . children against parents' – and even leads to executions. We can certainly infer that the prospect of death, following on from the splitting of families, made it necessary for the Marcan Christians to be securely grounded as resurrection people.

If the second half of the Gospel of Mark is dominated by one extended discourse (Mark 13), and it is, then the same applies to the first half, where the counterpart of Mark 13 is 4:1–34 (van Iersel 1998: 74). This parable section is dominated by the parable of the sower, which is said to be the key to all parables (v. 13), and is the only one to be provided with a point-by-point interpretation (vv. 14–20). That means that the interpretation must, like the final discourse, provide a specially clear access route to the Marcan Christian community. Now the parable itself is not a similitude describing something that *always* happens but a story-type parable – 'A sower went out to sow . . .' – with verbs in the past tense, and therefore with an expectation that the person in the story will experience something so extraordinary, something that happened *just once*, that the story is worth telling. It is like the two versions of the parable of the mustard seed: the Q version told of something extraordinary – once upon a time someone planted a mustard seed and up came a tree (Luke 13:18–19)! – but the Marcan version describes something that always happens – whenever you plant a mustard seed, up comes a shrub (Mark 4:30–1). In Mark's version of the parable of the sower, the extraordinary and astonishing thing was the yield, 'thirty and sixty and a hundredfold' (v. 8), which could only happen as a result of a special blessing from God (see Genesis 26:12: 'And Isaac sowed seed in that land, and in that year reaped a hundredfold: the Lord blessed him'). With that impressive climax to the parable, it is likely that the three unsuccessful sowings (vv. 4–7) are intended simply to set the scene: they are not essentially distinguished from one another, they are variations on the single theme of unfruitfulness, they use the 'law of three' in order to build up a presentation with unqualified intensity.

But what did the parable originally mean, with its stark contrast between useless sowing in unsuitable ground and special divinely-achieved successful sowing in good ground? It is hardly clear, and therefore an interpretation was needed. And Mark's interpretation or application – not entirely coherent in itself, in that 'the seed' starts off as 'the word' but immediately changes to become symbolic of different sorts of people who receive 'the word' (vv. 15, 16, 18–19) – Mark's application proceeds by distinguishing the three sorts of threat to the success of the sown seed: the supernatural (Satan, v. 15), the human/external (tribulation or persecution, v. 17), and the human/internal ('the cares of the world, and the lure of wealth, and the desire for other things', v. 19). The first and the third might count as problems that are part of the fabric of things: they are always there. The second is different: tribulation and persecution are not always there as part of the unchanging fabric of things. Therefore their presence in Mark's text and Mark's world is well and truly meaningful. For the evangelist it is significant (i) that the term 'tribulation' is used only here and in the pre-Marcan leaflet (13:19, 24), which he took over in order to address his own current situation; (ii) that the word 'persecution' is used only here and in a promise of the reward – which might be thought more than a little inappropriate – offered 'in this present time' to those who have left persons and possessions for Jesus' sake, and who have been, as it were, re-socialised in a replacement family (10:30). That must mean that persecution is the setting in which the new family life is experienced. It begins to sound very much like the scenario of 13:9–13. And it does all the more when the connection is observed between the criticism of those who wilt in the face of trouble and persecution as 'enduring only for a while' (4:17) and the concluding observation in 13:9–13 that 'the one who endures to the end will be saved'.

Reading the Marcan text in 4:1–34 is further enriching if account be taken of some narrative-critical evidence. By means of his characteristic sandwich structure Mark injects the 'reason for parables' tradition (4:10–12) between the parable of the sower and its interpretation (4:3–9, 13–20). By this means he sets up a sharp contrast between 'those who were around him along with the twelve' and those 'outside' (vv. 10, 11). Those who are 'around him' have just been contrasted with those 'outside' in 3:31–5, itself part of another sandwich structure, 3:20–1, 22–30, 31–5. And immediately before that the evangelist has positioned the call of the twelve tradition in 3:13–19. Prior to 4:10 there is no other reference to the twelve, and in the whole of Mark there is no other reference to a crowd of listeners 'around him' (περί αὐτόν). It is therefore clear that 3:13–19; 3:20–35; 4:1–20 (34) form a triptych. And if 4:10–12 combines the references to personnel in the other two, there is a very stark antithesis between the two groups – the family of Jesus, together with the scribes from Jerusalem *versus* the crowd and the twelve (Barton 1994: 72). Now the family of Jesus consists of his mother, brothers and sisters (3:32), and they are not incorporated into the 'new' family – far from it, they are sharply distinguished from it. That same sharp distinction will reappear in Mark 6:1–6a. When the residents of Nazareth ask, 'Is not this the carpenter, the son of Mary, and brother of James and Joses and Judas and Simon, and are not his sisters here with us?' there is no clear indication of whether the family share their scepticism and take offence, but when Jesus observes that 'a prophet is not without honour, except in his own hometown, *and among his own kin, and in his own house*', the implications of this 'especially rhetorical and emphatic' formulation (Barton 1994: 90) could not be clearer. The proverbial saying does not require any but the first community to be mentioned (cf. Luke 4:24; John 4:44); it is mildly surprising that a Christian document should mention both first and third (cf. Matthew 13:57); it is positively electrifying when first, second and third are brought together (Mark 6:4). The Marcan Jesus – this is clear beyond all peradventure – pursues his mission in spite of being dogged by the rejection of his immediate family (Barton 1994: 74). So the tension between the vulnerable Christians of the Marcan community, facing the reality of being 'handed over' by family members, has already been anticipated in the tension experienced by Jesus, himself written off by his mother and his siblings with an adverse interpretation of his endowment with the Spirit. Mark 3:13–4:20 sets out a paradigm that 13:12 will endorse.

MARCAN WOMEN AND MEN

Marcan editorial work on the pre-Marcan tradition of the women's experience at the tomb of Jesus brings the disciple group back into view. 'But go, tell the disciples and Peter that he is going ahead of you to Galilee; there you will see him, just as he told you,' said the angel (Mark 16:7). And what, according to Marcan redaction, did the women do about that? Answer: 'they said nothing to anyone, for they were afraid' (Mark 16:8b).

If the Marcan narrative had closed, as those of Matthew (28:8) and Luke (24:9) were to do later, with the women explicitly reporting to the disciples, how much trouble would have been avoided! As it is, the apparent break in transmission of the message of the angel to the disciple group feeds the suspicion that a dark plan is afoot, and that Mark's narrative is heavily tendentious, to put it mildly. Fearful disobedience on the part of the women means, so it is suggested, no reception of the angelic message, and therefore no return to Galilee, no meeting with the risen Jesus, no restoration after the fateful events of Mark 14:50, 66–72, no re-commissioning, and therefore no authority to exercise leadership within the nascent Christian church! Mark's dark plan, which is fed by the seemingly negative treatment of the disciples throughout his story, could be designed to put down the position of the Jewish-Christian community in Jerusalem and to promote instead the position of another community standing four-square in the Pauline tradition, committed to gentile mission and celebrating open table fellowship (Telford 1999: 137–51). Can this be right, in part or in whole? I suggest not.

First, the angelic message about the journey to Galilee is, as verse 7 insists, a repetition of a *saying of Jesus* to the disciples in 14:28. Therefore the disciples and Peter are not dependent on the women for the instruction to go there. 'I will go ahead of you' is a prediction, with no conditionality: *this is what is going to happen*. The reader is bound to assume that this prediction, like all Jesus' predictions, will in due course be realised. That means that, for Mark's readers, the disciples and Peter did indeed follow Jesus to Galilee.

Second, the silence of the women is arguably not intended

by Mark to be absolute and total. Yes, it sounds like that – 'they said nothing to anyone, for they were afraid' – but then the precise same phraseology was used in the story of the encounter of Jesus with the leper in Mark 1:40–5: 'See that you say nothing to anyone; but go, show yourself to the priest, and offer for your cleansing what Moses commanded, for a testimony to them' (v. 44). MarkR is widely recognised in 'See that you say nothing to anyone . . . for a testimony to them', and similarly in what follows concerning the former leper's disobedience: 'But he went out and began to proclaim it freely, and to spread the word . . .' (v. 45a). In the mind of Mark, therefore, the idea of keeping totally silent is, first, the antithesis of widespread public proclamation (κηρύσσειν . . . διαφημίζειν τὸν λόγον) and, second, not exclusive of communication with certain specified individuals. The implication for Mark 16:7, 8b is that the women did not engage in widespread public communication, but they did tell the disciples and Peter. The net effect is that the public proclamation of the Christian gospel is the responsibility of specially selected men, and it does not suffer from the supposed inhibition of stemming from a group of women. The proclamation derives, not from women who saw an angel and an empty tomb, but from men who saw Jesus. We note in passing that the effect of MarkR is slightly to lower the status of the women.

This interpretation is admittedly controversial and has encountered powerful opposition (Lincoln 1995: 231–3). It needs to be protected against the alternative argument that 'fear' in verse 8b should be understood negatively, viewed as a wrong attitude, and not assimilated to 'trembling and astonishment' (τρόμος καὶ ἔκστασις) in verse 8a. In the Marcan narrative, so runs the argument, 'fear . . . usually does not depict a proper response of faith'. The only exception to this rule is said to be the woman suffering from haemorrhage (5:33), whose faith had made her well. 'Not only is the women's fear associated with the disobedience of their silence, but it is also in the context

Resurrection People

of the failure of their flight. The mention of their flight (ἔφυγον, 16:8) inevitably recalls that of the disciples and the young man in 14:50, 52 (ἔφυγον, ἔφυγεν)'(Lincoln 1995: 233). Once again we must ask: Can this be right, in part or in whole? Again, I suggest not.

First, Mark's narrative strategy conditions the reader in advance to view the three women very favourably indeed, and in no way prepares for disobedience on their part. (i) The passion narrative, stretching over 14:1–16:8, is framed by two anointing stories, 14:3–9; 16:1–8. The praise lavished on the woman of Bethany for anointing the body of Jesus 'beforehand', itself by no means a substitute for a later anointing, recognises that later anointing as definitive and sets up an association which places the intended action of the women in 16:1 in the most favourable light possible. (ii) While 16:1 gives the three women for the first time an active role, it presumes the careful briefing which has been given to the reader in the MarkR 15:40–1. According to that briefing, they were lastingly involved in following (ἠκολούθουν) – here we learn for the first time that the group definitively attached to Jesus included women. They were also lastingly committed to serving him (διηκόνουν). That is, they exhibited the pattern – Peter's mother-in-law was the prototype (1:31) – which was twice laid out by Jesus under the heading of the Son of Man's passion experience: 'Whoever wants to be first must be last of all and servant of all' (9:35), and 'Whoever wishes to become great among you must be your servant . . . for the Son of man came . . . to serve' (10:43, 45). Leaving aside the irrelevant angels (1:13), no one in the story as told by Mark engages in serving apart from the Son of Man and the female followers. Notably, these female followers were representative of the many Galilean women who had come up (συναναβᾶσαι) to Jerusalem. The term used combines in a sort of pun the terminology of Mark 10:32 – 'he began to tell them what was about to *happen* [συμβαίνειν] to him' – and that of Mark 10:32–3 – 'they were on the road, *going up* [ἀναβαίνοντες] to Jerusalem . . . "See, we are going up [ἀναβαίνομεν] to Jerusalem" ' – and therefore the women have already confronted the fearful mystery of the passion, the prediction of death and the promise of resurrection. So the depiction of the three women is skilfully contrived to achieve the reader's sympathetic recognition and respect.

Second, the flight of the women should be kept as far away from the flight of the disciples (14:50, 52) as the 'young man' in 16:5 should be kept separate from the 'young man' who only just escaped from Gethsemane: flight in the one case, but not the other, is to escape arrest, and the 'young man' in the one case, but not the other, is human and non-angelic. But much more important than that is the significance of the attachment of verse 8b to verse 8a. This requires the (redactional) 'fear' to be a synonym for the (traditional) 'trembling and astonishment'. Consequently and inevitably the Marcan text resonates with recollections of the countless texts which combine 'fear and trembling'. But the tradition represented by those texts describes with virtual uniformity a reaction to the transcendent, or to its effective intervention, which is regarded as wholly appropriate. If the evangelist disapproved of the flight and the silence of the women, he would need to have disapproved of the triad of trembling, astonishment and fear which for him explain that three-in-one reaction. To rely upon a standard formula and simultaneously to reject its standard connotations would be a very strange strategy. One has to ask: was it appropriate for 'fear and trembling' to be exhibited by the nocturnal dreamer disturbed by a passing spirit (Job 4:13, 14), or by the nations and kings who were warned to 'Serve the Lord with fear, with trembling kiss his feet' (Psalm 2:11–12), or by Darius' subject nations required to 'tremble and fear before the God of Daniel' (Daniel 6:26), or by Daniel himself in the face of the heavenly vision (Daniel 10:11–12), or by Daniel's companions who in the same context feared and fled (Daniel 10:7), and inappropriate when exhibited by the women?

This brings us to a wider discussion of the fear motif in Mark, and its recurrent function in the story Mark sets himself to tell.

First, it is true that the disciples are rebuked for lack of faith in 4:40, but that refers back to their cry in the face of the storm, 'Teacher, do you not care that we are perishing?' (4:38). Their intense fear (ἐφοβήθησαν φόβον μέγαν) follows the stilling of the storm, and gives rise to the question which from Mark's point of view is wholly appropriate, 'Who then is this, that even wind and sea obey him?' (4:41). If the question is right, so is the fear.

Second, it is also true that those who have seen what Jesus has done to the demoniac go on to ask him to leave their neighbourhood (5:17), but the text does not see that as an expression of their fear: rather, the repetition of the summary of the sick man's condition serves to highlight the cure, which is in itself and by itself the cause of the fear (5:15). The cure has involved the exercise of transcendent power. To that there can be only one right response: fear.

Third, the case of the woman with the haemorrhage is specially important, since it is the only Marcan instance of 'fearing and trembling' (φοβηθεῖσα καὶ τρέμουσα) apart from 16:7, 8, and it is set within the story of the raising of Jairus' daughter, where the only Marcan instance of 'amazement' (ἔκστασις) apart from 16:8 occurs. The woman's reaction is grounded in her 'knowing what had happened to her' (5:33), which picks up the earlier statement that 'she knew in her body that she was healed' (5:29), which is in turn matched by Jesus' 'knowing that power had gone forth from him' (5:30). While her faith (5:34) produced the confident expectation *in advance* that healing would occur, fear and trembling are the altogether appropriate reaction to transcendent power in action *after* the cure has taken place. As for the witnesses' reaction of 'amazement' at the successful raising (*sic*) of the twelve-year-old girl, it plainly falls within the Marcan range of approved reactions to Jesus' displays of power.

There follows one of the two Marcan examples of persons being told *not* to fear. When Jesus says to the synagogue leader, 'Do not fear, only believe' (5:36), the situation is somewhat different. Believing/faith is the key connection between the two stories which are combined in a typically Marcan sandwich structure, so the synagogue leader is being asked to show faith *in advance of* a cure, in just the way that the woman had done. His fear is, however, not the same as the fear and trembling of the woman – not a response to a supernatural happening, but rather a typical and wholly normal concern in the face of death, cf. Hagar (Genesis 21:17), or Gideon (Judges 6:23), or Ichabod's mother (1 Samuel 4:20), or David (1 Samuel 22:23; 23:17), or Tobiah (Tobit 6:18). That fear is to be dispelled by the prospect of a saving act.

Fourth, the other Marcan example of persons being told *not* to fear involves the disciples as they face with Jesus walking on the sea (6:47–52). Here the situation is the same. The reaction of the disciples to the unnerving 'ghost' (φάντασμα), as they supposed, is underscored by the narrator as being provoked by the as yet unidentified person they see, and emphatically not by the storm (vv. 49–50a, leading to v. 50b: 'Take heart, it is I; do not fear'). Their reaction to this person aligns them with the extended succession of those who *entirely normally* react to the supernatural in its too immediate proximity and are then told 'Do not fear' as the preface to a promise of divine action: from Abraham (Genesis 15:1), Isaac (Genesis 26:24), and Jacob (Genesis 28:13 LXX), through to Daniel (10:12, 19), Tobit and Tobiah (Tobit 12:16–17). The standard human reaction in all these cases, including that of the disciples, is seen as normal and not a matter for negativity. While the story ends with the utter astonishment and incomprehension of the disciples (6:51b, 52), that should not be assimilated to the fear: the one is a reaction *afterwards* to the calming of the storm (6:51a), while the other is a reaction *beforehand* to the person who would, as things turned out, perform the calming.

Resurrection People

Fifth, Peter's fearful reaction to the three heavenly beings, the transfigured Jesus, Elijah and Moses (9:6b), certainly provokes uncomprehending speech (9:5–6a), but again we have to ask whether the evangelist regards that reaction as appropriate or inappropriate. Given the cause of the fear, the metamorphosis of Jesus and the 'appearance' of Elijah and Moses (9:2, 4), that reaction must surely be intended to be typical and representative of what always happens in such epiphanic circumstances. In terms of story-telling within a biblical tradition, Peter's reaction must count as appropriate.

Finally, if we set aside the indeterminate cases of human fear of humans – thus, Herod in relation to John (6:20) and the Jerusalem authorities in relation to Jesus and the crowd (11:18, 32) – there remain the two cases of fear on the way to Jerusalem (9:32; 10:32). Fear is here certainly associated with lack of understanding, but in a carefully nuanced way. The narrative continuity of the section beginning with the Caesarea Philippi watershed is structured by three passion predictions (8:31; 9:31; 10:33–4). In the first, Peter objects, and the focus of objection is plainly the prediction of death – not resurrection. Before we reach the second, the evangelist records that the disciples 'questioned what this rising from the dead could mean' (9:10), and the emphasis begins to shift very subtly to something which is a mystery outside human comprehension and therefore a divine intervention. With the disciples' lack of understanding and fear about further enquiry (9:32), the sense of mystery is increased, and all the more so since the handing over of the Son of Man is a divine act (παραδίδοται), and the persons to whom he is handed over are defined no further than 'human' (cf. the sharp contrast between the 'human' and the 'divine' in 8:33). As the journey continues, the sense of atmospheric heaviness intensifies: amazement and fear are produced as Jesus simply walks ahead of them to Jerusalem (10:32), and his companions have to come to terms immediately with a third prediction which draws together all the features of the first two. So while death in Jerusalem is assuredly a focus of the unsettling sense of mystery, the resurrection is equally the focus – underlined by a stylised formula 'killed . . . and after three days he will rise again'. The scene is set for a further act in the drama in which the announcement 'Jesus of Nazareth . . . crucified . . . raised', signalled by the emptiness of a tomb, and now reformulated using the divine passive of 'to raise' (only 14:28 and 16:6), makes just as strong an impact on the astonished trio of women as the angelic appearance itself. In sum, the fear and incomprehension of 9:32, 10:32, conditioned already by the same bafflement in 9:10, serve to turn the spotlight towards the empty tomb and the interpretative word of the angel as well as the appearing angel himself. Our earlier impression is confirmed: there is no negativity directed towards the women: they merely play their part – a crucially important part – in highlighting the mind-blowing reality to which they are the first to be exposed, that is, that God has intervened.

The evangelist therefore asks his readers to identify with and applaud the women who first discovered the emptiness of the tomb, and who passed on (so I have argued) the divinely authorised explanation of its emptiness. There may be traces of a patriarchal instinct in the presentation of their relationship to the male disciples, but there is no doubt that they are very special people indeed.

MARCAN CHRISTIANS AND MARCAN DISCIPLES

There remains another piece still to be put in the interpretative jigsaw of Mark 16:1–8, a piece whose shape is affected by the conclusion suggested concerning the role of the women. It concerns the status and authority of those to whom they passed their message – 'the disciples and Peter'.

First, any subversion of the authority of the disciples and Peter is excluded by the fact that the angel issues the instruction that they should be told. That means that from the perspective of heaven, the disciples in general and Peter in particular remain within the divine design. They have been scandalised, which is what happens when persecution and tribulation overtake people (cf. 4:17); they have been scattered at the same time that their shepherd is struck by God (14:27), which is what happened when they left him (14:50), or denied him (14:72), and thus fell within the scope of the chilling declaration, 'Those who are ashamed of me and my words . . ., of them will the Son of Man also be ashamed when he comes in the glory of his Father and with the holy angels' (Mark 8:38). Scattered, scandalised, and in peril of final condemnation they may have been, but divine disclosure declares them now to be rehabilitated and restored. And that means that their original and special status and function are unchanged. The reality is not dependent upon anything or anybody: what the angel says, God says, and what the women say (or, as some would prefer, do not say) is irrelevant.

Second, readers of the Gospel of Mark are made keenly aware of the disciples' difficulties in penetrating to the true and inner meaning of Jesus. When an understanding of the key miracle eludes them they are vulnerable to the same assessment as applied to the outsiders when the key parable was explained: 'Why are you talking about having no bread? Do you still not perceive or understand? Are your hearts hardened? Do you have eyes, and fail to see? Do you have ears, and fail to hear?' (8:17–18, cf. 4:11–12) – and more of the same, some of it bad but less serious (obstructing children's access to Jesus, 10:13), and some of it as bad as could be and exceedingly grave ('Get behind me, Satan! For you are setting your mind not on divine things but on human things', 8:33). But perhaps the true explanation is provided by talk of the 'mystery' (4:11), and the opposition of 'divine things . . . human things'. Both point to the intrinsic and essential contrast between two worlds, and to the nature of the process of disclosure to the one world of what intrinsically belongs to the other. In a sense, the disciples as representatives of humankind not only *do* have difficulties in understanding, they *must* have difficulties in understanding. Their difficulties are testimony to the essential character of all that they are witnessing. They are not being attacked – far from it! – they are witnesses of divine disclosure and parties to a divine encounter, and all that in spite of themselves. Hardly surprising therefore that there is another side to the coin: although readers of Mark are keenly aware of the disciples' difficulties, they are constantly given reason and encouragement to identify with, and not distance themselves from, the disciples.

Identification can be detected in the saying about the present this-worldly experience of the Marcan Christians, 'Truly I tell you, there is no one who has left house or brothers . . . who will not receive a hundredfold now in this age . . . with persecutions . . .' (Mark 10:29–30), the preface of which is almost certainly Marcan redaction: 'Peter began to say to him, "Look, we have left everything and followed you" ' (Mark 10:28). The pattern of leaving all and following Jesus is a model which becomes standard by constant repetition – the cases of the two pairs of brothers, of Levi, and (intended, even if not realised) the rich ruler. Peter, representing all followers, is the person to whom the generalised saying is directed. The readers of Mark could not but identify with him.

Identification is implicit when the same four who heard the initial call (1:16–20) reappear as a quartet only to receive the farewell discourse (13:3). By definition, such a discourse presupposes an identification between those addressed *in* the narrative and those addressed *by* the narrative, a presupposition which is made explicit at the end, 'And what I say *to you* I say *to all*: Watch' (13:37). Indeed, throughout the discourse, there is the hortatory refrain, 'Look' (vv. 5, 9, 23, 33) and 'watch' (vv. 34, 35, 37), with the equivalence of the two being made very clear by the same reasoning being attached to each, 'for you do not know when . . .' (vv. 33, 35). So explicitly and implicitly, the Marcan audience assimilates mentally to the disciple quartet.

Such an assimilation, or identification, could not but occur when attention is given to controversial issues which define the existence of a mixed Jew-gentile Christian community. Thus the disciples who infringe a Pharisaic *halakah* (legal ruling) on the sabbath are defended by Jesus (2:23–8), who proceeds in a secondarily attached story (3:1–5) to infringe another *halakah* himself. The two stories are clamped together very firmly by the evangelist, and therefore when the outcome is a developing conspiracy against Jesus (3:6) the disciples are in a sense implicated. The seriousness of the situation facing him is an indicator of how they are themselves, *by virtue of identification with Jesus*, at risk for infringing a *halakah*. And the readers of Mark, themselves in jeopardy from synagogue authorities (13:9) – how could they but look in the mirror of stories like 2:23–3:5 and, in the disciples, see the reflection of themselves? In similar vein, the issue of unrestricted table fellowship is explored on the basis of the conduct of the disciples (7:1–23). No matter that the transition from *how* one eats (vv. 2, 5) to *what* one eats (v. 15) is not logical! No matter that the background information about the conduct of 'the Pharisees and all the Jews' (vv. 3–4) may not be accurate! The point is that an author who views 'the Jews' from a distance for the benefit of readers who are plainly not all Jews, presumes an identification between his ethnically mixed community and disciples who distance themselves from the alleged *halakah*. The readers of Mark, again using a story as a mirror – how could they but see in the disciples a reflection of themselves? Association, not dissociation, is what it is all about.

There remains something very special about the twelve, and this allows dependence upon them to amplify the idea of identification with them. The Marcan narrative builds a commitment to mission into the call of the disciples (1:17), and this is effected in their being 'sent to preach and exorcise' (3:14–15; 6:7, 12–13) and their being formally appointed as 'apostles' (3:16). Their position is from the start a matter of being 'with him' (3:14) – thus, already in 1:21, when the scene is being set for an episode in which Jesus alone is active, the presence of the disciples is hinted at by a plural verb, '*they* went to Capernaum' (van Iersel 1998: 133). This being 'with him' makes them 'the authorised links with Jesus and his life story' (van Iersel 1998: 165), participants in a period which was unique and is now past (cf. 2:19), and also, as we have already seen, the nucleus of a group which is distinct from the family of Jesus and others 'outside'. It is therefore a mistake to associate the disciples of Jesus with his family. Rather, within the polarised and antithetical confrontation of opposed groups, the disciples are on the side of light rather than darkness. They are insiders, initiated, the possessors of the supreme secret (4:10–12). Doubtless, this scheme was designed to legitimate the Marcan Christian community (Watson 1985: 60–3), but it can only do that if the community sees itself in those upon whom it depends – 'those who were around him along with the twelve'. Of course, they need to be instructed in secret, but that need is not itself culpable. It is the corollary of their being singled out to receive divine revelation, or, as a later passage will put it, 'divine things rather than human things' (8:33).

Perhaps the most crucial consideration affecting the disciples in general, and Peter in particular, is that they voice the conclusions about Jesus which Mark's Gospel is devoted to promoting, and which Mark's readers are being pressed to maintain.

First, in all discussion of the term 'Messiah', and of whether or not Mark views it approvingly, three things should be remembered. (i) The first words of the Gospel, 'The beginning of the gospel of Jesus the Messiah . . .' (1:1), make clear how fundamental and foundational that definition is. After 1:1 the evangelist can hardly play down such an idea because of possible triumphalist nuances, as has been tentatively suggested (Telford 1999: 50–4). (ii) The taunting of the crucified Jesus, for all its irony, involves contemptuous dismissal of what Jesus has in fact said (14:61–2), and which the reader therefore believes to be true. The heavy emphasis on 'internal' connotations, that is, language used by Jewish persons to Jewish persons about all things Jewish, – 'the Messiah, the King of *Israel*' – does not encourage the thought that Mark wishes to open up a gap between Christian belief and traditional Jewish thinking. Rather, the resurrection will incorporate, as well as adjust, such thinking. (iii) Within the Marcan community there were clearly Jewish persons – why else would there be proceedings against them in synagogues (13:9)? – and for such persons a purely Hellenistic 'Son of God' christology, divorced from the messianic idea (thus Telford 1999: 52), would not meet their need for a salvation-historical fulfilment in Jesus of their traditional hopes and concepts.

When, therefore, Peter, speaking on behalf of the disciple group as a whole, acknowledges Jesus as the Messiah (8:29), he speaks the Marcan truth. (i) Formally, the contrast between the preceding inadequate or just plain wrong assessments of Jesus (8:28) requires that his assessment should be correct. (ii) Narrative-critically, the story here reaches its halfway turning point, and at such a juncture a confession, concerning which the evangelist is hesitant, would be unthinkable. (iii) The ensuing command to silence brings the story alongside other stories in which such a command is voiced, and in those stories there is no sense that what is to be kept secret is in any way incorrect – thus, the order to the demons who have supernatural insight and are quite correct in what they say: 'Whenever the unclean spirits saw him, they fell down before him and shouted, "You are the Son of God!" But he sternly ordered them not to make him known' (3:11–12).

Second, what of 'Son of David' language? Is this the triumphalist and nationalist thinking that Mark wishes to keep at arm's length or even reject, a christology, which with its associated attitudes, is placed by Mark on the lips of disciples, who are then shown to be blind to Jesus' true significance and in need of re-education (Telford 1999: 41, 50–1)? Three 'Son of David' traditions call for consideration.

The blind man, who calls out, 'Son of David, have mercy upon me!' (10:47–8), tends in modern Marcan studies to acquire guilt by association with the only other blind man healed by Jesus in the Gospel of Mark (8:22–6), and to have his confession of Jesus treated as the equivalent of initial but defective 'sight' concerning the truth about Jesus. But (i) his appeal to Jesus gains credibility by his being rebuked by 'many' – an unacceptable rebuke, echoing within the continuity of the narrative the recent and unacceptable rebuke of those who would bring children to Jesus (10:13). (ii) It is unlikely that any reader of the story as a separate unit would infer from it that the blind man's view of Jesus was wrong. (iii) The term 'Son of David' here grounds christology in miracle working, not in triumphalism or nationalism, so such an association of ideas is not *apropos*.

The following incident, which develops the Davidic theme by associating 'the coming one' with 'the coming kingdom of our father David' (11:9–10), can be seen in narrative-critical terms to be linked very closely indeed to the Bartimaeus incident: thus, the discipleship word 'follow' (10:52; 11:9), and 'the way' (10:52; 11:8), as well as the Davidic language (10:47–8; 11:10). And not the least important thing about the entry into Jerusalem from Mark's point of view is that the whole event was engineered by Jesus (using the same *modus operandi* as when arranging the final Passover supper in 14:12–16), designed to activate the Zechariah 9:9 expectation, 'Shout aloud, O daughter Jerusalem! Lo, your king comes to you; triumphant [*sic!*] and victorious is he, humble and riding on a donkey . . .', and accomplished from start to finish by means of the disciples. They, so the evangelist implies, are quite right in what they think and do because they are quite in line with Jesus. No hesitations! No equivocations! No Marcan reservations!

The final 'Son of David' tradition (12:35–7) is probably by itself responsible for all the sowing of doubt concerning Mark's attitude to that term. The double question asked by Jesus, 'How can the scribes say that the Messiah is the son of David? . . . from where [πόθεν] is he his son?' seems fatally to torpedo the very idea. Not so! (i) It is the scribes, not scripture, who are introduced as the source. That means that the scriptural reality, which can hardly be gainsaid (Jeremiah 23:5–6; Ezekiel 37:24–5; cf. *Psalms of Solomon* 17:21), is a matter of interpretation, and the question is: which is the right interpretation? It is the same situation as in 9:11–13. There the disciples ask, 'Why do the scribes say that Elijah must come first?', in answer to which question Jesus first confirms that the scribes are right, and then goes on to give the sense in which their correct belief should be interpreted, that is, with reference to John the Baptist. (ii) In 12:35–7 the concluding question has to do with the basis (πόθεν) of the idea of the Messiah as David's Son. The word in question occurs twice elsewhere in Mark, and usefully for our purpose in 6:2: 'Where [πόθεν] did this man get all this? What is this wisdom that has been given to him? What deeds of power are being done by his hands! Is not this the son of Mary . . .?' The point is surely that it would be wrong to understand the phenomena in question, which are real and not in dispute, as grounded within the earthly human order. Their origin is in a transcendent order. Similarly in 12:37 the concluding question points to an answer within the sphere of transcendence. And that is just what the Psalm 110:1 text in Mark 12:36 is about, as the further quotation in the answer to the high priest will confirm, 'You will see the Son of Man seated at the right hand of the Power, and coming . . .'. So this little unit is ultimately about how two texts can be synthesised in scribal style, and its message is that the Messiah Jesus is indeed Son of David by virtue of his exaltation, which, for readers of Mark, means the truth about the resurrected Jesus. And that truth, still future at the time of the entry into Jerusalem, is what the disciples were encouraged to recognise. They were right – which is just another way of saying that the Jewish Christians in the Marcan community can and should identify with those same disciples!

Third, the disciples were, above all, right in their recognition of Jesus as the one who, to use the term which qualifies all messianic language, is 'Son of God'. Given Mark's equation between 'Messiah' and 'Son of God', every time the former crops up explicitly in the narrative the latter is implicit. Yet not once is it used by disciples – only by God, the demons, Jesus himself, the centurion (echoing Jesus), and the evangelist! Those who recognise Jesus as such a transcendent being are able to do so on the 'spirit comprehends spirit, and only spirit can do so' principle (Wrede 1971: 25). But that explicit recognition by transcendent beings is acknowledged implicitly by the wholly appropriate reaction of the disciples. Faced with Jesus and all he does, they are repeatedly overcome with awe, amazement, fear, and bewilderment, and they recognise that what he does provokes christological questioning: 'Who then is this that even wind and sea obey him?' (4:41). Their experiences of Jesus are encounters with the divine, and a fear which *follows* an exhibition of transcendent power is not a fear to be dismissed as culpable cowardice – indeed, in such a situation to be fear-less would be culpable.

In conclusion, then, what of the dark plan, fed by the seemingly negative treatment of the disciples throughout Mark's story, a plan conceivably designed to put down the position of the Jewish-Christian community in Jerusalem and to promote instead the position of another community standing four-square in the Pauline tradition, committed to gentile mission and celebrating open table fellowship? What can we say now by way of summary concerning the angelic message given to the women for the disciples?

The answer is that an alternative reconstruction seems preferable. According to this, the disciples were restored after their plumbing of the depths of unfaithfulness, and they were led back to Galilee as a company of followers giving allegiance to the risen one. The angelic message *did* get through to them, prior to their vision of Jesus and the reactivation of their prophetic commission to preach. Their gospel was the same gospel which had been preached by Jesus of Nazareth, but it was also now, in the light of his crucifixion and resurrection, even more intensely centred upon him. As the original witnesses of a transcendent intervention of God in the world, their position was privileged, and the Marcan community acknowledged its dependence upon them for its defining and validating tradition.

This community, ethnically mixed and united in confessing the risen one and celebrating table fellowship, belonged within the Pauline tradition. The critical stance it adopted towards the family of Jesus could in principle be informed by the recollection of the leadership of the Jerusalem Christians by James the brother of Jesus. This would still allow a more appreciative view of Peter, who although he had exercised a leading missionary role from a Jerusalem base, had adopted a more accommodating (even if unstable!) position on the Pauline gospel. But it is equally plausible that the negative treatment of Jesus' family, including his mother, was informed by the historical reality that they had indeed been antagonistic to his mission, and thus could function as the prototypes of the anti-Christian relatives of the Marcan Christians. These suffering believers were resurrection people in a double sense. On the one hand, every affirmation of someone whom they named Messiah, Son of David and Son of God, was an affirmation of what the resurrection had confirmed. On the other, every dark experience of persecution and martyrdom was made bright by the confident hope that his way was their way, his destiny their destiny, and his resurrection their everything.

Chapter Two

A PALESTINIAN WORD AND ITS ENDLESS FALL-OUT: TRACING RESURRECTION PATTERNS WITH MATTHEW

INTRODUCTION

Some twenty-three years ago, in 1977, the Welsh priest-poet R. S. Thomas penned a short poem entitled 'Nuclear'. It needs to be read in the light of two of his recurrent and sometimes brooding preoccupations – a passionate loathing of nuclear weapons, and a dark sense of the silent remoteness of the invisible God. In that short poem, however, there is something arresting in his affirmation not simply of a 'God who is' but also of a 'God who speaks', and particularly in the bold use of a metaphor deriving from an area of keen antipathy and heartfelt repugnance.

> It is not that he can't speak;
> who created languages
> but God? Nor that he won't;
> to say that is to imply
> malice. It is just that
> he doesn't, or does so at times
> when we are not listening, in
> ways we have yet to recognise
>
> as speech. We call him the dumb

God with an effrontery beyond
pardon. Whose silence so eloquent
as his? What word so explosive
as that one Palestinian
word with the endlessness of its fall-out?

There we have it: Jesus certainly, the teaching of Jesus of Nazareth probably, and the influence of Jesus of Nazareth perpetually and irresistibly through space and time. Jesus of Nazareth, the eloquent and explosive speech of that God whose relationship to humans is never predictable and ever paradoxical. Matthew would have loved it!

Matthew ended his Gospel with a story which all else in that Gospel had flagged. Among commentators there is virtual unanimity that Matthew 28:16-20 picks up the threads of the evangelist's favourite traditions. The favoured metaphors may vary – maybe a 'grand finale' (Stanton 1992: 345), maybe 'like a large terminal railway station in which many lines converge' (Luz 1995: 5) – but a shared sense is everywhere apparent that this last story contains in a nutshell all that Matthew believes Jesus means to the community of faith.

> [16]Now the eleven disciples went to the mountain to which Jesus had directed them. [17]When they saw him, they worshipped him; but some doubted. [18]And Jesus came and said to them, 'All authority in heaven and on earth has been given to me. [19]Go therefore and make disciples of all the nations, baptising them in the name of the Father and of the Son and of the Holy Spirit, [20]and teaching them to obey everything that I have commanded you. And lo, I am with you always, to the end of the age.'

Famous last words indeed! The risen Jesus insists on the continuing validity of all he had taught prior to resurrection, and insists as well that the fall-out of those Palestinian words should, as it were, infect the world. But, as we shall see, the little phrase

---

'all the nations' takes us to the problematic heart of Matthean Christianity.

EN ROUTE TO THE GALILEAN RENDEZVOUS

Matthew's narrative route from the burial of Jesus in Joseph's tomb to the appearance of Jesus on the Galilean mountain is traced out in a unique and distinctive way. The tradition of the women's visit to the tomb is drastically changed, the most significant additions being the fear-inspiring descent of the angel of the Lord (28:2–4), and the postscript according to which Jesus himself appeared to Mary Magdalene and 'the other Mary' (28:9–10). Alongside the additions there are subtractions, notably the dropping of some of the Marcan redactional changes to the pre-Marcan version of the tradition – thus, no intention to anoint the body of Jesus (Mark 16:1), no conversation about the problem of the stone at the tomb (Mark 16:3, 4b), and no subsequent silence of the women (Mark 16:8b). Some of these changes call for comment.

First, the descent of the angel, now explicitly 'from heaven', makes the stone the focus of interest. The rolling away of that stone, and the angel's sitting on it in 'an elevated posture of triumph' (Davies/Allison 1997: 665), represent the devastation of the plans and precautions of the authorities (27:62–6) and a literal 'terrorising' of their agents. For Matthew the removal of the stone is not, as it was for Mark, a means to the end of allowing the women to enter a tomb in which they will see an angel: it is the means to a quite different end, the confrontation between the soldiers and an angel who, in that gesture of authority, sits on their carefully placed stone in its new position away from the tomb. Although the soldiers are present while everything described in verses 5–10 happens – thus, 'While they [the two Marys] were going, some of the guard went into the city and told the chief priests everything that had happened' (v. 11) – nothing is said to them by the angel, who addresses the women alone. As far as the guards are concerned, they are simply faced with an overwhelming and wordless angelophany centring on an act of heavenly power. Inevitably they exhibit the classic and necessary reaction, fear. The reader notes that no reference has been made to the women's having feared, but in an emphatic formation they are told, 'Do not *you* fear' (v. 5). By contrast, the angel says nothing to the guards, and their fear remains unrelieved (Davies/ Allison 1997: 667). And the intensity of that terror is plain: with a striking use of dramatic irony, the evangelist assimilates their shaking (ἐσείσθησαν) with fear to the accompanying earth-quake (σεισμός), and writes of how those who watch over the tomb of a dead man become like the dead (ὡς νεκροί) – we note that when the announcement of the resurrection is made, Matthew adds the words 'from the dead' (ἀπὸ τῶν νεκρῶν) to 'he has been raised' (v. 7). The distance between them and an authentic resurrection experience is immense.

Second, among the collection of MarkR additions to the pre-Marcan tradition the one which did not fall a victim to Matthew's editorial process was the message to the disciples about the Galilean vision of Jesus. Matthew uses it twice (vv. 7, 10): a message from the angel, and later a message from Jesus himself, no less! The origin of this message in MarkR is important for a decision about the origin of the story of the two Marys' encounter with Jesus. The story has, I believe, no sustainable claim to be a separate and pre-Matthean tradition. Rather, it should be credited to the evangelist alone (Neirynck 1968: 176–90). (i) The story is a construction out of, and a postscript/appendix to, verses 1–8. The identification of the women (v. 9) is dependent on what was said in verse 1, and the greeting of Jesus (χαίρετε) picks up the joy (χαρά) with which they rushed from the tomb (v. 8). (ii) The experience of the women is preliminary and subordinate to the experience which is in store for the eleven male disciples, and in this respect a typical Matthean reflex comes into view. There had been biblical precedent for a preliminary, incomplete and subordinate appearance to a woman (cf. the mother of Samson in Judges 13:2–14), and the mind of Matthew was wholly traditional, immune to the attractions of an 'equal rights' theology, and unconcerned to redress any gender imbalance (cf. Wire 1991: 103). The mind behind Matthew 28:9–10 is none other than his. (iii) The worship of the women, amplified by their taking hold of Jesus' feet – we are reminded of how worship and the taking hold of the feet of a person possessing divine authority are combined in the approach of the Shunammite woman to Elisha (2 Kings 4:27, 37) – conforms to the pattern of worshipful approach to Jesus which MattR so often introduces. Thus, the magi and (although hypothetically and hypocritically) Herod, the leper, the synagogue ruler, the disciples, the Canaanite woman and – a *tour de force* of political incorrectness! – 'the mother of the sons of Zebedee' (Matthew 2:2, 8, 11; 8:2; 9:18; 14:33; 15:25; 20:20). It also begins to build a bridge towards the final meeting in Galilee where, we are told, 'they worshipped him, but some doubted' (Matthew 28:17). That statement is itself likely to be MattR: in the entire New Testament Matthew alone uses that particular word 'to doubt' ($\delta\iota\sigma\tau\acute{\alpha}\zeta\omega$), in Jesus' question to frightened Peter, 'You of little faith, why did you doubt?' (14:31), and in close association there, as here, with the MattR theme of worship of the Son of God (14:33 diff. Mark 6:51). (iv) The story has no concern other than with the message for the disciples, and could scarcely exist without it. And that message, apart from the change from 'disciples' to the typically Matthean synonym 'my brothers' (12:49; 23:8; 25:40), is identical to the one given by the angel to the women. For that Matthean message MarkR is ultimately and exclusively responsible.

What function, then, does the Matthean postscript to the visit of the women to the tomb serve? First, a christological purpose: the association of the 'angel from heaven' and the risen Jesus. Second, an indication of the appropriate response to the risen one – worship, which will be the immediate reaction of the eleven when subsequently they meet Jesus on the Galilean mountain (v. 17). Third, a build-up in the tension, so that the Matthean readership waits all the more eagerly for that Galilean meeting. It could scarcely be clearer that for Matthew everything hangs on the story of that final meeting.

THE OUTREACH TO 'ALL THE NATIONS' AND ITS IMPLICATIONS

If there is one phrase in that final story which has huge implications for the reading of Matthew as a whole, and for the understanding of the 'resurrection people' about whom and for whom he writes, it is the phrase 'all the nations'. The term has been interpreted very differently, and the religio-historical context in which it and the whole Gospel should be set equally diversely. Does it stand for all the nations of the world, including Israel? Does it stand for all the nations of the world, apart from Israel? In the first case, it might mean that a Jewish mission continues at the time of Matthew's writing. In the second case, there are at least two alternatives which have been proposed: *either* that Matthew's Christian community has abandoned a mission to the Jews and instead turned towards the gentiles, *or* that the mission to the gentiles is recognised and respected but regarded as the responsibility of other people, while Matthew and his community continue with a restricted mission to the Jews alone (Sim 1998: 28, 243). Whichever of these possibilities has most probability, there is another complication: in the wings of the stage on which the Matthean drama is played out, there lurks a ghost, the ghost of Paul!

Most probably not the initiator of the gentile mission in early Christianity, Paul with his towering intellect, his theological acumen, his strategic sharpness, and his fearless readiness for inner-Christian controversy nevertheless maintained the engine room, as it were, of that mission. Matthew's 'all the nations' outlook necessarily involved him in taking a position on the Pauline version of Christianity. We found ourselves drawn in the last chapter to the view that Mark belongs to the Pauline tradition of Christianity. For Marçan Christians, Paul 'bestrode the narrow world like a Colossus'. When Matthew recast Mark's story of Jesus, then, he had to decide whether the re-telling would involve deviation from or endorsement of Mark's Paulinism? There was no way out of it.

Now the essence of Pauline Christianity, and therefore the reality determining absolutely everything in the community experience of the Pauline Christians, is set out in the baptismal reunification formula (Meeks 1974: 180–3):

> As many of you as were baptised into Christ have clothed yourselves with Christ.
>> There is no longer Jew nor Greek;
>> There is no longer slave nor free;
>> There is no longer 'male and female';
> For all of you are one in Christ Jesus.

This formula, readily recoverable from Galatians 3:27–8, 1 Corinthians 12:13, Colossians 3:10–11, sets out a position to which all Christians in the Pauline tradition were committed by virtue of their baptism. They saw themselves as belonging to a new world or community within which salvation-historical distinctions, gender distinctions, and socio-political distinctions had no place. In this new world – a world brought into being by the resurrection of Christ following the ending of the old world in his death – in this new world it was possible to celebrate the bringing together of hitherto opposed parties within the corporate Christ (Martyn 1997: 118–23). That bringing together was exhibited most clearly and indeed most controversially in the sharing of table fellowship between Jews and gentiles, a sharing which was not possible within the traditional Jewish parameters.

While controversy continues to rage over the extent to which

Paul saw his gospel as threatening the authority of the laws within the Torah, there can be little doubt that for him and for the members of his communities commitment to monotheism was fundamental – 1 Thessalonians 1:9–10 adopts and adapts a traditional scheme employed by Jewish apologists in their contacts with gentiles, and superimposes the resurrection of the Son, Jesus, on that emphatically monotheistic material – while circumcision, observance of food laws and the sabbath law were emphatically marginalised. How could it be otherwise if the people of God, with gentiles as full and by no means second-class members, was now defined as the corporate Christ, the body of the risen one? The insertion of divisive wedges, even wedges sanctified by covenant history, wedges which affirmed and insisted upon the primariness of the Jews within the community of faith, could not be tolerated. For the defence of those convictions Paul paid a very high price, as the letter to the Galatians attests. An early victory for his position on circumcision, and therefore implicitly on the other so-called 'boundary markers', can be inferred with virtual certainty from his account of the Jerusalem conference in Galatians 2:1–10: even allowing for his keen personal interest, it is hard to deny the essential accuracy of his main thrust. And he won! But the sequel in the Syrian capital, Antioch on the Orontes, was different: there, according to Galatians 2:11–14, Paul's opponents snatched victory from the jaws of their earlier defeat, and delivered a knock-out blow to Paul's authority. Faced with a renewed insistence that gentile Christians be circumcised if their status was to be that of full members of the people of God, and fractured in respect of table fellowship, the Antiochene community was brought emphatically under the authority of the Jerusalem leadership. Paul fought a lone battle, argued from the basics of the gospel (as he understood it), struggled against the exercise of centralised ecclesiastical power – and lost! Had he won, he could and would have announced the victory when dealing with much the same problem in the Galatian letter. He said nothing. Never was a silence so eloquent. He lost, indeed, and left!

And what has this to do with Matthew? Answer: this Gospel may well have been designed some thirty or so years after the fatal Paul versus Peter confrontation for that very same Christian community in Antioch on the Orontes, the community which had in turn been Pauline and then non-Pauline. Matthean specialists are not of one mind on this issue. One writes that 'the evidence is far from conclusive' and maintains 'our inability to locate the city in which the evangelist wrote', but still envisages a move by the community across from Palestine to Syria (Stanton 1992: 85–6, 109, 281). Another concludes that 'the great city of Antioch on the Orontes is only the most probable of many hypotheses' (Luz 1995: 18), while a third assembles a comprehensive case in Antioch's favour – 'by far the most probable place where Matthew composed his Gospel' (Sim 1998: 40–62). And if a setting in Antioch is a strong possibility, then history dictated that the ghost of Paul would figure in the drama reflected in Matthew's script.

A study of Matthew's references to gentiles favours the conclusion that, while aware of the traditional *distinction* between them and Jewish people, he is even more keenly aware that, through the gospel, Jesus has had the effect of bringing them together. Resistant to the message, and indeed the messengers, they may be, but receptive to both they may equally become.

First, Matthew subtly redacts and expands the Marcan introduction to the mission of Jesus, which in Mark had read, 'Now after John was arrested, Jesus came to Galilee . . .' (Mark 1:14a). In Matthew's hands this becomes, 'Now when Jesus heard that John had been arrested, he withdrew to Galilee. He left Nazareth and made his home in Capernaum by the sea, in the territory of Zebulun and Naphtali', and there follows the quotation of Isaiah 9:1–2 (4:12–16). It is striking that a coming to Galilee should involve leaving Nazareth, for the evangelist is well aware that Nazareth in fact belongs to Galilee (2:22–3). Evidently, there is something special about Jesus' destination being Capernaum within Galilee: set in the territory of Naphtali (Davies/Allison 1988: 377), it alone enables the Old Testament quotation to define Jesus' sphere of operation as 'Galilee of the gentiles'. That phrase must therefore be extremely important to Matthew. What that importance is can be deduced from 4:23–5, itself a substantially modified summary of the Galilean mission (cf. Mark 1:28, 32–4, 39; 3:7–8) and a commentary on 4:13–16. For 'the surrounding region of Galilee', the area touched by reports of Jesus, we are asked to substitute 'all Syria'. In place of Idumea, Tyre and Sidon in the list of places from which people came to Jesus, the mixed Jew-gentile Hellenistic cities of the Decapolis in the Roman province of Syria are among those providing followers of Jesus. For Matthew the theologically strategic position of a Capernaum-centred mission in Galilee seems to be that Jesus can work in Israel and make an impact outside it. Jews and gentiles are together those upon whom 'light has dawned'. If Israel is special, so too is Syria (Luz 1990: 206).

Second, by an unmistakable signal Matthew hooks up the mission of the disciples in 10:1–42 to the mission of Jesus in 4:12–17, 23–5. In both contexts it is said that 'Jesus went throughout Galilee, teaching in their synagogues and proclaiming the gospel of the kingdom and curing every disease and every sickness among the people' (4:23; 9:35). Matthew's readers are evidently being asked to remember the first summary – and its associated commentary – when reading the second. What follows is a tapestry, prima facie a tangle, in which some of the threads are fiercely exclusive in colouring and others firmly inclusive. The exclusive sayings are: 'Go nowhere among the gentiles, and enter no town of the Samaritans, but go rather to the lost sheep of the house of Israel . . . you will not have gone through all the towns of Israel before the Son of Man comes' (10:5b–6, 23b). They frame the basic instructions on mission – but those basic instructions also include: 'Beware of them, for they will hand you over to councils and flog you in their synagogues; and you will be dragged before governors and kings because of me, as a testimony to them *and the gentiles*' (10:17–18/Mark 13:9, 10).

What sense can we make of this apparent tangle? (i) The 'traditionalist' outlook of the introductory verses 5b–6 may be compared with the same outlook in 23:2–3, which is introductory to the discourse against the Pharisees, 'The scribes and Pharisees sit on Moses' seat; therefore do whatever they teach you and follow it; but do not do as they do, for they do not practise what they teach.' In view of what follows in Matthew 23, this introductory saying has to be seen as Jesus' initial premise, and an accurate summary of *some* of what he said by way of amplification, but because of its one-sidedness a premise which is overtaken by other considerations. Similarly, Matthew 10:5b–6 can be read as an initial premise, but not a principle which covers all that follows. (ii) From Matthew's standpoint, verse 23b must imply that a mission to Israel still continues, and indeed will continue until the time of the Son of Man's coming – and that, at the time of writing, is still awaited. (iii) The concern with 'the lost sheep of the house of Israel' will in due course recur in Jesus' encounter with the Canaanite woman (cf. 15:24). Using redaction criticism we are struck by subtle but significant changes made by Matthew to the story of that encounter in Mark 7:24–30. First, the saying about Jesus' exclusive mission to 'the lost sheep of the house of Israel' is set in a private conversation between him and the disciples (vv. 23, 24), and the woman consequently has to repeat her appeal for help (vv. 22, 25). Second, in Jesus' dialogue with her Matthew drops his saying, 'Let the children be fed first', thus excluding the idea that a mission to Israel is for a first phase, and an outreach to the gentiles for a second. And third, within the continuity of the Matthean narrative the distinctive ending of this story – ' "Woman, great is your faith! Let it be done for you as you wish." And her daughter was healed from that hour' – requires the reader to interpret the whole story in the light of the distinctive ending of the story of the healing of the centurion's

Resurrection People

servant – ' "Go let it be done for you according to your faith." And the servant was healed in that hour' (Matthew 8:13). In combination, therefore, the stories suggest that salvation–historical principles are respected in the mission of Jesus and the teaching he gives disciples; that Israel and the gentiles are part of a unified programme of simultaneous mission rather than a programme in which one precedes or even excludes the other; and that wherever and whenever faith in Jesus as 'lord' (κύριος) is forthcoming, then inclusiveness reigns supreme.

Third, when Matthew resumed his re-telling of the Marcan story in the Marcan order, and had covered the two sabbath controversies (Matthew 12:1–14/Mark 2:23–3:6), he reached the summary of Jesus' healing activity in Mark 3:7–12. But of that Marcan summary very little remained unused by Matthew after his narrative constructions in 4:23–5 and 9:35. Reading the text redaction-critically, however, we are able to treat this third rewriting of Mark 3:7–12 in Matthew 12:15–21 as the equivalent of the other two. And that means giving maximum possible weight to the extended quotation, the longest in the whole of the Gospel, from Isaiah 42:1–4. Like the other summary statements it is clearly intended to characterise Jesus' total mission: 'my beloved, with whom I am well pleased . . . I will put my Spirit upon him' echoes the tradition of Jesus' baptism which manifestly defines his total mission. In that setting much hangs on the double reference to gentiles: 'he will proclaim judgement to the gentiles [τὰ ἔθνη] . . . and in his name the gentiles [τὰ ἔθνη] will hope'. It is a moot point whether τὰ ἔθνη should be translated 'the gentiles', that is, everyone other than Israel, or 'the nations', that is, everyone including Israel. In the light of the earlier summaries, the second would be preferable. It is also a moot point whether 'judgement' (κρίσις) should be understood as justice, that is, the equivalent of Matthew's favourite 'righteousness', or as the final assize. Again the second would be preferable from the point of view of a narrative-critical respect for order, given that all previous allusions to κρίσις have had that final judgement in mind (cf. 5:21, 22; 10:15; 11:22, 24; and shortly afterwards, 12:36, 41, 42). But, whichever choice one makes, Jesus' mission has a universal dimension, gentiles are included, and hope is offered to all. Not unnaturally, the minds of commentators travel from this passage to the climax of Jesus' teaching in the apocalyptic discourse of Matthew 25:31–46. To cut a very long story very short indeed, one may boldly suggest that when the judge speaks of 'one of the least of these my brothers' he is using Matthean language for Christian disciples (Stanton 1992: 214–18), and therefore he is engaged not in assessing the gentiles on the basis of how they have treated Israel, but all the nations including Israel (πάντα τὰ ἔθνη) on the basis of how they have treated the Christian community in general and probably its missionaries in particular. That means two things: first, that everyone, whether Jews or gentiles, has been touched by the Christian mission; second, that to everyone, whether Jews or gentiles, the term 'righteous' may be applied; and third, that for everyone, whether Jews or gentiles, there is hope of the kingdom of God and eternal life (25:34, 46; cf. 12:21). Inclusiveness is evidently the keynote.

Fourth, the MarkR supplement (13:9–13) to the pre-Marcan memorandum, which we noted while investigating the Gospel of Mark, is not entirely transposed by Matthew into his version of the mission charge in Matthew 10. Matthew 24:9–14 also reuses it. Reminiscences of the earlier text in the later one require us, using narrative criticism, to interpret the one in the light of the other. Hatred 'by all' now becomes hatred 'by all the nations' (Matthew 24:9 diff. Mark 13:13), which clearly means those who are represented by councils and synagogues, that is, gentile and Jewish personnel. After the reference to the end (τέλος) in 'but the one who endures to the τέλος will be saved' (Matthew 24:13; 10:22b/Mark 13:13b), and before a MattR addition, 'and then the τέλος will come' (Matthew 24:14), there is set a slightly revised version of Mark 13:10, now reformulated by Matthew as 'and this gospel of the kingdom

Resurrection People

will be proclaimed throughout the world [οἰκουμένη] as a testimony to all the nations'. That the equivalence of the οἰκουμένη and 'all the nations' is consciously and deliberately affirmed by Matthew will be confirmed a little later when again he retains from Mark the saying of Jesus in the home of Simon the leper about how this gospel will be proclaimed in the whole world (κόσμος). It is plain, therefore, that the preaching of the gospel is to touch all nations, neither gentiles to the exclusion of Jews, nor vice versa.

In the light of this extended investigation we can return to the final story in Matthew's narrative (28:16–20). If that story draws together the threads of all that has gone before – and it does – then the evangelist is tracing back to the risen Jesus a mission which covers Jews and gentiles. All are to be brought to acknowledge his authority by becoming disciples, undergoing baptism, and obeying the teaching of the pre-Easter Jesus – *Matthew's* pre-Easter Jesus.

Now this conclusion immediately eases what might otherwise have been a serious problem: an Antioch-centred mission to non-Jews had not in fact been initiated by the resurrection, but a Jerusalem-centred mission to Jews which ultimately expanded to include 'all the nations' had been. That means that mission for Matthew is placed in the tradition of the Jerusalem church, and on that basis Matthew 28:18–20 makes sense. But if one problem is solved, another threatens, and that second problem is all to do with the spectre in the wings, the ghost of Paul! The problem can be defined in a question: when the Matthean Christians tried in the name of the resurrected Jesus to make inroads among gentiles, did they say that faith in Jesus as Lord was sufficient to bring full and complete membership of the people of God, or did they say that it was necessary for gentiles not only to acknowledge Jesus as Lord but also in effect to become Jews if they were to enjoy that full membership and the table fellowship which uniquely expressed it? Were they

'Christians' or 'Christian Jews'? Did they stand for or against Paul?

JUDAISM, CHRISTIANITY AND THE RELIGION OF MATTHEW

A valedictory speech calling for obedience to 'everything that I have commanded you' resonates with echoes of Moses' valedictory speech:

> 'Assemble the people . . . so they may hear and learn to fear the Lord your God and to observe diligently *all the words of this law.* . . . Take to heart *all* the words that I am giving in witness against you today; give them as a command to your children, so that they may diligently observe *all the words of this law.'* (Deuteronomy 31:12; 32:46)

The atmosphere on the Galilean mountain, the scene of the appearance of the one who has several times been painted in Mosaic colours, is more than a little Deuteronomic (Segal 1991: 8). And Deuteronomy is, of course, seriously concerned with the tendency of Israel to be led astray from authentic religious observance (4:19; 11:28; 13:6; 30:17). Again, not a million miles from Matthew, especially since unqualified obedience to the commands of Jesus is nothing less than unqualified obedience to the commands of Moses!

The Mosaic colouring of this climactic passage makes this a suitable stage at which to consider two contrasting reconstructions of Matthean community experience, each standing in a well-established tradition of interpretation, and each having an important bearing on how Matthew sees the Jesus/Moses relationship with its huge implications for the mission to 'all the nations'.

According to the first reconstruction (Stanton 1992), Matthew's religion is Christianity. A break with Judaism and the local synagogue communities has occurred after a prolonged period of hostility – hence the scattered references to 'their/your synagogues' and to the transference of the kingdom 'to a people that produces the fruits of the kingdom' (21:43). As far as the community of Judaism is concerned, therefore, Matthew's Christians are *extra muros*. The breakaway groups thus formed, most of whose members are Jewish, but some of whom are gentile, constitute a *tertium genus*. They are intent on establishing themselves over against their former co-religionists. Controversy continues to rage between the representatives of Matthean Christianity and Judaism, and from the Christian side it is necessary to try and rebut allegations that the authority of Moses has been set aside. When therefore the Matthean Jesus urges, 'Do not think that I came to destroy the law and the prophets' (5:17) – which could be paraphrased 'Don't think, as the scribes and Pharisees allege, that I have come to destroy the law and the prophets . . .' – it is not in the interests of some inner-Christian doctrinal dispute, as if some Christians are actually thinking that he had done: rather a polemical misinterpretation put out by the leaders of the synagogue community (who sail under the flag of 'the Pharisees') is being rejected. These leaders, and these alone, are the opponents whom Matthew has in his sights. In similar vein, when the Matthean Jesus, acting as the final judge, denounces some charismatic-prophetic figures and banishes them for their lawlessness (ἀνομία), it is not that there are actual prophetic persons advocating an allegedly antinomian position in Matthew's community: rather a message is being conveyed to the Christian readers of the Gospel that moral slackness and failure to keep the law is to be avoided at all costs, indeed at the ultimate cost of final banishment from the presence of the Lord (7:21–3). Unfaithful Christians will, so Matthew threatens, share the experience of judgement with the hypocrites, that is, the scribes and Pharisees. As far as the mission of the Matthean community is concerned, the risen Jesus had directed it to both Jews and gentiles, the latter being accepted freely, and the former being the objects of a dogged hope that the defence of Christianity over against non-Christian Judaism might cause at least some individuals to convert. And the relationship of Matthew to Pauline Christianity? The answer is that 'Matthew's gospel as a whole is neither anti-Pauline, nor has it been strongly influenced by Paul's writings; it is simply un-Pauline' (Stanton 1992: 314).

The second reconstruction sees Matthew's religion as Judaism: 'the religion of the Matthean community was not Christianity but Judaism' (Sim 1998: 163). A break with local synagogues has occurred, but (so runs the argument) a break from the synagogues is not the same as a break from Judaism. So 'it seems more appropriate to speak of a Jewish sect within Judaism than of a Christian sect outside Judaism' (Sim 1998: 5). In setting out the faith of Christian Judaism Matthew writes for the community in Antioch which had been brought back under the control of the Jerusalem church after the parting with Paul (Galatians 2:11–14). Now, despite the intervening deaths of those who had figured in that momentous debate, this community expressed its continuing loyalty to the Jerusalem tradition by making Peter its key authority figure and also – here's the rub! – attacking the position of Pauline Christians in the sayings material which appears to frame the sermon on the mount (5:17–19; 7:21–3). As far as the mission of the Matthean community was concerned, it was directed exclusively to Jews, and regarded gentiles with instinctive hostility, the gentile world as 'a foreign place with foreign practices' (Sim 1998: 231), and gentile converts as distinctly unusual, while respecting and recognising that for other Christians an outreach to gentiles in line with the commission of the risen Jesus was a primary obligation. 'The common understanding of the Gospel as open to Gentiles and advocating a gentile mission is wrong on both counts' (Sim 1998: 28). So if we again raise the question of the relationship of Matthew to Pauline Christianity, the answer is that 'the evangelist is engaged in an anti-Pauline polemic' (Sim 1998: 8).

There, then, are two sharply contrasting views of where the Matthean community stands in relation to Torah-centred Judaism, the mission to 'all the nations', and the legacy of Paul. How may we inch forward to a conclusion about the impact of the authority of the risen Jesus on his 'resurrection people'?

First, it is necessary to retrace our steps to the definitive message of Jesus in his Capernaum-centred mission, that is, in 'Galilee of the nations', as set out in 4:17, 'Repent, for the kingdom of heaven has come near.' That shortened version of Mark 1:15 is what is meant by 'the gospel of the kingdom' which Jesus preached in Galilee, and on the basis of which crowds from Galilee and elsewhere followed him (4:23, 25). Those same crowds formed the audience of the sermon on the mount (MattR: 'seeing the crowds', 5:1). Now that shortened version of Mark 1:15 had already been put into the mouth of John the Baptist: 'In those days John the Baptist appeared in the wilderness of Judea, proclaiming, "Repent, for the kingdom of God has come near" ' (Matthew 3:1–2). The effect, in narrative-critical terms, is that the detail of John's proclamation has to be seen as commentary on the theme of the near kingdom, and therefore to be implied and included when Jesus proclaims that near kingdom. Consequently we are hardly surprised to find Jesus saying Baptistic things from time to time in Matthew's Gospel – and not the least bit surprised that the teaching for the crowds gathered on the mountain after hearing 'the gospel of the kingdom' should include one such saying, the warning to false prophets that 'every tree that does not bear good fruit is cut down and thrown into the fire' (Matthew 7:19; cf. 3:10). Yet the false prophets are hardly the same as the Pharisees and Sadducees who bore the brunt of John's ferocious attack (Matthew 3:7 diff. Luke 3:7). So John's prophetic preaching sets out a position that can be used flexibly for different sorts of audience.

The John-echoing statement that 'every tree that does not bear good fruit is cut down and thrown into the fire' is a MattR addition to a cluster of sayings about good/bad fruit coming only from good/bad plants and trees (vv. 16b–18), with the saying 'You will know them by their fruits' acting as an *inclusio* (vv. 16a, 20). The word 'their' cannot but refer back to the false prophets of verse 15. Since the formulation 'Beware of [certain persons]' elsewhere in Matthew refers to a real, existent threat – as in 10:17, 'Beware of men: they will hand you over to councils . . .' – in respect of persons and/or their teaching (cf. 6:1; 16:6, 11, 12), it emerges that Matthew's community is in actual fact faced with the threat of prophetic 'invaders', about whom Matthew knows enough to denounce them for inner rottenness. Of course, we note the evangelist's use of a time-honoured polemical strategy of personal attack rather than rational argument – but Matthew was not the first to follow this strategy, and his successors are alive and well and with us to this day!

The John-echoing statement that 'every tree that does not bear good fruit is cut down and thrown into the fire' has another very important function. In 7:21–3 Christian prophets defend themselves by protestations of their charismatic activities – prophecy, exorcism and miracle-working, all in the name of Jesus – and are then provided with an explanation of their dismissal by the judge: they are evildoers (οἱ ἐργαζόμενοι τὴν ἀνομίαν). But how do they come to defend themselves? Something has clearly been said to cause them to protest. In the apocalyptic discourse in Matthew 25:31–46 there was a protestation (vv. 38–9, 44) and an explanation (vv. 35–6, 40; vv. 42–3, 45), but prior to both there was a formal statement of the judge's decision (vv. 34, 41). Of that there is no explicit counterpart in 7:21–3. Therefore, on formal grounds, that judicial decision seems to be implicit in the talk of being cut down and thrown into the fire (cf. Matthew 25:41). And the common concern with false prophets and with 'doing' (ποιεῖν) reinforces the reader's sense that 7:15–20, 21–3 constitute a single section. Now, while we listen to Matthew's attack on these persons, we have also to ask about the self-understanding of the prophets themselves. They set store on the confession of Jesus as Lord (κύριος) – note the ironic and even sarcastic repetition in Matthew's quotation: 'Not everyone who says to me, "Lord, Lord, . . ." ' – and on their prophetic-charismatic gifts, but we have to presume that they would not see themselves as advocates of ἀνομία in the sense of moral disobedience, nor as hypocrites bereft of integrity. Therefore what is at stake between them and Matthew (who, by the way, is quite keen on prophets as such for the furtherance of Christian mission, cf. 10:41; 23:34) is a difference of opinion about how the will of God should be defined. Do the charismatic prophets define the will of God as Paul did? That is not clear from the data of Matthew 7:15–23. All we can say is that a Pauline connection is perfectly possible in view of the use of the itinerant prophet model, the appeal to acts of power (Galatians 3:5), and the claim that acknowledgement of Jesus as Lord would bring salvation (Romans 10:9–10). But, it has to be acknowledged, a Pauline connection is not exclusively demanded.

Second, the sermon on the mountain, which defines the will of God in the light of the kingdom preaching of John and Jesus, is dominated by the two sections 5:21–48 and 6:2–18, which are in turn controlled by their headings, 5:17–19 and 5:20/6:1. In 5:17, the introductory 'Do not think that I came . . .' is arguably a reference to something that is actually being thought by Christians, in just the same way as 'Do not think that I came to bring peace to the earth . . .' (Matthew 10:34) is arguably being thought by Christians who are mindful of traditional Jewish expectations of the era to come (cf. Isaiah 2:2; 9:5; 52:7) and unprepared for intra-family division provoked by Christian allegiance, or who take seriously the function of peace greetings in the mission of Jesus and the disciples (Matthew 10:13). The immediately following insistence on the permanent authority of every law, however apparently trivial, contains reinforcement by the arguably synonymous 'until heaven and earth pass away . . . until all these things have taken place'. That synonymous parallelism is involved is shown by Matthew 24:34–5:

> 'Truly I tell you, this generation will not pass away *until all these things have taken place. Heaven and earth will pass away,* but my words will not pass away.'

Once the reader of Matthew 5:18 has reached 24:34–5 s/he can be in little doubt that whatever applies to Jesus' sayings applies to Moses' sayings, and vice versa. And then there is Matthew 5:19, a MattR addition to the preceding Q saying (cf. Luke 16:17), and one which, by the intensity of its warning against the loosening of 'one of the least of these commandments' *and the teaching of others to do the same,* most probably envisages a threat posed from within Christianity by those with a teaching function. This saying, presented by Matthew as the necessary inference from the preceding saying – note the 'therefore' (οὖν, v. 19) and the 'for' (γάρ, v. 18) which ground 5:19 as well as 5:17 in 5:18 – should not, I believe, be played down as 'a very conservative saying which is somewhat out of character with 5:17, 18, 20 and with Matthew's emphases elsewhere' (Stanton 1992: 300–1). It forms a pair with 5:17, both sayings providing commentary on 5:18. And unless real persons and a real threat are involved it is hard to see why Matthew 5:18 should be so aggressively intensified by the addition of Matthew 5:19. The persons concerned therefore teach and act at variance with the law. While it would certainly be possible that Matthew had in mind only to correct Pharisaic misinterpretation of the Christian position by stressing the orthopraxy and the orthodoxy of the approved leaders of his own community (thus, Stanton 1992: 49), the strength of the attack on teachers seems more likely to require a real Christian threat than a Jewish misunderstanding. And if so, it is not difficult to correlate the two sections which essentially frame the body of the sermon, 5:17–19 and 7:15–23.

Third, to describe the Christian persons who embody the threat to Matthew's conservative Torah-based community as antinomians would risk exaggeration. The term 'lawlessness' (ἀνομία), both in general usage and in the specific passage in Psalm 6:9(8) which is quoted by the judge, requires no more than a sense of disobedience to the Torah: it is 'a comprehensive term encompassing any position which falls short of true obedience to the law and its demands' (Sim 1998: 205). But to go further and allow the possibility of a theologically purposeful and selective abandonment of certain specific laws would be a position for which there was, of course, precedent, and against which the principle that while time endures 'not one letter, not one stroke of a letter, will pass from the law' would be relentlessly opposed. No one who respected that principle could tolerate the setting aside of circumcision, or the food and sabbath laws, as the condition for gentile entry into the people of God. So at the very least we are pressed towards the conclusion that Matthean Christianity is fundamentally at variance with Pauline Christianity, and that the real Christian threat which concerns the evangelist may well come from the direction of the Pauline tradition. This would fit the terms in which the section 7:15–23 is introduced: 'Beware of false prophets, who come to you in sheep's clothing but inwardly are ravenous wolves.' This suggests a concrete situation within the community (Overman 1990: 118), but not one provoked by prophets who are within the community. They are an unqualified menace, and they 'come to you' from outside.

In order that the wheel may come full circle, the critical issues of circumcision, food laws and sabbath have now to be tackled. These are the make-or-break issues: with them the argument about Matthew's relationship to Judaism should finally be settled.

Matthew makes no direct reference to circumcision. However, what his attitude was to flexibility in the demand for circumcision may be guessed in the light of the story of King Izates under pressure from Eleazar, the Galilean Pharisee:

'In your ignorance, O king, you are guilty of the greatest

offence against the law and thereby against God. For you ought not merely to read the law but also, and even more, to do what is commanded in it. How long will you continue to be uncircumcised? If you have not yet read the law concerning this matter, read it now, so that you may know what an impiety it is that you commit.' (Josephus, *Antiquities* 20:44–5)

Matthew's similar attitude to any flexibility in the demand for circumcision may be guessed when (as we have just noted) his Jesus thunders forth, 'Whoever relaxes one of the least of these commandments, and teaches others to do the same, will be called least in the kingdom of heaven.' Circumcision was far from 'one of the least' of the Mosaic commandments. So we can hardly doubt that on circumcision the Matthean Jesus, and therefore Matthew, adopts a conservative 'no surrender' approach in the best Paisleyite style: to liberalism, woolly or otherwise, he will not give the time of day.

As far as the food laws are concerned, Matthew takes the opportunity to include in the discussion in Matthew 15:1–20 the most savage attack on the good faith and legitimacy of the Pharisees – 'Every plant that my heavenly Father has not planted will be uprooted' (15:13) – but refuses to treat Jesus' ruling on cleanness as 'making all food clean' (thus Mark 7:19).

As far as the sabbath is concerned, the position set out in Matthew 12:1–14/Mark 2:23–3:6 is more complex. Built into the first sabbath controversy is the rebuke, 'But if you had known what this means, "I desire mercy and not sacrifice", you would not have condemned the guiltless.' This is not, strictly speaking, part of the logical argument in the specific setting. Positively, of course, it introduces 'a dramatic new hermeneutical filter that necessitates a rereading of everything in the Law in the light of the dominant imperative of mercy' (Hays 1996: 100). But, almost more importantly, and applying negatively in view of its polemical thrust, it is a general criticism, applicable in all settings, and spelling out why the Pharisees have (allegedly) gone wrong.

They have neglected mercy, that is, commitment to meeting human need, whether in action or in assessment of other people's actions. The earlier use of the same text, Hosea 6:6, in the story of the call of Levi/Matthew (Matthew 9:9–13/Mark 2:13–17) demonstrated the priority and the meaning of mercy as action to meet human need: sacrifice as such was not an issue, but only the positive definition of what the will of God is. If Matthew was aware, as is probable, that Hosea 6:6 was being used by the successors of the Pharisees in their work of reconstruction following the demise of the sacrificial system (cf. Hays 1996: 99), his use of that same text would involve a certain brutal ferocity. The cherished text of scripture, to which the leaders of Judaism turned for solace, was being thrown in their faces: the charge is that they do not know what it means.

Leaving aside for a moment the polemical use of Hosea 6:6, we note that each of the sabbath controversies ends with a pronouncement by Jesus: 'The Son of Man is lord of the sabbath . . . It is lawful to do good on the sabbath' (Matthew 12:8, 12). Neither pronouncement should be read as an abandonment of the sabbath in principle or an encouragement to abrogate the sabbath in practice. Just as the terms 'lord of the harvest' and 'lord of heaven and earth' (Matthew 9:38; 11:25) point to permanent spheres in which lordship is exercised, so too with the term 'lord of the sabbath': the sabbath is a sphere in which the Son of Man's authority is and continues to be exercised, and in the exercise of that authority he declares what sort of action is appropriate on that day. The Matthean Christians therefore keep the sabbath, but not in the way that the Pharisaic critics (Matthew 12:1, 14) believe to be right. The arguments of the Matthean Jesus in support of his particular rulings are (i) addressed to situations of human need, (ii) distinctly *ad hominem* in style, (iii) couched in terms of the 'from the lesser to the greater' rule, and (iv) set within the framework of 'it is lawful . . . on the sabbath' language (vv. 2, 10, 12). They depend heavily on MattR and represent a distinct shift away from an argument from precedent (even though the case of David in 1 Samuel 21:1–6 remains – but, someone might ask, was he right or was he wrong in doing what he did?) and from creation ('The sabbath was made for humankind, not humankind for the sabbath', Mark 2:27). The first of the new arguments is that the same law as affirms the sabbath also allows a breach of the sabbath in a specified place. That is, the interests of that place/institution take precedence over the sabbath, and technical breaches of the sabbath in that place/institution incur no guilt: how much more is this the case in the sphere of the authority of the one who is greater than the holy place? The second of the new arguments is an appeal to what anyone would do ('Which of you . . .?') to rescue an animal in difficulty, no matter what day it might be. It combines with the first argument to make the meeting of human need the starting point and the cardinal principle under-girding the will of God in the sphere of Jesus' authority.

So we are drawn to the conclusion that Matthew was in deadly earnest when he laid down the principle that relaxing in deed or word even the least, let alone the heaviest, of the commandments in the Torah was *streng verboten*. Circumcision was obligatory. The food laws were not in jeopardy. The sabbath was sacred time to be hallowed in the way that 'the lord of the sabbath' had determined. None of the boundary markers of the people of God had been moved. The religion of Matthew was, from this perspective, Christian Judaism.

SPOTLIGHT ON THE SON

If none of the boundary markers of the people of God had been moved as far as Matthew and his Christian community were concerned, why was there such a problem in relations with the Jewish synagogue? Why had relations been strained to the point of breakage, with mutual hostility and recrimination the outcome? There must have been some cause célèbre which brought about so dire a situation. Perhaps the tradition of the final meeting between Jesus and the eleven disciples may provide the clue. Sonship christology is the core of the story. Could a Jewish sect within Judaism (Sim 1998: 5) take the theological liberties that were inherent in such an acclamation of the risen Jesus? And if the answer is 'no', then the religion of Matthew will begin to look like Christianity.

Just before Matthew's narrative brings us to the final meeting between Jesus and the eleven disciples we are alerted by some subtle editorial work to the serious part played by the Sonship idea in relations between Jews and Christians. While Jesus' claim to be the king of Israel – Son of David christology *in nuce* – provokes a sceptical demand for proof as death approaches (Matthew 27:42/Mark 15:32), even that claim is subsumed in talk of divine Sonship. Twice the calls for death to be kept at bay and the cross to be vacated are adjusted, first by the addition of 'if you are the Son of God' in Matthew 27:40 and then more lengthily in Matthew 27:43: 'He trusts in God; let God deliver him now if he wants to; for he said, "I am God's Son." ' The reference back can only be to the confession before Caiaphas, which brought a sentence of death for blasphemy. While it is certainly right that the term Son of David had regularly been given the leading role in the conflict between Jesus and his adversaries (Verseput 1987: 533–7), nevertheless the ultimate denouement saw even Davidic sonship subsumed within divine Sonship. This was the ultimate problem for the opponents of Jesus, but it was soon demonstrated to be the ultimate truth. Faced with the first of two earthquakes, the execution squad could not forbear to acknowledge this truth (Matthew 27:54). The occurrence of a second earthquake not many hours afterwards (Matthew 28:2) implies that everything to do with the resurrection has to do with Jesus as the divinely confirmed Son. That is the perspective from which the evangelist wishes the final chapter of his Gospel to be read.

It is also, one may add, the perspective which he encouraged in his readers when he edited the parable of the wicked tenants (Matthew 21:33–43). Of Matthew 21:43, the saying Matthew attaches at the end of that parable, 'Therefore I tell you, the kingdom of God will be taken away from you and given to a people that produces the fruits of the kingdom' it has been said that it is 'as important as any other verse in the Gospel for our understanding of the relationship between Matthew's community and Judaism' (Stanton 1992: 118). That being so, it is significant that the identity of the person whose rejection brings about the transfer of the kingdom is defined as 'his son' (Matthew 21:37).

When Matthew's narrative does finally bring us to the meeting between Jesus and the eleven, we with our knowledge of other related Gospel traditions, as well as the family of traditions to which they belong, are in a strong position to gauge what was being conveyed by the central affirmation of the Sonship of Jesus. The appearance of Jesus to the disciple group is the best attested of all the appearance traditions. The pre-Pauline tradition mentions it twice (1 Corinthians 15:5, 7), Mark is aware of it (Mark 16:7), and Luke has an alternative version which can be set alongside Matthew 28:16–20. Luke's version of the shared themes includes the appearance of Jesus (Luke 24:36), the re-action of the disciples (Luke 24:37) and specifically their doubts (Luke 24:37–8), an assertion of resurrection-based authority (Luke 24:46), and a commissioning speech by Jesus (Luke 24:44–9) which opens up a universal mission centred on the Jewish community and probably envisaging baptism: 'repentance and forgiveness of sins is to be proclaimed in [the Messiah's] name' (Luke 24:47, cf. 3:4). Additionally the Lucan Jesus associates the Father and the Spirit with himself in the final promise, 'And see, I am sending upon you the promise of my Father; so stay here in the city until you have been clothed with power from on high' (Luke 24:49). From these Matthew/Luke parallels it is evident that Matthew is depending upon a pre-Matthean tradition in fashioning the great climax of his story of Jesus.

In their various ways Matthew and Luke, and therefore their

traditional source, tell about a commissioning, and thereby they set their stories in the tradition of commissioning stories in which the Old Testament abounds. The standard form of a commissioning story often involves a self-disclosure by the commissioning person, as well as a reassurance to the commissioned person/s (Hubbard 1974: 62–4). Matthew's distinctive handling of this standard form is in line with his most characteristic instincts and reflects some of his deepest convictions. In particular, we find him, as we would expect, turning the spotlight on Jesus himself – the authority given to him, the baptism administered in his name, and the promise of his timeless presence.

The self-announcement, 'All authority in heaven and on earth has been given to me', is the equivalent of the oft recurring divine I-formula of earlier stories – thus, to Jacob, 'I am the Lord, the God of Abraham your father and the God of Isaac' (Genesis 28:13), or to Moses, 'I am the God of your father, the God of Abraham, the God of Isaac, and the God of Jacob' (Exodus 3:6). This time, however, the self-announcement is at one and the same time a disclosure of both exaltation and subordination. Supreme authority 'has been given', and is therefore to be exercised by an agent within a religious context of uncompromising monotheism. The risen Jesus presents himself as God's chief agent, in rank superior to all other heavenly beings, and second only to God himself, yet in no way threatening the lonely eminence of the one God. Christologically, this involves, of course, releasing the resources of Jewish reflection, itself always uncompromisingly monotheistic, on such agency in whatever form it takes – divine attributes like wisdom, exalted patriarchs like Moses, and principal angels like Michael or Melchizedek (Hurtado 1998: 17–92).

Matthew doubtless wished this self-disclosure formula to be heard in the light of indications earlier in his Gospel. Together 'heaven and earth' represent the entire creation (Matthew 5:18; 24:35), the sphere of the royal sovereignty and lordship of God

(5:35; 11:25); separately, heaven is where God's will *is* done, and earth where it *should be* done and doubtless *will be* done when the kingdom comes, as the MattR expansion of the Lord's prayer suggests: 'Your will be done, as in heaven, so also on earth' (Matthew 6:10). Present and future are there both brought into view. Very noticeably, the heaven/earth sayings in Matthew draw particular attention to an exercise of authority which is experienced in the revelation of secrets, to which we shall turn shortly, and the forgiveness of sins. The healing of the paralytic (Matthew 9:1–6/Mark 2:1–12) is retold in such a way as to omit the scribes' question, 'Who can forgive sins but God alone?' (Mark 2:7), to introduce for the only time in Matthean miracle stories the reaction of fear to what has been said and done (Matthew 9:8), and to find in the exercise of authority by a unique individual an implicit conferral of authority upon 'human beings'. Human beings are thus, as it were, caught up in the earthly authority of the (implicitly heavenly) Son of Man – and that authority is experienced in forgiving and being forgiven. From here it is a small step to the forgiveness of sins exercised by Peter and the community (16:19; 18:18, 19). When the risen one discloses his supreme authority in heaven as well as on earth, this has powerful community implications: Matthew's understanding of the church is of a body where forgiveness is experienced on earth and endorsed by the risen one. That this is a matter of controversy between Jews and Christians is evident from the scribal suggestion that it is blasphemy, and the counter-attack that they are thinking 'evil things' (Matthew 9:4 diff. Mark 2:8), aided by the observation that recognition of the forgiving authority of the Son of Man was part of a glorifying of God (Matthew 9:8). In other words, the Christians' community claims and experience do not threaten monotheism in the slightest degree.

The self-disclosure of the risen one, the announcement of his universal authority, has, as we have seen, a strongly participationist dimension: statements about him are implicitly statements about the Matthean community. It is a community which acts with his authority and also *makes* real in itself that which *is* real – a sort of Pauline view, whether or not Matthew would have welcomed such a parallel! The same participationist theme is presented powerfully in the commission which depends upon the preceding self-disclosure: 'Go *therefore* and make disciples of all nations, baptising them in the name of the Father and of the Son and of the Holy Spirit . . .'

Historically, Christian baptism had been 'in the name of Jesus/Christ' before the Matthean community – and Matthew 28:20 must document community practice rather than an individual evangelist's redaction – changed to the triadic formula. In formalising the triadic reference in this way, the community was doubtless stimulated by the common Christian conviction that baptism opened up a filial relationship to God as Father, and also brought endowment with the Spirit of God. It was easy for the Matthean Christians to read and use the tradition of the baptism of Jesus himself (Matthew 3:16–17) in this way, especially as Matthean theology so stressed continuity between John the Baptist and Jesus. Nevertheless, the triadic formula went rather further. The selection of the term 'the Son' for Jesus, the description of God as 'the Father', and the use of the singular 'the name' to draw together Father, Son and Spirit – all carried huge christological implications, though not, of course, any echoes of Trinitarian thinking, the introduction of which could only be anachronistic. At the very least, initiation into the Matthean Christian community – thus 'make disciples . . . baptising' – meant experiencing the supreme God and his Spirit as an experience of his Son. While the idea of divine agency had frequently been employed in a severely monotheistic setting, it is understandable that the opponents of a Christian community understanding itself in this way should believe that the boundaries of monotheism had been overstepped.

That 'the Father and the Son' should together be experienced thus as a consequence of the Easter exaltation of the one who announces that 'all authority in heaven and on earth has been given to me' could not but drive this Christian community back to traditions in the centre of the Gospel, where just such an association of ideas had already been employed: Matthew 11: 2–30. The later text, as it were, drew into itself the earlier one. And that earlier one (Matthew 11:27/Luke 10:22) read:

> 'All things have been handed over to me by my Father, and no one knows the Son except the Father, and no one knows the Father except the Son and anyone to whom the Son chooses to reveal him.'

Throughout Matthew 11 the evangelist has been sticking fairly closely to the text of his Q source. If we also bear in mind that on the whole Matthew is prepared to move Q material around, whereas Luke does so only rarely, then we can detect the following editorial changes: (i) the insertion of the phrase 'the works of the Messiah' (Matthew 11:2 diff. Luke 7:18), and the change from 'Wisdom is justified by her children' (Luke 7:35) to 'Wisdom is justified by her works' (Matthew 11:19); (ii) the insertion of the saying about violence to the kingdom, with an attached commentary (Matthew 11:12–14), in place of a narrative statement about the reaction of various groups to John the Baptist (Luke 7.29–30); (iii) the movement away from the mission charge and into this context of the woes on the cities of Galilee (Matthew 11:20–4/Luke 10:13–15).

Of these changes the most important for our purpose is the first, in which we find a section consisting of several distinct units held together by an *inclusio*: 'the deeds of the Messiah . . . the deeds of Wisdom'. It is extremely tempting to infer from this double description of the deeds of Jesus that Matthew is promoting an equation: Jesus = the Messiah = Wisdom (thus, Deutsch 1987: 103), and it is a temptation for which I must admit I have fallen in past times. However, a more restrained inference which takes Jesus the Messiah to be the agent of Wisdom has several points in its favour. (i) Contrary to the claim that Matthew presents Jesus as Wisdom incarnate (Deutsch 1987:

130), this Gospel stands apart from those texts, first Jewish and then Christian, which develop the idea of a heavenly person, pre-existent in the presence of God and active in the work of creation, and then entering the world from outside. The evangelist does not build into his story of Jesus either pre-existence or incarnation. (ii) Texts describing Wisdom's involvement in human/Israelite affairs by means of agents can be set alongside Matthew 11:2–19: thus, with reference to the signs and wonders carried out by Moses, 'she entered the soul of a servant of the Lord, and withstood dread kings with wonders and signs' (Wisdom 10:16), doubtless effecting the general principle that 'in every generation she passes into holy souls and makes them friends of God and prophets' (Wisdom 7:27), or in connection with Mosaic happenings in the desert, 'Wisdom prospered their works by the hand of a holy prophet' (Wisdom 11:1); reverting to Adam, Wisdom 'gave him strength to rule all things' (Wisdom 10:2), that is, to effect her own rule, or to Noah, the builder of the ark, yes, but 'Wisdom was the artisan who built it' (Wisdom 14:2); and turning to the prayer of the supreme exemplar, Solomon, 'Send her forth . . . that she may labour at my side . . . For she knows and understands all things, and she will guide me wisely in my actions' (Wisdom 9:10–11). In all these cases, and arguably in the case of Jesus, it is not a personal equation but agency which the text presents.

In Matthew 11:25–30, a section with three parts, a significant history of tradition can be uncovered. The prayer in Matthew 11:25–6, 'I thank you, Father, Lord of heaven and earth . . .' provides several themes for the quite distinct proclamation which follows in Matthew 11:27: God as Father, universal sovereignty, a transcendent plan, and a revelation for certain selected persons. There is, therefore, a thematic continuity from the one to the other. But there is also what might be called a seismic shift from one to the other: first, the sovereignty is transferred from the Father to the Son; second, whereas the petitioner is addressing God as any Jewish person would who enjoyed a sense that the God of Israel is father of all Israelites, the proclamation gives the Son a quite unique status and relationship with the Father; third, whereas the distinction between those who are inside or outside the scope of revelation stems from the will of the Father in Matthew 11:26, it is a matter of the decision of the Son in Matthew 11:27; and finally, in Matthew 11:25 what is revealed is 'these things', i.e. the meaning of the mission of Jesus as a whole, but in Matthew 11:27 it is nothing less than the knowledge of God himself which is now attainable exclusively through the Son. The shift from the prayer to the proclamation makes the latter a 'commentary saying' (Wanke 1980: 218), but not in the sense of the proclamation's drawing out meaning which is genuinely inherent in the prayer. The 'commentary' imposes new meaning, dictates how what was originally said must now be heard – and, in the light of the parallel between 'all things have been delivered to me by my Father' and 'all authority in heaven and on earth has been given to me', 'now' means for Matthew 'in the era of the resurrection, and in the experience of those who can count themselves as resurrection people'.

The effect of Matthew 11:27 upon Matthew 11:25–6 was doubtless very significant already before Matthew and in Q, but at the Matthean stage that effect was reinforced by the attachment of the saying about the easy yoke (Matthew 11:28–30). Matthew very probably redacted an earlier saying (Stanton 1992: 340–1), which read:

> 'Come to me, all you that are weary and are carrying heavy burdens, and I will give you rest. Take my yoke upon you, and you will find rest for your souls. For my yoke is easy, and my burden is light.'

This saying is exactly the sort of thing Wisdom says, and according to Sirach 6:18–37 and 51:13–20, had said (Deutsch 1987: 130), and therefore exactly the sort of thing that a person acting as mouthpiece for Wisdom could appropriately and on her behalf say again. And the heavy burdens stand for the interpretations of the Torah by the Pharisees (cf. Matthew 23:4), impossible burdens dictated by 'the wise and prudent' from whom the decisive revelation has been withheld (Matthew 11:25). The alternative, supremely authoritative, teaching is what the risen Jesus lays down, the one who as a result of MattR adds, 'and learn from me, because I am meek and humble in heart' (11:29). This is the Messianic king speaking (cf. Matthew 21:5), and speaking to the closed community circle of Matthean Christians. If they are resurrection people, they are committed to the recognition of his transcendent and royal authority by unswerving obedience to his teaching. But his teaching is not the burden that the leaders of the contemporary synagogue are intent on laying on the shoulders of the Jewish community. The Christians observe the Torah, but according to the knowledge disclosed by the risen Jesus.

All in all, it is clear that Matthew 11:27, once it is brought under the control of Matthew 28:19, points to a belief pattern which was inevitably going to alienate traditional Jews. That Jesus should, on the basis of resurrection, be assimilated to the Father and the Spirit within a single name; that he should be entrusted with unrestricted cosmic authority of the sort possessed only by God; that he should as the risen one be worshipped – all of that was bound to provoke an irreconcilable conflict of ideas and a polarisation of communities. From the synagogue side it was intolerable that former members of their community should form themselves into a group which (i) affirmed their own exclusive possession of the knowledge of God, implicitly denying it to the parent community, and (ii) set aside the restraints of the agency scheme, in which worship had never been offered, in favour of a new scheme in which 'they worshipped him saying, "Truly you are the Son of God" ', 'When they saw him, they worshipped him . . .' (14:33; 28:17). From the Christian side these insights into the significance of the risen Jesus were at the same time flashes of self-understanding.

Legitimation was to be found in their possession of secret knowledge that had now, in their view, been brought out into the open, but possessed by them and by them alone. Their crossing of a boundary line had taken place in baptism, which made forgiveness for the repentant effective, committed them to Sonship christology, and made them a community of taught disciples obedient to all those commands of the earthly Jesus which the resurrection had confirmed.

A PARADOXICAL PRESENCE

That the promise of the presence of the commissioning person, the risen Jesus, should be his last word to the eleven is no surprise. A standard part of the commissioning scheme, and 'by far the commonest expression of reassurance in the Hebrew Bible' (Hubbard 1974: 35), it had featured in the covenant with, and/or commissioning of, a succession of figures in the Jewish hall of fame: Abraham, Isaac, Jacob, Moses, Joshua, Gideon, Isaiah (Genesis 17:4; 26:3, 24; 28:15; 46:4; Exodus 3:12; 4:12, 15; Deuteronomy 31:23; Joshua 1:5, 9; Judges 6:16; Isaiah 6:8). Tailored to the particular task and circumstances, fears and hesitations of each person to whom it was conveyed, the promise of presence nevertheless contained certain standard ideas: protection from human threats, participation in the providential plan of God for his people, endowment with power, and the assurance of ultimate success. Doubtless these were intended to be implicit in the promise to the eleven, to whom the Matthean community looked back. This community was convinced that it occupied a key position within the providence of God, that its opponents and persecutors would not prevail, and that its mission to the world would be granted good success. It *had* to believe those things: whether such beliefs were realistic and borne out in experience, only time would tell. What is of particular interest to students of Matthew's Gospel and community is the special way in which the idea of 'the presence' is shaped within the parameters which apply to all such community/commissioning promises. And here we are drawn back to the two other traditions which, together with the resurrection encounter, overarch and control the Matthean story, that is, the story of the birth of Jesus (1:18–25) and the community rule (18:15–22).

The story of the birth of Jesus touches many Christian people at a deep emotional level, and what follows may make some uneasy. At the same time, I hope it may come to other readers as a liberation. However that may be, the place to begin is the evidence that the story fairly clearly has a pre-history, a point proved by its internal tensions (cf. Soares Prabhu 1976: 243–53).

First, the purpose of 'the birth of Jesus the Messiah took place in this way' (v. 18a) is to connect the following story to the language and the key idea of the preceding genealogy. Apart from the name Jesus, it is not a necessary part of the distinct pre-Matthean unit of tradition telling the story of the birth.

Second, the phrase 'from the Holy Spirit' (v. 18b) tells the readers in advance what would – indeed should – have maximum impact if the angel were left to disclose it: it makes verse 20b 'redundant, anticlimactic and nonrevelatory' (Schaberg 1995: 45), it tends to distract the reader's attention towards Mary and away from Joseph in his distress, and it should be assigned to MattR.

Third, that Joseph was 'her husband' is a repetition of the earlier definition of the Joseph/Mary relationship – technically correct, of course, since engagement implied the legal status of husband and wife, even though the wife would remain under her father's authority in the parental home, and the couple would not be sexually active. Since the central person in the story is Joseph, and the reader is meant to enter into his pain, it is probable that 'and unwilling to expose her to public disgrace . . . secretly' is also there only because of MattR. The issue is not *how* divorce proceedings should be effected – could they realistically be kept secret? – but *whether* they should be, and that is what the story is about. Joseph is a law-abiding person, which means he is wholly in line with Torah in deciding to get rid of his fiancée. That is only prevented by an angelic intervention. We may add that he is also a fearful person (cf. 'Do not be afraid . . .', v. 20b), and the fear is not in this case, as we would expect, fear provoked by the encounter with the angel. It is fear concerning the effect on his honour caused by marriage to a woman, the timing of the birth of whose child would reflect gravely and shamefully on his conduct in respecting the conventional restraint on sexual contact during the engagement period.

Fourth, the address to Joseph as 'son of David' is another connective with traditions on either side of this one (cf. 1:1–17; 2:4–6), and is shown by its absence from later angelic addresses to Joseph (2:13, 19) to be unnecessary. It too should be assigned to MattR.

Fifth, the smooth flow of the narrative would be rescued if we were to marginalise verses 22, 23. Without those verses the angel's instructions to Joseph (vv. 20b, 21) are straightforwardly put into practice by Joseph (vv. 24, 25): he is told to consummate the engagement with his pregnant fiancée and to name the child Jesus, and he does exactly that. Moreover the double naming – a different name, conferred by different persons ('*they* shall call his name . . .') – complicates and to an extent distracts. When we hear that '*all* this took place in order that . . .' we realise that it is the total event, and not just what has been described up to that point in the story, which is the basis for the 'Emmanuel . . . God with us' interpretation. So in the wholly characteristic Matthean allusion to prophecy there is superimposed in both literary and theological terms something which was no part of the original story.

Sixth, the insistence on Joseph's having 'had no sexual relations with her until . . .' (v. 25) is something of an interruption in the narrative concerning how Joseph did what the angel had ordered, that is, (i) taking Mary as his wife and (ii) giving the newborn baby the divinely chosen name.

This enables the pre-Matthean story to emerge from Matthew 1:18–25, whose MattR changes are here italicised:

> 18bWhen Mary the mother [of Jesus] had been engaged to Joseph, but before they lived together, she was found to be pregnant *from the Holy Spirit.* 19Joseph, being a righteous man, *and unwilling to expose her to public disgrace,* planned to divorce her *quietly.* 20But when he had resolved to do this, an angel of the Lord appeared to him in a dream and said, '*Joseph, son of David,* do not be afraid to take Mary as your wife, for the child conceived in her is from the Holy Spirit. 21She will bear a son, and you are to name him Jesus, for he will save his people from their sins.' 22*All this took place to fulfil what had been spoken by the Lord through the prophet:* 23'*Look, the virgin shall conceive and bear a son, and they shall name him Emmanuel.'* 24When Joseph awoke from sleep, he did as the angel of the Lord commanded him; he took her as his wife, 25a*but had no marital relations with her until* 25band she bore a son; and he named him Jesus.

The story begins with a very problematic pregnancy, the result of a liaison to which Joseph is not a party. His fiancée is to be divorced, not executed, that is, we seem to be in the area where a sharp distinction is drawn between a liaison into which an engaged woman has entered voluntarily (cf. Deuteronomy 22:23–4), and one into which she has been forced involuntarily (Deuteronomy 22:25–7). For the first the penalty is death by stoning; for the second, there is no penalty because she was wronged, rather than guilty of wrongdoing. The human tragedy is that she has to live with the loss of her personal honour, about which Philo wrote humanely and compassionately that she deserves 'mercy and sympathy' (*On the Special Laws* 3:76). But, as in the crisis faced by Joseph, the virtual equivalence of the immediate premarital situation and marriage makes divorce the right term for a decision by the prospective husband to release the engaged woman.

The story continues with the angel's encountering Joseph and tackling his problem head on. The purpose is to protect the planned marriage, as a result of which the new baby will not be born out of wedlock and will, in legal terms, have a father. Paternity and 'ownership' are to be established by Joseph's naming of the child, the name itself bringing both present dilemma and future role within the scope of the providence of God: 'you are to name him Jesus, for he will save his people from their sins.' To bring the present dilemma within the paradoxical providence of God is what was also intended by the angel's explanation that 'the child conceived in [Mary] is of the Holy Spirit'. Contrary to the physicalising interpretation of these words, an interpretation which has (I believe) had such unfortunate consequences for Christian theology, and which leaves Jesus without a human father and therefore with only a qualified identification with humankind, two arguments can be mounted. (i) The preposition 'of' in the phrase 'of the Holy Spirit' (ἐκ πνεύματός . . . ἁγίου) should be compared with its use in phrases like 'from heaven . . . from men' (ἐξ οὐρανου . . . ἐξ ἀνθρώπων), where the issue is the divine provenance and authorisation of a phenomenon in the world of human happenings (cf. Matthew 21:25). (ii) The angelic explanation must be set in the tradition of conceptions – conceptions as normal as normal can be – conceptions which are traced biologically to human parents and theologically to the providential involvement of God. One has only to think of (i) the conception and birth of Cain – 'I have produced a man with the help of the Lord', cries the mother (Genesis 4:1), notwithstanding the narrator's comment that 'the man knew his wife Eve' (4:1); or (ii) how 'the Lord raised up another seed' (*Jubilees* 4:7) in place of Cain from the Adam-Eve partnership (Genesis 5:3); or (iii) how the promise to Abraham that 'I will give you a son by her . . . I will surely return to you in due season, and your wife Sarah shall have a son' was fulfilled when 'the Lord dealt with Sarah as he had said' (Genesis 17:16; 18:10, 14, cf. *Jubilees* 16:12); or (iv) how it was said of both Leah and Rachel that 'the Lord opened her womb and she conceived and bore a son' (Genesis 29:31; 30:22–3); or how (v) the Targums use a heavenly voice to say of the pregnancy of the unfortunate Tamar with the deceitful Judah that 'It is from me that this thing comes from me/God' (Schaberg 1995: 24), while *Testament of Judah* 12:6 records that Judah's discovery of Tamar's pregnancy made him want to kill her, but he was prevented for it was 'from the Lord' (παρὰ κυρίου ἦν); or (vi) how in the story of Ruth 'Boaz took Ruth and she became his wife; when they came together, the Lord made her conceive, and she bore a son' (Ruth 4:13); or (vii) how the difference between conception and non-conception for the distressed and shamed Hannah, enjoying throughout normal sexual relations with her husband, was the change from 'the Lord had closed her womb' to 'the Lord remembered her' (1 Samuel 1:5–6, 19). In all such cases the intervention of God is effected through, not by circumventing, the normal process of procreation – and nothing in the pre-Matthean story of the birth of Jesus suggests anything different.

As is often the case in birth narratives, the climax is the baby's naming, which serves to define status or role or both. In the case of Jesus, again, the story proceeds on normal and predictable lines. 'He shall save his people from their sins' is a deliberate echo of Psalm 130:8, where it is said of God that 'he will redeem Israel from all its iniquities'. Doubtless the liberty taken at the pre-Matthean stage in the clarification of the name Jesus – more strictly, 'Yahweh is help' (Luz 1990: 117) – was thoroughly congenial to Matthew, for whom the forgiveness of the sins of God's people is a major preoccupation.

Matthew's own reworking of the earlier tradition is above all evident in his attaching it to the preceding genealogy – only in Matthew 1:1, 18 does he use the word 'birth' (γένεσις), thus making the tradition in 1:18–25 a sort of footnote to the genealogy – and in his injection of the formula quotation of Isaiah 7:14 in verses 22–3:

²²All this took place to fulfil what had been spoken by the Lord through the prophet: ²³"Look, the virgin shall conceive and bear a son, and they shall call his name Emmanuel.'

These two moves by the evangelist serve to confirm his agreement with the interpretation put forward above, specifically that there is present no idea of a birth brought about supernaturally by the Holy Spirit without the involvement of a male parent. First, that is not what Isaiah 7:14 is about, and it is important to note that in the worlds of both Isaiah and Matthew the term 'virgin' (παρθένος) refers to a person without sexual experience up to a particular moment in time, and includes any engaged or just married woman. Second, the enigmatic quartet of Tamar, Rahab, Ruth and Bathsheba, added to the genealogy have defied all efforts to discover a common characteristic which would connect them to Mary. To define them all as gentiles (Luz 1995: 26) is a frail possibility, though that frailty is exposed by several considerations: (i) Sarah, who would have been an excellent embodiment of the divine plan to include gentiles, is not mentioned; (ii) the main claim to fame of Tamar and Rahab is hardly gentile origin; (iii) to make Bathsheba in some way representative of the gentile world would require emphasis on the effect of her marriage to a Hittite – but then Ruth comes in the opposite direction and marries more than once into the Israelite community before becoming the mother of David's great-grandfather, while Bathsheba herself was married to David before the conception of Solomon (2 Samuel 12:24). So some alternative appears necessary. To define them all as sinners founders on the rock of Ruth's virtue – though what was she up to in the highly ambiguous episode at the threshing floor (Ruth 3:1–14)? – and it is a reasonable question: 'are the marriage of Ruth, the adultery of Bathsheba, and the betrothal of Mary really comparable?' (Luz 1990: 109) So perhaps the most cautious way forward may be, first, to acknowledge the failure of all attempts to find a single common thread in the stories of Tamar, Rahab,

Resurrection People

Ruth and Bathsheba; and, second, to recognise that *the most notable and notorious feature* of (i) the story of Tamar was that, even though she was a victim of injustice and exploitation, she was not married to Judah but was involved in sexual irregularity, and through that irregularity the line of descent was providentially secured, cf. Genesis 38:14, 26; Ruth 4:12; (ii) the story of Rahab, introduced quite gratuitously as the partner of Salmon and mother of Boaz in spite of belonging to the time of the conquest, that is, two hundred years earlier (Schaberg 1995: 25–6), was that she was a prostitute and was most naturally described as such, cf. Hebrews 11:31; James 2:25; and (iii) the story of Bathsheba was that although she was married to David at the time of the conception of Solomon (2 Samuel 12:24), she had been a victim of lust. The sexual irregularity of at least three out of the four women is not made irrelevant by the varied forms that it took, nor by the fact that no one of the three was in *precisely* the same predicament as Mary's: the important thing is that Matthew's choice of three paradigms of sexual irregularity in general establishes a line of continuity from them to Mary, and – even more important than that – the incorporation of such irregularities within the providential design of God for Israel. That providence is for Matthew all-inclusive and paradoxical, and it shows why he dares to say of the whole story that '*all* this happened to fulfil what had been spoken by the Lord . . .'.

And so it is a matter of 'Emmanuel . . . God with us'. God with whom, and what does 'with' mean? The whole texture of the story is the specialness of the Jewish people. Gentiles are not excluded, but if they are drawn in, it will be as those who share in the experience of the Jews. The drama of the Gospel will be played out with that in mind, the tensions and strains of the relationship between Jesus and the Jews notwithstanding. As to the 'with', it is a matter of a topic being put on the agenda but not exhaustively discussed and clarified until the whole story has been told. The name Emmanuel was not applied to Jesus as an historical personage in the way that Isaiah 7:14 envisaged, so the person through whom 'Emmanuel' becomes true is the whole Jesus, the one who comes to be acknowledged thus in the light of the resurrection. In this way the 'all this' of Matthew 1:22 will have to be expanded to cover not just the events of Matthew 1:18–25 but all those narrated in Matthew 1–28. This presence of God is a mediated rather than an immediate presence: it is a presence in the community gathered round and sustained by the risen one in their midst. Those community members are the persons who can and do call Jesus by his name.

That brings us very naturally to the third saying about a divine presence, not this time at either start or finish of this Gospel but rather close to its midpoint. The striking Matthean saying, 'For where two or three are gathered in my name, I am there among them', clearly has the risen Jesus in mind: no one else could be present 'wherever' any small grouping of Christian people might be found. Since time and space impose no limitations on him, he must be transcendent.

And the meaning of this striking saying must be sought by observing (i) the verbal connections which secure it to its context, as well as (ii) the adaptations which mark it out from the famous saying of *m. Aboth* 3:2:

'If two sit together and words of the Law [are spoken] between them, the Divine Presence rests between them. . . . If three have eaten at one table and have spoken over it words of the Law, it is as if they had eaten at the table of God.'

The structure of, and verbal connections within, Matthew 18: 15–22 open up an impressionistic view of the world of inter-Christian relationships in Matthew's community. (i) The controlling section, verses 15–17, details the procedure for tackling dislocations. The underlying principle is that of Leviticus 19:17, 'You shall not hate your brother in your heart; you shall reprove your neighbour . . .', which happens to be adjacent to the great command in Leviticus 19:18 that 'you shall love your neighbour as yourself'. (ii) Provoked by the reference, a very formal reference, to 'the church' in verse 17, Matthew introduces the 'binding and loosing' saying in verse 18, a MattR modification of the 'binding and loosing' saying which was attached to the only other reference to the church in 16:18. The conclusion of the abortive process of reconciliation had not involved formal exclusion in verse 17 – the verbs are singular, and the attitudes are those of the individual Christian person – but verse 18 makes it do so. (iii) Provoked by the reference to the 'two or three' in verse 16, Matthew attaches the saying about the two effectively praying persons, which has a very explicit logical basis. Their unanimous and effective prayer is grounded in the listening presence of the risen one. (iv) Provoked by the reference to the sinning of the non-gender-specific 'brother' in verse 15, Matthew attaches the requirement that sins, even those committed by obdurate Christians who will not be reconciled and have no thought of repentance – such sins are to be forgiven. Immensely difficult though any theological reflection on that will be, there is a simple but stirring conviction around in the Matthean air: Christians get all out of sorts with one another, they can legitimately set up all kinds of disciplinary processes to cope with their conflicts, but those who claim the risen presence, share the baptismal name, and participate in the table of the Lord, are above all the forgiven and forgiving ones. Grace and grudges are incompatible among resurrection people.

Thus the community lives healthily and in a way which is true to itself when loving and undamaged relationships exist among its members. And the experience of the two or three is a microcosm of the experience of the whole: where there is a living out of the shared baptism into the name of Jesus, then the presence of the risen one is enjoyed in just the same way as a living out of commitment to the Law allowed two or three Jewish persons to experience in microcosm the presence of the divine glory within the whole community of Israel.

WHAT FUTURE FOR MATTHEW'S RESURRECTION PEOPLE?

> What word so explosive
> as that one Palestinian
> word with the endlessness of its fall-out?

R.S. Thomas' question would certainly express Matthew's thoughts. The decisive and transforming moment in human history had occurred with and in Jesus – 'that one explosive Palestinian word'. And no one in any place or at any time was outside the range of 'the endlessness of its fall-out'. For this to be so there were two preconditions – the resurrection of Jesus and the formation of a community of 'resurrection people'. That is just what had happened to him and also to them. They were a people called to participate through baptism in the risen person, whose name, the Son, expressed the transcendence of his status and his identification with Father and Spirit. They were dependent for their faith on a mission which ultimately stemmed from 'the eleven', who in turn were commissioned by that risen Son. The time-space-transcending presence of the risen one had been promised as power and protection to the original missionaries, the success of whose work was embodied humanly in the Matthean community. There in a spirit of peace and mercy, forgiveness and love, his presence could continue to be experienced and cherished. The theory was that those who experienced it and cherished it would come from 'all the nations', and doubtless to some degree they did. But it is hard to believe there were many of gentile origin among them. And this is where we come upon what made Matthean Christianity problematic, its all-inclusive vision notwithstanding.

The ghost of Paul . . . here he is again! For Matthew universalism implied dutiful and determined mission, whose goal was faith-ful recognition of the resurrected Lord by persons of any and every ethnic background. To that extent the minds of Matthew and Paul were two minds with but a single thought. But when the implications of the lordship of Jesus came to be drawn out, their visions were in sharp contrast. Here one's dream would be the other's nightmare. For Matthew the pre-Easter Jesus, working within a traditional framework, had in no way threatened the tenets of Judaism or revised the understanding of the people of God. As a matter of fact, he was probably right in his view of the historical Jesus! But where he may or may not have been right was in his insistence that with the risen Jesus nothing had changed. And, however much his Gospel invested in a mission to non-Jews, it leaves behind a serious question about how far it could possibly have succeeded in drawing in any but Jews. To demand, in the name of a tradition that stretched back to the Jerusalem church, that gentiles who became Christians must become Jews if they were to be full members of the people of God, and to claim that as the intrinsic meaning of the resurrection, was almost certainly a strategy of dogged faithfulness leading to disastrous failure.

And so we come back to Paul. One of the leading Matthean specialists of our time has said that 'Matthew and Paul, had they known one another, would certainly not have struck up a strong friendship.' It would be hard to argue with that! And then he adds, 'for Paul, Judaism and Christianity are two fundamentally opposing principles', while Matthew 'sees no rupture between Judaism and Christianity' (Luz 1995: 148). And if that is right, which should we choose, Matthew or Paul? Unless we are going to endorse circumcision, food laws and sabbath as the boundary lines around the people of God – or alternatively compromise on the equality of the status of all persons of faith – the choice has been made for us. Matthew's interpretation of the life of the resurrection people is in many respects fine, but it is also flawed. Would he and the Antiochene community not have been better to stay with a corporate risen Christ in whom the polarities of human existence were overcome – 'no longer Jew or Greek, no

---

longer slave or free, no longer "male and female" ', but instead 'all one in Christ Jesus'?

A TALE OF TWO TRAVELLERS: THE
ANGELIC JESUS OF LUKE

INTRODUCTION

In his pungent and polemical preface to *Androcles and the Lion* George Bernard Shaw surveyed the pictures of Jesus painted by the four evangelists. No expert himself in Gospel criticism, Shaw nevertheless wrote with unrestrained self-confidence. Even if you disagree with 95 per cent of it, his survey is rather more than a good read. When it came to Luke's turn for review, this literary artist, as Shaw called him, was given perhaps the ultimate accolade. With special concentration on the infancy narratives, the tradition of Jesus' visit to Nazareth (4:16–30), and the revised version of the crucifixion story, Shaw declared, 'It is Luke's Jesus who has won our hearts.' Even if no more than 5 per cent of Shaw is right, that comment must be!

The Jesus of Luke is defined by colourful scenes and compelling sayings, by much power and many parables, by the atmosphere of faith in which his life begins and by the calm trustfulness with which it ends. And beyond the end...? Yes, the reader's imagination continues to be stirred by a combination of literary artistry and religious sensitivity – and never more so than in the tale of two, and then three, travellers en route to Emmaus. This story – truly described as 'a gem of literary art' (Fuller 1972: 104), and 'full of emotions subtly sketched'

(Johnson 1991: 398) – will be our special preoccupation as we observe the Lucan resurrection drama.

Before indulging that preoccupation, however, we should note that the high point in the drama is reached not in the disclosure to the travellers but in the subsequent commissioning of the witnesses. In Luke 24 the evangelist constructs a sort of triptych: three scenes involving events at the tomb in the morning (vv. 1–12), on the Emmaus road in the late afternoon (vv. 13–35), and in Jerusalem in the evening (vv. 36–53). The third of those scenes is itself another, a minor, triptych: the proving of Jesus' identity (vv. 36–43), the commissioning of the witnesses (vv. 44–9), and finally the ascension of Jesus (vv. 50–3). In one respect the three scenes in the major triptych are no different from one another: they each and all centre on the divine design which lays down suffering and death as the necessary route to resurrection and glory (vv. 6–7, 25–7, 44–6). Yet, quite unmistakably, there is development and progression as the drama moves from scene to scene and the plot rolls forward to its dénouement in the commissioning episode.

First, a group of named women appears at the beginning of the sequence, and they duly report what happens to them at Jesus' tomb. While the reader knows that their report is true and worthy of belief, LukeR ensures that the report is dismissed as rubbish by the recipients (v. 11). That dismissal is only partly retracted after Peter has personally checked the content of the tomb – grave clothes, yes, but anything else, no (v. 12) – so that the women's key claim to have seen 'a vision of angels who said that he was alive' (v. 24) remains the object of confused scepticism. That is still the position on the Emmaus road (vv. 22–4). But then the unexpected happens in Emmaus itself (v. 31) and, in parallel with that, in Jerusalem as well (v. 34): the disappeared one appears! So scene 1 is inconclusive: the reader waits for more, and more is indeed given in scene 2. By making scene 1 inconclusive Luke is able to stress with what difficulty and hesitation the apostles reached their own faith position.

Resurrection People

Second, if attention is switched from the women to Peter, the same sense of progression is gained. Peter moves from a first stage, bewilderment at the tomb (v. 12) and, as will be clarified shortly afterwards, no sight of Jesus (v. 24), to a second stage, the sight of Jesus which is the basis for the faith conviction of those associated with him (v. 34). But at that stage they have had no first-hand experience for themselves. Only in scene 3 does that happen.

Third, we shall see grounds – on which, more anon – for viewing the conversation about Jesus' identity (vv. 36–43) as an attempt to qualify and correct one aspect of the Emmaus road tradition. If that turns out to be correct, the evangelist meant to hurry the reader on from scene 2 to scene 3. And that done, the ground is prepared for the biggest of all the big moments, the moment when Jesus commissions witnesses for the world.

Fourth, the succession of statements about suffering and glory is so formulated as to make the final one particularly emphatic. (i) We move from no allusion at all to scripture, but a reminder of the teaching of the Galilean Jesus (vv. 6–8), to 'the prophets . . . Moses and all the prophets . . . all the scriptures' (vv. 25, 27), and then to the fullest and most formal description of scripture in the whole of the New Testament, 'everything written in the law of Moses, the prophets and the psalms', all of which is said to be the content of 'my words that I spoke to you while I was with you' (v. 44). In effect, the words to the women and the travellers are definitively pulled together in what Jesus says in scene 3. (ii) The third of the passion summaries (v. 46) draws upon and combines 'crucified, and on the third day rise again' from the first (v. 7) with 'the Messiah [must] suffer' from the second (v. 26). (iii) When the angelic quotation of the passion predictions of Jesus draws mainly on Luke 9:22 – of the three predictions the second (9:44) does not mention resurrection, which is the angel's main concern, and the third (18:31–3) is not set in Galilee – it passes over the list of Jewish groups responsible for action against Jesus and prefers to adopt and broaden the term used in 9:44: 'men' (ἄνθρωποι) become 'sinful men' (ἄνθρωποι ἁμαρτωλοί, cf. Mark 14:41, which Luke omitted in situ). While the Emmaus travellers show some interest in the opposing personnel, 'our chief priests and leaders' (v. 20), Jesus shows none, that is, not even as much interest as the angels had shown, and he maintains that position in the concluding explanation. Thus, the definitive kerygma, introduced to the duo and then formally confirmed in the presence of the apostles, concentrates with stark and undistracted simplicity on the divine, and not at all the human, action which is to be the content of future witness.

Having said all that, there is no doubt that within the developing sequence of this chapter, the narrative of the walk to Emmaus captures and excites our imagination as nothing else does. Luke is sensitive to this sort of thing: he must intend it so.

THE EMMAUS TRADITION: FIRST IMPRESSIONS

A veritable cluster of ideas specially favoured by Luke can be located in this story – the historical Jesus as 'a prophet mighty in deed and word before God and all the people', a death for which the hierarchy of the Jewish community in Jerusalem carry responsibility, Jerusalem as the focal point of God's dealings with his people, the suffering and glorified Messiah, and the definitive Christian community gathered around the eleven and most notably Peter. At the same time, however, there is an underlying scheme which is most definitely *not* favoured by Luke. Before unearthing it, we need to move briefly to the following story of the appearance to the disciple group.

The story of the appearance to the disciple group leans, as it were, on what has gone before. What happens, however, might as well be a first appearance – we note all the appropriate initial reactions of the recipients: 'They were startled and terrified, and thought they were seeing a ghost [πνεῦμα]' and Jesus' own question, 'Why are you frightened, and why do doubts arise in your hearts?' This question highlights those reactions. But he then proceeds to attempt to disabuse the assembled company of the idea that they were seeing a ghost, or (to put the matter positively) to demonstrate that the one they were seeing was indeed the one they had known (. . . ὅτι ἐγώ εἰμι αὐτός, v. 39). It is important that the attempt and the demonstration involve two stages: first, sight and touch, and second, observation of his eating food that they, the witnesses, have provided. The two stages are separated by the narrator's explanation that 'in their joy they were disbelieving and still wondering'. That the evangelist should stick a veneer of piety ('joy') on to their reaction should not divert the reader's attention from the two crucially revealing words 'disbelieving . . . wondering'. Exactly the same verb 'to disbelieve' was used by LukeR in 24:11 – and never elsewhere in his Gospel – to describe the scepticism with which the women's report from the tomb had been greeted, and exactly the same verb 'to wonder' was used in 24:12 to describe Peter's baffled and bewildered scepticism as he went back home from the tomb. In short, Jesus' first attempt to establish that he was not a ghost was a failure, and everything hung on the second attempt. Would eating succeed where sight and touch had not? Apparently, yes, but how and why?

The answer is to be found in the accumulating evidence that angelic beings were thought not to eat human food, and that those who ate human food were thereby proved not to be angels. Here is a sample of that evidence.

The ancient story in Genesis 18 of the visit of the mysterious trio to Abraham by the oaks of Mamre leaves no doubt that the offer of Abraham's hospitality, including the food, was accepted: 'he took the curds and milk and the calf that he had prepared, and set it before them; and he stood by them *while they ate*' (Genesis 18:8). Many years later, Philo exercised editorial muscle to revise the account. According to him, the three angels 'did not shrink from halting and receiving hospitality from men', and they would not have given the impression of feasting except as a sign of their sharing with their host the service of 'their master . . . the primal God'. Yet the giving of an impression was precisely what it was: 'though they neither ate nor drank they gave the appearance (παρέχειν φαντασίαν) of both eating and drinking' – and this from beings who 'though incorporeal . . . assumed human form (ἀσωμάτους ὄντας εἰς ἰδέαν ἀνθρώπων μεμορφῶσθαι)' (Philo, *On Abraham* 115–8). A few years later still, Josephus responded to the unequivocal statement of the Genesis text by producing the so-called 'docetic paraphrase': the visitors are again described explicitly as 'three angels' (τρεῖς ἄγγελοι), and as for their receipt of hospitality, 'they gave him to believe that they did eat (οἱ δὲ δόξαν αὐτῷ παρέσχον ἐσθιόντων)' (*Antiquities* 1:196–7).

The second piece of evidence also appears in a story involving Abraham, this time in the *Testament of Abraham*, a text belonging to the same period of time as Luke, or perhaps a little later. In it the archangel Michael visits Abraham in advance of his reception into the presence of God, and an elaborate ruse has to be devised so that the hospitality offered by Abraham may be accepted – and yet not accepted! The reason for the ruse is set out in Michael's own reminder to God, 'Lord, all the heavenly spirits are incorporeal, and they neither eat nor drink' (4:9, recension A: cf. Sanders 1983: 884).

The third piece of evidence is contained in a much earlier text, the apocryphal book of Tobit. It is the climax of the long story of Tobiah's journey in the company of the unrecognised angel (Tobit 5–12) and the enigmatic dog (6:2)! The reader is told what Tobiah does not know: the volunteer travelling companion, in appearance a 'young man' (νεανίσκος), is in fact the angel Raphael. Tobiah 'did not perceive that he was an angel of God' (5:4–5), and misleading information about the family background of the 'young man' made perception more rather than less difficult (cf. 5:6, 13). Naturally, provision for the journey was put together in advance (5:17), and Tobiah certainly enjoyed food in the course of his travels (6:6). Both he and the angel were offered and, after negotiation, accepted generous and extended hospitality from Raguel their host (7:9–14; 8:20; 10:7). More was to follow in the form of a second wedding reception after the return of Tobiah and his brand new wife in the company of the angel – not forgetting the dog (11:4)! – to the parental home (11:16–18). But it turned out that there was one non-participant in all the eating and drinking. In private, with the mission safely accomplished, the angel explained himself: 'I am Raphael, one of the seven angels who stand ready and enter before the glory of the Lord . . . Although you were watching me, I really did not eat or drink anything – but what you saw was a vision (ὅρασις)' (12:15, 19).

In the face of this evidence it is clear that Jesus' second attempt to dispel scepticism and establish his identity is, in very specific terms, an attempt to impose one particular understanding of risen-ness, and to banish with all possible firmness an alternative understanding. The risen Jesus could be, but in Luke's view should not be, understood as angelic. But, we may ask, how did the idea of the risen Jesus as angelic 'come on screen' in the first place? Answer: through the pre-Lucan version of the story of the walk to Emmaus!

At this point the problem arises as to whether a pre-Lucan version of that tradition ever existed, and if so how we may gain access to it. A minutely detailed word-statistical investigation of Luke 24:13–35 serves to demonstrate that Luke's own editorial fingerprints are everywhere to be seen: there is scarcely a word, or a turn of phrase, that is not typical of his style (Wanke 1973). Moreover, the theology of the story is on point after point his own theology (Dillon 1978). Luke is keen on the characterisation of the historical Jesus as 'a prophet mighty in deed and word before God and all the people'; he redacted the story of the proceedings against Jesus in such a way as to maximise the responsibility of 'our chief priests and leaders'; he worked hard with the thought that Jesus was 'the one to redeem Israel'; he showed some determination in following a Jerusalem-centred scheme and to that end remoulded anything which promoted any alternative scheme; he doubtless relished 'what had happened on the road', that is, the three-person seminar on the scriptural foundations of Jesus-focused belief in a suffering and glorified Messiah. On those grounds some declare the Emmaus story a Lucan creation! Such an inference would, however, be unjustified, for two reasons. (i) A study of Luke/Mark parallel passages throughout the Gospel shows how thoroughly Luke sometimes rewrites the material he draws from his sources: examples like the feeding of the crowds (9:10–17) or, nearer to hand, the visit of the women to the tomb (24:1–11), show substantial Lucan rewriting when it is clear that a source, in these cases Mark, is being used. (ii) Seams and competing climaxes are detectable within the present version of the story, and these point to the likely adjustment for Lucan purposes of a pre-Lucan story. While we can neither deny the thoroughness of the theologically motivated editing which has taken place, nor hope to isolate the *ipsissima verba* of the earlier story, we can at least discern its silhouette.

There are two particular components of the story which have aroused suspicion of being later additions to an earlier tradition.

The first is the second half of the two travellers' summary of recent events (vv. 21b–4). Without it, the first half (vv. 19b–21a) is formally complete: it describes what has happened – the career and the crucifixion of Jesus – and then, leaving what has happened behind, adds a personal evaluation in the form of a statement of disappointed hope. We would not ordinarily have expected anything else to follow. What does in fact follow recalls the timenote of verse 1, the women's encounter with the angels in verses 1–11, and then the perplexed and perplexing visit of Peter shortly afterwards in verse 12. The effect is that this second Lucan narrative is attached firmly to what precedes it. But such attachments would not be fitting in a self-contained and independent tradition, which the Emmaus tradition shows every

sign of being. Moreover, when it is said of Peter, using a generalising plural, that 'they did not see [Jesus]' there is a certain
anticipation of later events, for 'seeing Jesus' is not what Peter's
visit to the tomb is all about, but it certainly is what the climax
of the present version of the Emmaus story is about: 'The Lord
has risen indeed, and he has appeared to Simon!' (v. 34).

The second suspect component of the story is that announcement of the appearance to Simon. Not only does it interrupt
and, in doing so, depreciate the Emmaus travellers' exuberant
report of what has happened to them, taking the wind out of
their sails (Fuller 1972: 112) by making sure that the disciples in
Jerusalem make a report to them before receiving one from them –
it would be a smoother and more continuous narrative which
moved directly from verse 33 to verse 35. More seriously, it
competes with and overshadows the moment of mealtime recognition of Jesus with which the main story reaches its climax: 'he
took bread, blessed and broke it . . . their eyes were opened and
they recognised him; and he vanished from their sight . . . they
told what had happened on the road, and how he had been
made known to them in the breaking of bread' (vv. 30, 31, 35).

So there are in verses 21b–4, 34 two suspect elements which
would leave a formally more satisfactory narrative if they were
removed. But the case for a pre-Lucan tradition is not thereby
proved. We are being edged in that direction, but have not yet
arrived. It is the underlying scheme, which Luke sets out to
correct, which above all suggests such a conclusion.

My proposal is that the tradition of Jesus' walk to Emmaus
with Cleopas and another unnamed person finds a remarkably
clear analogy and parallel in the story of the journey of the
unrecognised angel Raphael with Tobiah in the book of Tobit.
As such, it is revealed as a very special case of the angelic
appearance pattern, and one to be distinguished from two other
variations on the epiphany theme: first, those in which a
heavenly person appears and then disappears in a very specific
location (thus, appearances to the patriarchs in Genesis 17:1–22

and 35:9–14, or to Gideon in Judges 6:11–24, or to the parents of the soon to be born Samson in Judges 13), and second, those in which a heavenly person or persons appear as journeying traveller/s to a designated and special person, but still in one specific location (thus, the appearance at Abraham's encampment of the three transcendent persons in the guise of travellers in Genesis 18, followed by the further appearance of two of the three in Sodom, that sink of moral perversion in which Lot allegedly 'tormented his righteous soul'). This second variation on the epiphany theme, which inspires the cautionary advice not to 'neglect to show hospitality to strangers, for by doing that some have entertained angels without knowing it' (Hebrews 13:2), comes close to the Tobit/Luke examples, most notably in the feature of the hidden identity of the angelic travellers, but it is not the same as a story of a journey shared by a human person (or persons) and an angel.

The salient and shared features of the two stories are as follows:

1. *A problem.* (a) Tobit, an exile in Nineveh, has suffered for four years from incurable blindness (Tobit 2:9–10); in Ecbatana in Media, Sarah, daughter of Raguel, suffers distress and the contempt of a household servant for having lost seven husbands to the wicked demon Asmodeus before any of the marriages could be consummated (Tobit 3:7–9). The seriousness of their respective problems is underlined by both Tobit's and Sarah's praying for death (Tobit 3:2–6, 10–15), and in Tobit's case by his making a farewell speech (Tobit 4:3–19). (b) The Emmaus travellers, for their part, are oppressed by the recollection of recent events in Jerusalem, and distraught with sadness (Luke 24:14–15).

2. *An angelic mission to solve the problem.* (a) Raphael is sent on a dual mission to bring sight to Tobit and freedom to Sarah. In achieving both purposes the human agent is Tobit's son, Tobiah, who acquires healing ointment for Tobit and successfully consummates a marriage with Sarah (Tobit 3:17).

(b) It is precisely in the circumstance of the Emmaus travellers' gloom and disappointment that Jesus joins them (Luke 24:15).

3. *A journey designed to achieve a human purpose.* (a) Tobiah is sent by Tobit to regain possession of money previously entrusted to his cousin Gabael who lives in Rages, also in Media (Tobit 1:14; 4:1, 20; 5:1–3). (b) The Emmaus travellers are simply going home (Luke 24:13, 28), but going home is symbolic of leaving Jerusalem, the focus of hopes of redemption.

4. *The start-point and end-point of the return journey are precisely defined.* (a) It stretches from Nineveh to Rages via Ecbatana, and back again. (b) The Emmaus travellers walk from Jerusalem to Emmaus and back again (Luke 24:13, 33).

5. *A companion is needed, and becomes available, for the journey.* (a) Tobiah's need of a travelling partner who knows the way is immediately satisfied by his encounter with Raphael (Tobit 5:4). (b) The Emmaus travellers do not need a companion for the purpose of safety or success, but their need of understanding is clear enough (Luke 24:25): in one sense they know, and suppose that their companion is ignorant, but in fact *he* knows and *they* are ignorant (Luke 24:18, 25). Without their fellow-traveller, things would have stayed that way.

6. *The true identity of the volunteer travelling companion is withheld but at the same time disclosed to the reader.* (a) Tobiah encounters Raphael but does 'not perceive that he [is] an angel of God' (Tobit 5:4), and the hiddenness of Raphael's identity and origin is underscored by a protracted and potentially irritating debate about his family and tribal antecedents (Tobit 5:5, 11–14). The reader has, however, been told in advance (Tobit 3:17), and now possesses the key to the understanding of all that follows. When Tobit affirms that an angel will make the journey safe and successful, using a notion present already in the comparable story of the mission of Abraham's

servant to find a wife for Isaac (Genesis 24:7, 40, cf. Moore 1996: 8–9, 188), he speaks better than he knows (Tobit 5:17, 22). (b) On the Emmaus road, 'their eyes were kept from recognising him' (Luke 24:16).

7. *The travelling companion possesses vital information about the solution to the problem, but even in affirming it authoritatively is not recognised.* (a) In response to Tobit's pathetic and self-pitying summary of his health problem, Raphael says, 'Take courage; the time is near for God to heal you; take courage' (Tobit 5:10). A little later Tobiah's compliance with the marriage-making strategy which will bring safety to Sarah, is achieved by instructions so insightful and so authoritative that the reader must feel some surprise that the identity of the instructor is not realised (Tobit 6:16–18). (b) In similar vein, the authoritative interpretation of scripture by Jesus is pursued, but still the Emmaus travellers do not recognise him (Luke 24:27).

8. *The companion provides the solution to the problem which dominates the journey.* (a) The fish, caught from the Tigris river by Tobiah, provides heart and liver which will be burnt to banish the oppressing demon, and gall which will provide healing ointment for Tobit's sight problem (Tobit 6:3–9). (b) For the Emmaus travellers, the same features as related to item 7 apply here.

9. *The solution to the problem is found within the Mosaic writings.* (a) Raphael engineers the marriage between Sarah and Tobiah with a particularly emphatic appeal to the Levirate marriage regulations (Tobit 6:11–13; cf. Deuteronomy 25:5–10). (b) It was in general the prophets who provided the biblical resources for the seminar on the Emmaus road (Luke 24:25), but this is then qualified as a survey of 'Moses and all the prophets', doubtless because the expectation of the Mosaic prophet of Deuteronomy 18:15 is being invoked (Luke 24:27).

10. *Each stage of the journey ends with the provision of hospitality*

and a celebratory meal. (a) Raguel lays on a celebratory meal
when the two travellers reach Ecbatana (Tobit 7:9), a
meal whose status is raised to a high plane by becoming
a marriage feast (Tobit 7:11–14; 8:1). A further feast celebrated the successful consummation of the marriage between
Tobiah and Sarah (Tobit 8:19–20), and on this occasion
Gabael was brought from Rages by Raphael to share in it
(Tobit 9). And on the return of the two travellers – not
forgetting the dog (Tobit 11:4)! – further celebratory feasting
in Nineveh stretched over no fewer than seven days (Tobit
11:18). (b) The climax of the journey to Emmaus is the
pressing offer of hospitality, so pressing that it has to overcome the impression that Jesus would travel further on
beyond them (Luke 24:28–9, cf. Genesis 18:3; Mark 6:48).

11. *An outpouring of emotion greets the solution of the problem.* (a)
The return of Tobit's sight, like the release of Sarah from
the demon, produces an outpouring of joy (Tobit 11:11–15).
(b) The Emmaus travellers subsequently recalled the burning
of their hearts which the teaching of Jesus had produced
(Luke 24:32).

12. *The identity of the fellow-traveller is disclosed.* (a) The two
leading characters in the narrative receive a private disclosure
of the truth of Raphael's identity (Tobit 12:6–15). (b) In
Emmaus the guest takes the role of the host, gives the two
travellers the bread he has blessed and broken – and then
the penny of recognition drops (Luke 24:30–1).

13. *The permanent influence of the experience is safeguarded.* (a)
Raphael orders a permanent record to be made of everything
that has happened (Tobit 12:20). (b) In Luke 24:13–35 this
is only implicit, but (i) the survival of the story itself and
(ii) its climax in the mealtime experience, which links the
story to the ongoing Christian experience of fellowship
meals, achieves the same outcome.

14. *The angel ascends to the presence of God and becomes invisible.*
(a) 'I am ascending to him who sent me,' said the angel, and

Tobit and Tobiah for their part could see him no more (Tobit 12:20–1). (b) Before the very eyes of the Emmaus travellers 'he vanished from their sight' (Luke 24:31).

15. *The reaction of the most affected persons is described.* (a) Tobit and Tobiah react in two stages: first, in the correct epiphanic manner to the disclosure, 'the two of them were shaken; they fell face down, for they were afraid' (Tobit 12:16), and then second, with ecstatic acclamation of God following the angel's disappearance: 'blessing God and singing his praises, they acknowledged God for these marvellous deeds of his, when an angel of God had appeared to them' (Tobit 12:22). (b) As for the Emmaus travellers, their reaction to the total experience brought them by Jesus, and their ready return to Jerusalem, undeterred by the lateness of the hour (Luke 24:29), tells its own tale.

This list of the defining features shared by the two stories suggests that beneath the surface of Luke 24:13–35 there is a pre-Lucan tradition which Luke manipulated, partly by interfering with its content and partly by setting it in a longer narrative context, in order to impose rather different ideas upon it. This conclusion needs to be developed in respect of some of the details of the story, a number of which can perhaps in spite of everything be reclaimed for the pre-Lucan stage of the tradition's history.

First, the most important inference from the schematic parallelism between the Raphael and the Jesus stories is that the risenness of Jesus is interpreted in angelic terms by Luke 24:13–35. When Jesus appears he comes, as it were, from the heavenly world where he has achieved 'glory' (Luke 24:26), and his present physicality has a docetic quality. That is not an interpretation with which Luke is the slightest bit happy. He resists it vigorously, as we have seen, in the following episode.

Second, the non-recognition of Jesus may pick up on earlier precedents (e.g. Numbers 22:22–35; 2 Kings 6:17; 3 Maccabees

5:27–8, cf. Wanke 1973: 36–7) or have, as one commentator after another observes, an affinity with the LukeR veiling of disciples' understanding of the second and third passion predictions (Luke 9:45; 18:34 diff. Mark 9:32; 10:32), but the schematic parallel – cf. item 6 above – demonstrates that this feature is of the very *esse* of the story. Its original place in the tradition is therefore reinforced. The agency of Satan is not involved (thus, Nolland 1993: 1201); nor are the travellers guilty of 'culpable failure' (thus, Tannehill 1996: 352). Without non-recognition at the start there could be no moment of recognition at the end.

Third, the destination of the two travellers is Emmaus, a sufficiently obscure place to frustrate the best efforts of commentators to locate it, and a detail which encourages many of them to allow it as evidence of a source (Wanke 1973: 37–42). But if the travelling is to Emmaus, what is more likely than that the tradition should specify the place where it started – cf. item 4 above – and therefore pinpoint Jerusalem? Of course, we know about Luke's preoccupation with Jerusalem (Wanke 1973: 48), but (i) not all Lucan journeys that begin in Jerusalem can on that account be deprived of that detail, cf. the journey to Jericho from Jerusalem in the parable of the good Samaritan (Luke 10:30); (ii) the reference to Jerusalem–Emmaus serves to distance the moment of recognition of Jesus from the capital city, something not exactly in line with Luke's instincts.

Fourth, if 'Emmaus' encourages many to envisage a pre-Lucan source, so too does 'Cleopas'. An otherwise unknown disciple of Jesus, and not one of the ecclesiastical heavyweights whose position was to be justified by a vision of the risen Jesus, his presence in the story is so markedly out of kilter with the imposed presence of Peter (Luke 24:34) that we cannot safely assign his presence to Lucan creativity.

Fifth, the food motif emerges as an original and integral part of the story, and by no means a cause of 'overload' or tension with the 'entertaining angels unawares' scheme in what went before (thus, Nolland 1993: 1199) – cf. items 10, 13 above. At the same time, it is handled in a strikingly different way in the Emmaus tradition from the following episode. In the latter Jesus is a guest throughout, and shares the food; in the former, Jesus is initially a guest but speedily changes role to that of host, presiding at a meal which his companions share but which he does not.

This inference, which has a bearing on whether the meal at Emmaus is intended to be eucharistic, needs to be justified. (i) When the Emmaus duo reported that 'he had been made known to them in the breaking of bread', they were describing the context in which – 'in' (ἐν) – and not the evidence upon which that knowledge was based. For the latter interpretation the natural preposition would have been 'from' (ἐκ), as in 'each tree is known by/from [ἐκ] its fruits' (Luke 6:44). Therefore recognition was brought about, not by the sharing of a whole meal (thus, Robinson 1984: 484) but instantaneously, at the moment when the process of distributing the bread was completed: 'he took bread, blessed and broke it, and was giving it [ἐπεδίδου] to them'. Recognition was not grounded in reminiscence, either, for those who had witnessed Jesus performing the same actions two days earlier were the apostles only (Luke 22:14–20a) and not a larger group including Cleopas and his companion. (ii) While the sequence of taking bread, blessing, breaking and distributing it could easily stimulate eucharistic thoughts in the minds of readers, especially since the developing tradition of the Christian community used just such a scheme (cf. Mark 14:22/Luke 22:19a), it is almost certainly necessary to distinguish between a eucharistic way of describing an event and a eucharistic event itself in the strict sense of a sacramental rite. The same potentially eucharistic sequence of taking, blessing, breaking and giving occurs in the tradition of the miracle of the loaves and fish (Luke 9:16), but, in spite of a powerful tendency among commentators, the event described has features which prevent its being a eucharistic or sacramental rite: first, its timing in advance of the inauguration of the rite on the last evening of Jesus' life; second, fish as part of the bread-and-fish combination

(Luke 9:13, 16) representing the basic Palestinian diet (cf. Matthew 7:9–10), and not the Passover/eucharistic bread-and-wine combination; third, the crowd of five thousand men (Luke 9:14); fourth, the concern to emphasise the huge amount of food left over (Luke 9:17); and fifth, the evident authorial intention to develop a 'Jesus is greater than Elisha' pattern (cf. 2 Kings 4:42–4). (iii) If we were to ask whether the bread which Jesus proceeded to give to the Emmaus duo had just been interpreted by means of the formula, 'This is my body' (Luke 22:19a), without which we can scarcely equate the meal with a eucharist, we would, I believe, have to say that such would be almost unimaginable: the moment of recognition is not brought on by such a self-referring word. Therefore the event may be described in a eucharistic way, but it was not a eucharist. (iv) Luke himself probably provides confirmation of this conclusion by setting up a bread-and-fish sequence in the two encounters between Jesus and the travellers and then the Jerusalem group, cf. Luke 24:30, 42. The two together recall the feeding of the five thousand, and neither that feeding nor the meal of fish are eucharists. In the latter, Jesus is from start to finish a guest, requesting fish from them that *he* might eat in *their* presence – a clear pointer to their being hosts at a meal which he shares, for all that *his* initial eating is the feature of greatest interest. When he asks whether they have any food available, the implication is that a meal is not already in progress, but his eating 'in their presence' suggests a shared meal involving him and them (cf. 2 Samuel 11:13; 1 Kings 1:25; Luke 13:26: cf. Tannehill 1996: 360) – both ordinary and extraordinary, but not eucharistic. The same conclusion can be drawn about the meal in Emmaus (Robinson 1984: 484–94, though with heavy recourse to Acts; Green 1997: 843).

Sixth, the reaction of the two travellers, and their return to Jerusalem, appear all the more naturally at home in the story in view of the schematic parallels – cf. items 4, 15 above. From a form-critical perspective, it is perfect that a report of these amazing happenings should be made to someone.

In terms of its overall scheme and structure, then, the pre-Lucan tradition of the walk to Emmaus corresponded roughly to what is left after verses 21b–4, 34 have been excised. The narrative described the return home by Cleopas and another – quite possibly, though not demonstrably, his wife in view of only Cleopas' name being provided, and their sharing the same home. Burdened by the problem of disappointed hope, following the apparent failure of the mission to Israel of the prophet Jesus, their problem is resolved by the intervention of a stranger, whose identity is unknown to them but known to the privileged reader/hearer – none other than Jesus himself! Hospitality having been offered persuasively and accepted at the end of the homeward journey, it is immediately transcended by a climactic reversal: the guest becomes the host, and the hosts become the guests. At the moment of reception – not a moment earlier, not a moment later – there arrives the moment of recognition. And having been recognised, the angelic Jesus, for his part, does what angels ultimately always do: he disappears. And the Emmaus duo, for their part, cannot but reflect and report on a life-transforming experience which rescues, renews and revitalises their hope of Israel's redemption. The story in its essence gives them, that duo of Cleopas and his partner, a role which, in the light of later developments, is a refreshingly passive one. They are not commissioned to *do* anything of note, and they are not expected to *be* anyone of note: they and their story do not belong to the setting in which appearances of the risen Jesus are exploited for the purpose of personal ecclesiastical validation. That secondary purpose was what Luke tried – and he was not the first to follow such a line of thought – to impose.

We have seen how scene 2 in Luke 24 is overtaken, as it were, by scene 3 – but we must not forget how scene 2 took off from scene 1: the literary picture of some women who encountered scepticism, and some men, who were the sceptics. The experience and evidence of the women are plainly valued highly by the evangelist.

First, he, like Mark, mentions the Galilean provenance of the witnessing women (23:49, 55), but the significance of this only emerges when the angelic instruction to go to Galilee (Mark 16:7) is changed to a reminder of what Jesus had previously said in Galilee (24:6). In fact the specifically Galilean sayings about the passion of the Son of Man (24:7) were directed to 'the disciples' (Luke 9:18, 43/Mark 8:27; 9:31) as distinct from the non-Galilean saying directed to 'the twelve' (Luke 18:31/ Mark 10:32). That the women should be reminded of what had been said on those earlier occasions serves to establish them as genuinely representative of the 'followers' and to explain why the Emmaus travellers can refer to them as 'some women *of our group* [γυναῖκές τινες ἐξ ἡμῶν]'.

Second, the coming to faith of the women is presented in a truly remarkable way. For them the remembrance of Jesus' prophetic predictions, fortified now by what they (do not) see at the tomb, is enough. They require no appearance by Jesus (Seim 1994: 154–5). This point needs to be emphasised in the face of the suggestion that their 'remembering' falls short of faith, being no more than bare recall of those passion predictions in Luke 9:44, 18:31–3 whose meaning was veiled in mystery as far as the disciples were concerned (so, Dillon 1978: 51–3). Against this interpretation, (i) the two angels ask for no more than a remembering as a resolution of the women's perplexity, and Luke states explicitly that remembering is what happened; (ii) remembering elsewhere in Luke is seen as a unified combination of recall and insightful recognition, cf. the cases of Dives (16:25) and Peter (22:61/Mark 14:72); (iii) the allusion is exclusively to the passion prediction in 9:22 – in Galilee, and mentioning resurrection – and that one of the trio of passion predictions does not have a cloak of mystery thrown around it; (iv) if the disciples rubbish the testimony of the women, and they do, that testimony must have conveyed the faith-realisation of resurrection fact. So, we must conclude, the women are not entangled in a web of confusion, misunderstanding or unbelief. On the contrary, they are models of insight and understanding.

Third, Luke imposes a certain formality by repeating the fact that they reported (vv. 9, 10); by reminding the reader of the official position of those to whom the evidence was conveyed ('the eleven . . . the apostles', an echo of their official appointment as twelve apostles in 6:13 diff. Mark 3:14); and by saving the list of the women's names until that precise point, instead of taking his cue from Mark's threefold use and positioning of such lists. Moreover, in respect of the naming of the women it is important to note one small detail, namely the evangelist's precision. That precision, and therefore the store he sets on the role of the women, is made clear to (i) the continuous reader of Luke, who is aware of the change from 'Mary called Magdalene . . . and Joanna, the wife of Herod's steward Chuza, and Susanna' (8:2–3) to 'Mary Magdalene, Joanna, and Mary the mother of James' (24:10) among the Galilean female followers of Jesus (cf. 23:49, 55), and (ii) the reader with an eye for LukeR, who is aware of the change from 'Mary Magdalene, and Mary the mother of James, and Salome' (Mark 16:1).

Fourth, the women's claims are, after much toing and froing, vindicated. Luke's dramatis personae have in the end to acknowledge that the women were right – not that any of them say so explicitly! Thus far, on the whole, the position of the women is presented appreciatively.

There are, however, some subdued undercurrents, detectable

Resurrection People

in LukeR adjustments, which have the effect of subtly diminishing the standing of the women.

First, when Luke introduced in 23:49, 55 the female Galilean followers who watched the crucifixion and the burial (23:49, 55), he inserted a group of 'all Jesus' acquaintances [πάντες οἱ γνωστοὶ αὐτῷ]', who are distinguished from the women, mentioned in advance of them, and turn out to be the persons with whom the women followed (αἱ συνακολουθοῦσαι αὐτῷ) – in other words, the women followed along with the men, and not the other way round. The impression can hardly be missed: if all the followers of Jesus are equal, some (the men) are more equal than others.

This comes as no surprise to the perceptive reader of the Lucan text as a whole. The list of the women who visit the tomb – 'Mary Magdalene, and Joanna, and Mary the mother of James' – recalls the list of the women who formed a female penumbra around Jesus and the twelve during the Galilean mission – 'Mary Magdalene, . . . Joanna, the wife of Herod's steward Chuza, and Susanna' (8:1–3). Those women were defined primarily by their having benefited from healing. In the case of Mary Magdalene it was a release from total control by demonic forces, seven demons representing a dominance as complete as that of the seven invited in to repossess the previously exorcised person, whose 'last state will be worse than the first' (Luke 11:26). So Mary is an extreme case of the control by evil forces which Jesus' mission is designed to destroy, and she is therefore the most notable case of release in the whole Gospel – more notable than the demoniac in the synagogue, Peter's mother-in-law, and the other beneficiaries of Jesus' power during the inaugural day in Capernaum (4:31–44), and many another thereafter. As the most notable case of release, under the terms of the programme to 'proclaim release to the captives . . . and to let the oppressed go free' (4:18), Mary stands, as it were, on a pedestal as the most outstanding exhibit of all. Perhaps that is why she is placed first in both lists, the place of highest standing (Seim 1994: 33). But she, like her colleagues, and like Peter's mother-in-law (4:39), is freed and then committed to the traditional female role of service – and not just serving Jesus, but serving 'them', i.e. Jesus *and the twelve* (8:3, cf. 4:39/Mark 1:31: Seim 1994: 58–61). It happens that this trio of women, together with their associates, are not among the poor but have the resources out of which to provide the necessary support for those, i.e. Jesus and the twelve, who have voluntarily embraced poverty for the sake of the kingdom of God. When two of them reappear in the fresh trio of women who prepare spices and ointments for the last act of respect for the corpse of the dead Jesus, they are continuing to do what had become constant and habitual: 'they were serving (διηκόνουν) out of their resources'. But serving Jesus has already become inseparable from serving the twelve. By now, of course, the principle of mutual service as the true greatness has also been laid down for the twelve themselves, enhanced by being set in the final instructions of Jesus prior to the passion (22:24–7), and exemplified in Jesus himself. One could almost say that the women are thereby established as prototypes of the serving priority – almost, but not quite! For the paradigm for the twelve is Jesus, and Jesus alone, so in matters of social structure, within which women have an established and inferior position, Luke is a good straight-down-the-line conservative. Even within the Christian community, whose contours we can discern through the filter of Luke 24, the women give, but nothing is given to them. The eleven and their male colleagues stand first in honour and in function; the women stand where they had always stood, in supportive subordination. As has been pointedly observed, 'the new life becomes a variant of the old life', and 'there is no way to get round the fact that women are portrayed in Luke, sometimes *expressis verbis*, as serving and providing for men who benefit from their service' (Seim 1994: 71, 76). That means that in Lucan Christianity, even though the resurrection is so powerfully formative, the old patriarchal system and the tacit patriarchal assumptions are alive and well. They live on unaffected and unscathed.

Second, the double statement about the women's report introduces a conscious gender polarisation, with all the women standing over against all the men. Whereas 'the rest' in the sentence 'they told all this to the eleven and to all the rest [πᾶσιν τοῖς λοιποῖς]' could have been inclusive and gender-non-specific, it becomes clear from the second qualifying statement associating all the women (καὶ αἱ λοιπαὶ σὺν αὐταῖς) with the trio of Mary Magdalene, Joanna and Mary the mother of James that it is in fact gender-specific. Consequently, Luke wants to say that after the named trio have spoken to, and convinced, the other women, all the women in solidarity with one another, undertake the task of reporting, while all the men receive the report, and it is the men who proceed from an implicit position of superior authority to assess it. Of course, Luke's readers know that they assessed it wrongly, and that might be a reason to blame the men and praise the women. But that is not really Luke's strategy. For him, the men were harder to win over, and that fact gives steel to the faith to which they were eventually won. The people who really mattered got there in the end!

Third, the women fade from the narrative after giving their report. One can only harbour dark suspicions about that, because those to whom they report, and those to whom the Emmaus travellers report, are (in a line of literary continuity) those who receive the Lord's commission in scene 3. In view of the LukeR women-excluding reference to 'the eleven and all the rest' in verse 9, the commission emerges as the business of men only. A message, all-inclusive in ethnic terms, was to be delivered by messengers, defined non-inclusively in gender terms. If all we know about Luke suggests a broad theological sympathy with Paul, then we have to add that there were certain liberating convictions at the heart of the Pauline gospel to which, sadly, Luke's ears were deaf.

Fourth, the overall Lucan tendency to show appreciation of the role of women but at the same time to stay with the traditional male-dominated view of human and indeed ecclesiastical life is demonstrated by what may seem a surprising small – but how small? – detail. Throughout his Gospel Luke makes a habit of inserting the gender-specific word 'man' (ἀνήρ) in contexts where, even if it is strictly accurate, it is quite unnecessary. The list of such LukeR insertions is long and therefore reflective of a deliberate strategy: the lepers (5:12 diff. Mark 1:40; similarly 17:12) and the supporters of the paralytic (5:18 diff. Mark 2:3), the man with the withered hand (6:8 diff. Mark 3:3) and the demoniac Legion (8:27, 38 diff. Mark 5:2, 18), Jairus (8:41 diff. Mark 5:22), Moses and Elijah (9:30, 32 diff. Mark 9:4), and not a few others. Three particular cases might be singled out as specially significant: (i) the *men* who are invited to the great banquet, where women would not normally be present (Smith 1987: 623), and who decline in order to engage instead in characteristically male activities (14:24, cf. 14:18–20); (ii) the *men* of this generation who will be confronted and condemned in the judgement by the queen of the south (11:31 diff. Matthew 12:42; cf. 11:32/Matthew 12:41), and who can only be isolated as the recipients of a judgement which is in fact universal (cf. 17:34–5/Matthew 24:40–1) if they, the men, are tacitly assumed to determine the position of the women; and then above all (iii) Jesus himself – not just a prophet but 'a *man*, a prophet [ἀνὴρ προφήτης]' (24:19). Factually accurate, yes, but necessary? Not at all! There, at the heart of the Emmaus tradition, Luke's instinctive gender awareness appears for the last time but more heavily loaded than ever.

Resurrection People

The world of the Emmaus travellers is the world of Israel. Nothing and nobody causes readers of their story to pause and dwell on the existence of a wider world. The frame of reference is supplied by the capital city of Jerusalem, with all the immense salvation-historical resonance of that sacred place; the expectant longings of the travellers themselves are for the redemption of Israel; and the events which have jeopardised those longings have been initiated by 'the chief priests and *our* leaders'. They are the people who have handed Jesus over (παρέδωκαν). The hope of a better tomorrow for Israel has been undermined from within Israel. And having been undermined in such devastating style, what can be said of that hope from the standpoint of the resurrection? (i) Within the Emmaus tradition, has the centring of the divine programme on the necessary suffering and glorification of the Messiah – 'was it not necessary . . .?' – brought about the abandonment and replacement of the hope for Israel's redemption? Or is it merely a matter of the timing of something that will assuredly happen? And (ii) within the wider context in which the Emmaus tradition was set by Luke, has the suffering and resurrection of the Messiah, and the consequent proclamation of repentance and forgiveness 'to all nations', loosened the ties of the whole Jesus event to Israel?

When the two disconsolate travellers expose the hard core of their disappointment, 'We had hoped that he was the one who was about to redeem Israel [ὁ μέλλων λυτροῦσθαι τὸν Ἰσραήλ]', they speak directly to Jesus but indirectly and equally importantly to the reader. And the reader knows, as they do not, that such was the language of the Spirit-inspired and prophesying Zechariah, 'Blessed be the Lord God of Israel, for he has looked favourably on his people and redeemed them' (1:68). Not only so, the reader cannot but recollect from the same infancy narratives the part played by Anna, the inspired octogenarian widow, the female prophet matching the male prophet Zechariah, who acclaimed the child Jesus to 'all who were looking for the redemption of Jerusalem' (2:38). That same reader is being deliberately encouraged to recall and recognise the authority of all that was said and done in the world of the infancy narratives by several considerations.

First, apart from one solitary reference (21:28) there is nowhere else in the Gospel of Luke where the language of 'redemption' is heard apart from the infancy material (1:68; 2:38) and the Emmaus story (24:21).

Second, Zechariah and Anna are known by readers of the Gospel to be 'reliable witnesses', not persons whose views can be set aside as misconceived, for in both cases their speech is labelled prophetic and Spirit-inspired. That is, when they speak God speaks. Moreover, within the span of the whole Gospel they are as such rare phenomena – apart from them the only persons defined as prophets, or endowed with the divine Spirit, or both, are John the Baptist (1:15), Mary (1:35), Elizabeth (1:41, 47), Zechariah (1:67), Simeon (2:25–7), Anna (2:36) and preeminently Jesus (3:22; 4:1, 14, 18; 7:16, 39; 10:21) – that it is clear they are to be taken with maximum seriousness.

Third, by subtle means – here a hint, there a hint – the evangelist brings to mind in this his last chapter the mission of John the Baptist. Hint no. 1: The commission of the risen Jesus is a scripture-based proclamation of 'repentance with a view to the forgiveness of sins' in the name of the Messiah (24:47). Now the prophet Jesus frequently calls people to repent (cf. 5:32 diff. Mark 2:17; 10:13; 11:32; 15:7, 10), and the prophet Jesus unmistakably centres on forgiveness/release as his grand theme (cf. 4:18; 5:20–4; 7:47–9), but the stylised formula 'repentance with a view to the forgiveness of sins' has precedent only in the mission of the Baptist: 'He went into all the region around the Jordan, proclaiming a baptism of repentance with a view to the forgiveness of sins, as it is written in the book of the words of the prophet Isaiah . . .' (3:3–4). Hint no. 2: Almost the final sentence of the final speech of the risen Jesus to his designated agents is, 'And behold, I am sending the promise of my Father upon you' (24:49a), which is immediately clarified as the clothing with 'power from on high' (24:49b). While the triad of the Father, the Son and the implicit Spirit is a point of correspondence with the Matthean commissioning saying (Matthew 28:20), and doubtless therefore the legacy of earlier tradition, it needs to be set within the continuity of the total Lucan narrative. In this narrative the gift of the Spirit in response to prayer is introduced by LukeR (11:13 diff. Matthew 7:11) as a gift of the heavenly Father, a gift derived from his goodness, a gift far transcending the necessary food which an earthly father can be presumed to provide – would that this were so in the modern world! – and a gift about which Jesus authoritatively argues. But only in one place, and from the mouth of one speaker, is the experience of the Spirit brought about by the person who in the view of Luke (notwithstanding the likelihood that in Q that person was God) is Jesus: 'I baptize you with water; but one who is more powerful than I is coming . . . He will baptize you with the Holy Spirit and fire' (3:16). So the words in Luke 24:49 are words which belong to the risen Jesus, but the vocabulary as well as the uniquely defining idea belong to John. All this being so, the reader of the Emmaus story in its Lucan context is deliberately enticed back to where it all began when the story of Jesus absorbed the story of John.

The beginning of the story of John, which probably existed as a separate story carefully preserved among those devoted to his memory and convictions, can be uncovered by a 'textual dig' below the surface of Luke 1 (Vielhauer 1965). Once the lower level is discovered, not only can Luke's reasons for including such rich material concerning John be determined, but also the significance of the later and higher stratum of text, itself preoccupied with Jesus, can be understood.

As has so often been observed, the stories of John and Jesus run on parallel lines, that is, on lines so comparable that one story must almost certainly have been constructed in imitation of the other. And the story about John can hardly be the dependent and imitative one, since (i) it is quite untouched by Christian convictions except when a meeting between the two mothers-to-be (1:39–45, 56) causes the two stories to intersect, and (ii) it is out of line with at least two Lucan convictions. These two deviations are the use of the Elijah model for John (1:17), which Luke drops when he finds it in Mark (Mark 1:6, cf. 2 Kings 1:8; Mark 9:11–13), and then the idea of John as an Isaiah 40:3–type preparer for the Lord, who is 'the Lord their God' (1:15–17), rather than a preparer for the Lord, who is Jesus (3:4–6, 16; 7:27). So we are encouraged to dig below the surface of the Lucan text for pre-Lucan material about John. But how widely might such pre-Lucan material extend within Luke 1? The story of Gabriel's appearance to Zechariah, the subsequent pregnancy of Elizabeth, John's birth and naming, together with the ecstatic prophetic utterance of his father, which we know as the Benedictus – all that must have been included. But was that all? What about the song which we know as the Magnificat? If the text of Luke assigned that song to Mary it cannot have stemmed from the pre-Lucan material concerned with John, but . . . there are very strong reasons indeed for concluding that the song was assigned to Elizabeth! And if so, the pre-Lucan material would have consisted of a narrative looking forward to John's birth and culminating in a celebratory song by his mother (1:5–25, 46–55), and then a narrative following John's birth and culminating in a celebratory song by his father (1:57–79). What impressive and delightful coherence and symmetry such a source would have exhibited!

First, a minority of manuscripts of the introduction in Luke 1:46 read 'and Elizabeth said' in the face of the majority which read 'and Mary said'. Now a decision about the original text is never made by a majority/minority vote. The *lectio difficilior* principle has to operate here as elsewhere, and that principle favours the Elizabeth reading. Put another way, we can well imagine copyists changing 'and Elizabeth said' to 'and Mary said' for theological reasons, the same reasons as cause some still to cling tenaciously to the theory that the Magnificat is a song of the historical Mary: we can hardly imagine change in the opposite direction.

Second, immediately after the Magnificat has ended, the narrative continues, 'And Mary remained with her . . .' (1:56). Had Mary been the singer, the smooth flow of the narrative would have demanded, 'And she remained with Elizabeth . . .' Given the precise formulation of 1:56, the manuscript evidence for which is not in doubt, the song must have been Elizabeth's.

Third, the content of the Magnificat establishes several strong connections with the surrounding story of Elizabeth.

(i) Commenting on her pregnancy, Elizabeth declares, 'This is what the Lord has done for me in the days when he looked on me [ἐπεῖδεν] to remove my shame [ὄνειδος] among men' (1:25). A straight line leads from this declaration to 'he has looked on [ἐπέβλεψεν] the humiliation [ταπείνωσις] of his servant' (1:48). By contrast, a very crooked line indeed is needed to connect Mary's situation with ταπείνωσις. It is significant that on this issue a most distinguished conservative-critical commentator, evidently conscious of the pressure of Roman Catholic belief, found himself conceding that ταπείνωσις is 'a term more obviously appropriate to the OT barren woman than to the NT young virgin' (Brown 1993: 361). There is no exit route to be found by translating the term ταπείνωσις as 'lowliness' or 'humility', for the term stands for a condition from which release is desperately needed, so 'humiliation' it is, and 'humiliation' it must be. Equally, there is no exit route from the problem via a claim that she faces the humiliation of being a single mother, for that is not a 'humiliation' from which the Lord has released her: rather, it is one into which the Lord has brought her. Finally, there is no viable exit route from the problem of her ταπείνωσις via literary critical surgery, that is, by the excision of 1:48 as an unoriginal LukeR insertion into the text (so, Brown

1993: 356–60). The word ταπείνωσις stands alone in the first-person part of the Magnificat (vv. 47–50) as a definition of the problem which God has resolved: it can hardly be dispensed with. Moreover, everyone agrees that the Magnificat is so fashioned as to echo the song of Hannah in 1 Samuel 2:1–10, itself a joyful song celebrating deliverance from childlessness and the answer to the prayer that God 'may look on [ἐπιβλέψῃς] the humiliation [ταπείνωσις] of your servant' (1 Samuel 1:11). The naturalness and appropriateness of such verbal echoes can be no surprise to anyone who takes seriously the Hannah/Elizabeth parallelism, coupled with the manifest Hannah/Mary non-parallelism.

(ii) The structure of the Magnificat, as already indicated, falls into a first-person section (vv. 47–50) which shades into a third-person section (vv. 51–5). The key term used in each to describe what is being celebrated now, and then set in the long-term context of God's faithfulness, is the rare (in Luke) term 'mercy' (vv. 50, 54). Not only is that also the key term in the song of John's father, the Benedictus (vv. 72, 78), but the intervening narrative has the neighbours and relatives of Elizabeth (sic) hearing 'that the Lord had magnified his mercy to her, and they rejoiced with her' (v. 58). There is no biblical precedent that I have been able to discover for the use of the term 'mercy' in connection with a pregnancy and birth, so the choice of such a word here must be intended to echo and apply what was said just previously. Further, the shared joy recalls 'my spirit rejoices in God my Saviour' (v. 47) and also Gabriel's prediction to Zechariah: 'You will have joy [χαρά] and gladness, and many will rejoice [χαρήσονται] at his birth' (1:14) – in both cases the primary joy of the parent expanded to include the joy of others over a very special birth.

If the pre-Lucan tradition in Luke 1 covered the announce-ment of John's birth (vv. 5–25), the Magnificat (vv. 46–55), the actual birth and its sequel (vv. 57–66), and the Benedictus (vv. 67–79), our interest in it is focused on its treatment of Israel and the gentiles. The same interest can then be pursued with reference to the Jesus narrative which is initially interwoven with the John narrative (vv. 26–45) and then developed at length in the following chapter.

A more classical profile of Jewish piety than that of Zechariah and Elizabeth could scarcely be imagined: a priest and the daughter of a priest, both of them 'righteous before God, living blamelessly according to all the commandments and regulations of the Lord', but with the dark shadow of the shame of childlessness falling across the life of Elizabeth (vv. 7, 25). With the biological clock ticking mercilessly away as this couple head for old age (vv. 7, 18), there is effectively no prospect of that shadow's passing. Into that situation comes hope in the form of Gabriel, bringing the promise of a child who will, like Samuel, be a holiness-driven ascetic (cf. Numbers 6), and who will through a Spirit-driven mission start a spiritual revolution in Israel, the people of God. The programme outlined tersely by Gabriel receives amplification through the two songs of the parents, the Magnificat and the Benedictus. Those two songs combine in chiastic style: the focus shifts from the person (vv. 47–50) to the people (vv. 51–5), and then from the people (vv. 68–75) to the person (vv. 76–9). Both insist that the mercy which has been experienced – past tenses serving to express the certainty of what is to happen in the near future – is the content of the promise made sure by the Abrahamic covenant. This is redemption. This is salvation. This is forgiveness. This is holiness and peace. This is the paradoxical freedom from fear (of enemies) which is offered to those who do fear (God). This is spiritual renewal and social revolution. For inter-generational tension between parents and children will be relieved (v. 17; cf. Sirach 48:10), nothing less than a return to God and wise law-keeping by his people will be achieved, and so will that reversal of which Elizabeth is the paradigm as her humiliation (ταπείνωσις) and shame give way to honour and joyful acclamation (vv. 25, 48, 52). Spelt out in detail, it means the relief of poverty and hunger, with a matching negative prospect for the powerful, the proud and the prosperous. And who is the person whose agent John will be in this addressing of the plight of the people of God? Answer: 'the Lord God of Israel' (v. 68). Thus the parameters of divine action are set out with limpid clarity: that divine action is in and for Israel.

What then of the later layer of material superimposed by Luke? It demonstrates how congenial the evangelist found his source material. For him the Jesus-pattern could be grounded naturally and without tension upon the John-pattern. With regard to substance, themes central to the one could be adopted into the other: the context of scrupulous spiritual devotion in which the child's life is set from the very beginning (2:22–4, 39), the child's own dedication to the Lord (2:22–3), the programme of transformation of the people whose identity is defined patriarchally as 'the house of Jacob' (1:33), the bringing of salvation (2:30) and peace (2:14) to the chosen people. With regard to strategy, angelic proclamation and Spirit-inspired prophecy by a wonderfully faithful pair, a man and a woman, Simeon and Anna (2:25, 36), give divine authority to the plan. At the same time the superiority of Jesus over John could be affirmed: Elizabeth is made into a Christian who acknowledges 'my Lord' (1:43); the unborn John, indwelt by the Spirit from the womb of his mother (1:15), recognises with joyful excitement the status of the second baby (1:41, 44), a prenatal movement as meaningful as the struggle of the twins in the womb of Rebecca (Genesis 25:22–3); above all, Jesus is repeatedly defined as the special Davidide and therefore in royal terms 'the Son of God' (1:32–3, 35; 2:11), a king for Israel and a figure of note for the whole of humanity. For the purpose of our study of that theme of Israel and the gentiles it is important to note three things: (i) that Jesus is from the outset set in the context of universal human experience, 'salvation . . . prepared in the presence of all peoples'; (ii) that even when the universal range of his influence is affirmed, it is 'glory for your people Israel' that is seen as the supreme climax; (iii) that precisely when the theme of opposition is introduced, indeed division in and damage to the nation, the accent is placed in the position of hope, for it is not the rising and the falling but 'the falling and rising of many in Israel' that is in view (2:34). The end term is a rising, emphatically not a falling.

An implicit endorsement of all that John the Baptist stood for is conveyed, not simply by the incorporation within his infancy story of the infancy story of Jesus, but also by the way the whole life story of Jesus unfolds from beginning to end, pausing from time to time to renew the reader's acquaintance with key themes. Only in one respect, to which we shall come, is there a partial retreat from the Baptist's position.

The Magnificat moved from Elizabeth's experience of release from shame and humiliation to the matching revolution in the situation of the nation, whose plight is embodied in that of the poor and hungry. Those same poor and hungry came to be exemplified in, but not limited to, Jesus' disciples. Thus, the original version of the beatitudes affirmed the same revolution which the Magnificat had celebrated:

> 'Blessed are the poor, for theirs is the kingdom of God;
> blessed are the mourners, for they shall be comforted;
> blessed are the hungry, for they shall be filled.'

Under the influence of LukeR, these three beatitudes were reapplied to 'you' (that is, the disciples, cf. Luke 6:20a) rather than 'them', and reordered, so that hunger stood alongside poverty, with tears/laughter replacing mourning/comfort in the final saying in the trio. Thus was a bridge built, via the idea of laughter as a gesture of triumph over enemies (cf. Psalm 2:4), into the long beatitude on the Christian victims of Jewish persecution (Catchpole 1993a: 81–7). In this way, the Jesus of Luke kept those fires of hope burning which had been lit by Elizabeth in her joyful celebration of the removal of her (alleged) shame. The realisation of that hope was still something for the future.

Without any restriction to the disciples, and therefore pointing to a broad programme, the inaugural proclamation by the Lucan Jesus in the Nazareth synagogue is a blend of promise and warning. The warning is a critical reminder that according to two biblical precedents God has showed himself free in his liberating and healing interventions: just as need within Israel was bypassed by both Elijah and Elisha, so a repetition in Nazareth of those miracles already carried out in Capernaum cannot be taken for granted. The logic of the argument in Luke 4:23–7 is not 'first Israel, and second (after rejection in Israel) the gentiles', but 'gentiles and not Israel', and therefore 'Capernaum and not Nazareth' (Catchpole 1993b: 236–40). Yet the story of Jesus is a story of constant attention to the needs of the people of Israel, and even when he moves outside the confines of Israel he is persuaded to do so by the argument that a non-Israelite deserves his attention because he has done good things to a local community within Israel (Luke 7:3–5)! So the closest parallel for the logic of the argument put forward in Nazareth is to be found in the prophetic preaching of division and judgement by none other than John the Baptist: 'Bear fruits worthy of repentance. Do not begin to say to yourselves, "We have Abraham for our ancestor"; for I tell you, God is able from these stones to raise up children to Abraham' (Luke 3:8/Matthew 3:8–9). So much for the warning. The promise, on the other hand, is set out in a carefully constructed literary pastiche of texts from Isaiah, a promise that leaves not the faintest scintilla of doubt that the essence of the mission of Jesus is a gospel of liberation for Israel, a nation whose poor are all too easily marginalised by compatriots but who are never less than the priority concern of Israel's God. Prophetically endowed with the anointing of the Lord's Spirit, Jesus defines his role in such a way as to prove that the Emmaus disciples made no error in their disconsolate reflection that 'we hoped that he was the one who was . . . to redeem Israel'. His own carefully structured mission statement had implied just that:

'to evangelise the poor he has *sent* me;

to *preach* release to the captives and recovery of sight to the blind;

to *send* release to the oppressed;

to *preach* the year of the Lord's favour.'

In this keynote speech the evangelist signals the commitment of Jesus to Israel, a community approached by way of its poor and sick members, and at the same time a community placed under critical scrutiny, a community unwise to take its God for granted.

The question has now to be faced: Has the course of Jesus' mission, and particularly his rejection by some Jewish personnel, brought about a revision of this hope of liberation through a programme of national renewal? Has the drama of Israel turned itself into a tragedy, the tragedy of the awakening and subsequent dashing of hope of an earthly messianic kingdom because of Jerusalem's rejection of its messianic king (Tannehill 1986: 8, 26)? In the light of some sophisticated redactional work by Luke on traditions concerned with the ending of the long march to Jerusalem by Jesus and his companions, the answer would seem to be 'no'. And in that case, in answer to the related question of whether the Emmaus disciples were wrong to look to Jesus for the redemption of Israel, we shall again be able to say 'no'. They were correct – except in one particular, their short-termism: 'We had hoped that he was the one who *was about to* redeem Israel.'

In the Marcan narrative of Jesus' approach to Jerusalem, the third passion prediction and the discussion of greatness (Mark 10:32–4, 35–45) are followed by the healing of Bartimaeus (Mark 10:46–52), the entry into Jerusalem (Mark 11:1–11) and the two-in-one 'sandwich structure' involving the cursing of the fig tree and the action in the Temple (Mark 11:12–25). More significant than what Luke moves or removes – the discussion of future greatness (cf. 22:24–7), and the cursing of the fig-tree (cf. 13.6–9) – is what he inserts – the 'saving' of the 'lost'

Zacchaeus (19:1–10) and the parable of the pounds (19:11–27) in advance of the entry into Jerusalem, and the prediction of Jerusalem's destruction (19:39–44) in advance of the action in the Temple.

(i) The reason for the insertion of the Zacchaeus tradition emerges from the matching pair of announcements by Jesus, 'Today it is necessary for me to stay in your house . . . Today salvation has taken place in this house, because he too is a son of Abraham' (19:5, 9). Not for the first or only time is the apparently insignificant word 'too' (καί) in fact more than a little significant: here it signals insistently the membership of the scorned tax-collector/sinner in the wider community of Abraham (Tannehill 1986: 125), and the essential purpose (δεῖ: v. 5) of Jesus' mission as the renewal of that community as a community of 'salvation'. That last term provides both the catchword connection with the preceding Bartimaeus miracle – 'Your faith has *saved* you' (18:42) – and the key to the concluding punchline of this story – 'The Son of Man came to seek out and *save* the lost' (19:10). If confirmation were needed that the parable of the lost sheep was about inclusiveness and the priority of repentance (15:3–7), or that table-fellowship is both the means and the end to the achievement of that inclusion (7:34), or that the people of Abraham remain Jesus' unshaken priority, or that the strategy set out in the Nazareth manifesto remains intact, here it is. This is doubtless the context in which the following parable of the pounds and the entry to Jerusalem are to be set.

(ii) The parable of the pounds is a close relative of the parable of the faithful and wise servant (Luke 12:42–6/Matthew 24:45–51): both envisage a transfer of responsibility by an employer (κύριος) to a servant or servants prior to his departure elsewhere, the choice between faithfulness and faithlessness which faced the servant, and the return and subsequent effecting of judgement by the employer. If the setting of the one parable was a delay in the coming of the κύριος, a delay so serious that the coming was itself made doubtful (cf. the servant's conduct which presupposes no day of reckoning at all, because 'My lord delays to come', Luke 12:45/Matthew 24:48), that was very probably also the setting of the other one. Whereas both parables originally *assumed* a delay and set about filling the interval with faithfulness, Luke used the second one to *affirm* a delay in the realisation of overheated hope: 'He was near Jerusalem, and they supposed that the kingdom of God was to appear immediately' (19:11). Both parables, given that they are Christian constructions not attributable to the historical Jesus, also tacitly imply that the departing and returning κύριος is Jesus, but only the second one, and (it must be underlined) only the Lucan version of the second one, make the departure a matter for considered reflection: Jesus' departure is necessary in order that he may receive somewhere else and from someone else a royal status. In the strict sense he was not a king when he left, merely a person of note and standing, but he would be a king when he came back (v. 15: 'he returned, having received royal power'), and he would proceed to exercise that royal power irresistibly. Therefore, whenever in the subsequent narrative Jesus is acclaimed as a king (cf. 19:38 diff. Mark 11:10), that kingship must be understood in future rather than present terms. It remains to be ratified by higher authority. A prophetic miracle worker is what he *is* (19:37 diff. Mark 11:9), a king is what he *will be*.

The prediction of the destruction of Jerusalem (19:39–44) illustrates the bifocal view of the city which is part of the Lucan vision. The critique of the 'citizens' who set about resisting the royal accession of Jesus the κύριος (vv. 14, 27) is quickly targeted at the Pharisees, who want the disciples' kingly demonstration stopped in its tracks (19:39), and shortly afterwards at the chief priests and the scribes (19:47; 20:1, 19). They are both the representatives *of* the people and distinct *from* the people in relation to Jesus (cf. 19:47–8). Put the other way round, the people are both embodied in their leaders, who reject Jesus and his kingship, and separated from them by their acceptance of him. In the same way, Jerusalem is the community which in blind ignorance rejects the visitation of God/Jesus, the city whose stones will be reduced to rubble – 'your enemies . . . will not leave one stone upon another' (19:43–4) – and yet at the same time the city whose stones would acclaim Jesus if the disciples were silenced – 'If these [disciples] were silent, the stones would shout out' (19:40). Two such adjacent allusions to stones must be intended to condition one another. If so, the position of Jerusalem is less clear-cut than talk of 'the place quintessentially opposed to God and his will' (Sanders 1987: 32) would imply. Rather it is ambiguous, and it would be misleading to relax or remove that ambiguity. The disaster of the Jewish war is, as it were, a punishing word of judgement from God in response to the opposition to Jesus, but it is not the only word. There is still to be heard the voice of God in the voices of those who look for 'the redemption of Jerusalem'.

The key word in the Emmaus travellers' summary of shattered hope is often passed over in English translations, with misleading effect. 'We had hoped that he was the one who *was about to* [μέλλων] redeem Israel.' Very occasionally drawn from one of Luke's sources, it is far more often introduced by LukeR. In the first group are the imminent wrath which, according to the Baptist, is *about to* engulf the sons of Abraham (3:7), and the signs that will indicate that final events are *about to* take place (21:7, 36/Mark 13:4). In the second group are the centurion's servant's being *about to* die (7:2), the exodus which Jesus was *about to* fulfil in Jerusalem (9:31), the imminent passion of the Son of Man (9:44 diff. Mark 9:31), the mission of the disciples in places where Jesus was *about to* follow (10:1), the one extra year of grace in which the barren fig tree might bear fruit (13:9), Jesus' being *about to* pass Zacchaeus in Jericho (19:4), the imminent betrayal of Jesus by Judas (22:23) – and the two remaining examples which begin to resemble one another rather obviously: 'They supposed that the kingdom of God was immediately *about to* appear' (19:11) and 'We had hoped that he was the one who was *about to* redeem Israel' (24:21).

In the context of Luke's own thought the hope of the Emmaus travellers was in substance not misplaced. But an adjustment in timing was necessary. When their unknown companion shifted the centre of gravity of their reflections to the suffering and glorification of the Messiah (24:26), the intention was not to set aside the hope of redemption, nor to play down what had been done in an anticipatory way by 'the prophet mighty in deed and word before God and all the people'. Rather, it was to set up a sequence: first, the prophetic mission of liberation; second, the suffering; third, the glorification in exaltation and resurrection; fifth, the return from heaven of the royal redeemer; and then, sixth, the redemption of Israel and Jerusalem. The one missing element is the fourth, the protracted proclamation of repentance and forgiveness – the message of John in the name of Jesus – to all the nations, 'beginning from Jerusalem' (24:47). The formulation 'beginning from' (ἀρξάμενοι ἀπό) is an inclusive one: Jesus' exposition to the Emmaus travellers of all the scriptures 'beginning with Moses' (ἀρξάμενος ἀπὸ Μωυσέως) manifestly included Mosaic texts, and similarly the proclamation to all the nations 'beginning from Jerusalem' evidently includes Jerusalem. So just as all, both Jews and gentiles, are brought by the gospel within earshot of John the Baptist – all that he said, and all that he stood for – so too all, both Jews and gentiles, Jerusalem and places far beyond, are brought by the gospel within the influence of the resurrection. The royal rule of the exalted Christ will become visible at some unspecified later time, but the gospel calls for that rule to be recognised in advance by those who thus become the resurrection people of God.

THE EMMAUS TRADITION IN LUCAN PERSPECTIVE:
JESUS

The Jesus of the Emmaus road chose to concentrate his conversation with his companions on the Messiah's suffering and entrance into glory (v. 26). In so doing, he was not, as we have already seen, setting aside the dynamic mission he had carried out as a prophet. The authenticity of that mission, said the travellers, bore the ultimate seal of being prophetic 'in the sight of God and all the people' (v. 19). The two concepts are not opposed in respect of substance but, in Luke's view, to be distinguished in respect of strategy. The public profile and provisional status of Jesus is that of a prophet; his ultimate, but secret, status is that of the Messiah – secret, that is, until after the resurrection.

The term 'Messiah' does not appear very often in Luke, but from the start its appropriateness for Jesus is made clear. Angels – short of God himself, the ultimately reliable witnesses – acclaim him as such (2:11), the Holy Spirit prepares the old man Simeon for the meeting with Jesus in precisely those terms (2:26), and the demons who belong to the supernatural world cry out, 'You are the Son of God', because, says the redactionally active evangelist, they knew him to be the Messiah (4:41 diff. Mark 1:34). Between those events and the encounter with the chief priests the only whisper concerning Messiahship is the teaching unit defining Messiahship in terms of heavenly session (20:41) – apart, that is, from Luke's version of Peter's confession (9:18–22). Very crucially, there too Lucan redaction brings about a significant development. In Mark's account the incident essentially splits into two halves: first, the confession and the following secrecy command (Mark 8:27–30), and second, the dialogue about the passion of the Son of Man (Mark 8:31–3). In Luke's account there are not two halves. The passion saying is integrated with the exceedingly strict secrecy command: 'He sternly ordered and commanded them not to tell anyone, *saying*, "The Son of Man must undergo great suffering . . ."' (9:21–2). The Messiahship of Jesus is a secret cloaked in the passion. Now we have already seen that the angelic reminder to the women at the tomb requires and achieves an insightful recollection of precisely and pre-eminently that saying. So the sub-text of the angelic reminder is that the resurrection has not only ratified but also

Resurrection People

made possible a public disclosure and demonstration of what has hitherto been a secret. The way to this conclusion – a provisional and public prophetic role, to be overtaken by a heavenly royal role – is smoothed by the LukeR modification of the exchange with the assembly of Israel's elders (22:66–71). Not for Luke the straight two-in-one question, 'Are you the Messiah, the Son of the Blessed?' and its unwavering answer, 'I am, and you will see the Son of Man seated ... and coming ...', but instead a splitting away of Messiah from 'Son of God', with the question, 'Are you, then, the Son of God?' presented as an inference from the assertion about a heavenly session, and the request for information about Jesus' Messiahship parried in the prophetic style of Jeremiah: 'If I tell you, you will not believe; and if I question you, you will not answer' (22:67–8, cf. Jeremiah 38:15). In other words, the formal title of the Messiah, the anointed one, is best not used until after the resurrection, though we, the readers, know that the informal non-titular idea of anointing is wholly appropriate for the one who used it just once and decisively: 'The Spirit of the Lord is upon me, because he has anointed me ...' (4:18).

This sense that Messiahship is in the air throughout the resurrection-focused events of Luke 24 is reinforced by a further visit to the LukeR remodelling in the parable of the pounds. Tediously familiar though the tendency of interpreters to refer to the story of Archelaus may be, it does provide an important yardstick by means of which to measure the Lucan story of Jesus (Josephus, *Antiquities* 17:194–317; *Jewish War* 1:668–70; 2:1–93). Archelaus, son and designated successor of Herod the Great, had a problem. He wanted to be king, was acclaimed as king, found himself forced by popular turmoil to act in advance as if he were king, but could only become king if Augustus sanctioned it. In mounting a case before the emperor in favour of his being granted the kingship, Archelaus found that he had played into the hands of his opponents by having unadvisedly accepted royal plaudits after a formal entrance into the Temple, where he sat on a golden throne and then later, when the going got tough, acting with merciless severity to put down unrest. The golden throne incident proved a golden opportunity for all his opponents, whether supporters of rival candidates or advocates of direct Roman rule. Their efforts rewarded, he left Rome with, from his point of view, a second-best decision: ethnarchy only, and a promise that kingship might be awarded later if a probationary period confirmed the adequacy of his rule. The Archelaus/Jesus parallels are obvious: a formal entrance to Jerusalem and the Temple to the accompaniment of royal greetings, but (by virtue of the previously inserted parable) a journey to receive kingship in the teeth of fierce opposition, kingship conferred by the only one in a position to give it, God in heaven. And then three non-parallels become just as important: (i) the departing Jesus, unlike Archelaus, is already at the time in an ultimate sense, even if not in the public sphere, a kingly person; (ii) the members of his community know on the basis of his resurrection that his kingship is incontrovertible; (iii) kingship is bestowed on Jesus without reservation. So the kingship which has already been anticipated and experienced in the acts of power (cf. Luke 19:37 diff. Mark 11:9: 'the whole multitude of the disciples began to praise God joyfully for all the deeds of power that they had seen, saying, "Blessed is the king who comes . . ." ') has to do with authority to exercise the functions relating to the office, most notably the function of judgement, and to do so in the public sphere. And the entry to city and Temple, while exhibiting a true state of affairs, does so provisionally.

The risen Jesus, whose still future return to exercise that judicial power is ratified by his resurrection, is the person to whom the hope of his community is attached. Following the resurrection, and prior to the return, the representatives of his community have seen what will eventually be seen by all. And the authority which will be seen by all is prepared for by the preaching of a gospel which is itself in a legal sense the act of witness to all (Luke 24:48). It is moreover a royal function which will be passed on by a chain of authority to his table-companions who have special responsibility for the special people. It can be none other than the Messiah of Israel who, from the perspective of his universal rule, declares: 'You who sit at my table in my kingdom will sit on thrones judging the twelve tribes of Israel' (Luke 22:29–30).

Now let us recall that the Jesus of the Emmaus road is an angelic figure. He therefore appears from heaven, walks and talks incognito, and finally disappears. He can participate in the world of space and time, but he is not bound by it. For Luke, however, that way of understanding the state of resurrection is inadequate – hence the stage-by-stage demonstration of non-angelic physicality in the first part of scene 3 in the drama of Luke 24. What a rod Luke thereby created for his back, not to mention the backs of all those who have subsequently reflected on the meaning of resurrection – and, for their pains, squirmed with embarrassment at the last part of scene 3! What can we make of the ascension?

In biblical literature the ascent motif usually occurs at the end of an epiphany scene: a heavenly person appears, speaks or acts, and then 'goes up'. Many epiphany texts have no conclusion as such, and therefore have no need of one, so the 'going up' is merely a making explicit of what would otherwise be implicit, a signal that the event has come to an end. Thus 'when he had finished talking with him God *went up* from Abraham' (Genesis 17:22), or 'God *went up* from [Jacob] at the place where he had spoken with him' (Genesis 35:13), or in the angelic epiphany to the parents of Samson, 'the angel of the Lord *ascended* in the flame of the fire while Manoah and his wife looked on' (Judges 13:20), or the classic announcement by Raphael to Tobit and Tobias that 'I am *ascending* to him who sent me', after which 'he ascended' (Tobit 12:20). Two biblical antecedents of the climactic moment for the Emmaus travellers serve to show that we do not have to wait for the Bethany scene to meet an ascent. After Gideon had provided meat and unleavened cakes as sacrifice in line with the angel's requirement, and after the angel had caused the food to be burnt, 'the angel of the Lord vanished from his sight, and (then) Gideon perceived that it was an angel of the Lord' (Judges 6:19–22). In similar vein, after Manoah had provided a kid and a grain offering, and the angel of the Lord had ascended, then 'Manoah realised that it was the angel of the Lord'. The combination of motifs – the food, the vanishing or ascent, and the recognition – serve to show that an ascent is implicit already when 'he took bread, blessed and broke it, and gave it to them . . . Then their eyes were opened, and they recognised him; and he vanished from their sight' (Luke 24:30–1). The angelic Jesus has appeared from heaven and finally gone back up again.

If Luke allowed his readers to interpret the ascent of Jesus in the context of this family of traditions, talk of ascension would be nothing more than talk of resurrection appearance – and all the better for that! But Luke is resolutely physicalising the resurrection appearance tradition, with drastic consequences for all talk of ascension. Ascension, in short, now achieves separation from, and independence of, resurrection.

In biblical literature the ascent motif also occasionally occurs in stories about the ending of a person's earthly life. An ambiguous example, though one which some later writers adopted and deprived of any trace of ambiguity by insisting that he did not die, is Enoch – 'he walked with God; then he was no more, because God took him' (Genesis 5:24; cf. Hebrews 11:5). An entirely unambiguous example is Elijah, received up into heaven, and bequeathing his prophetic spirit to his protégé Elisha (2 Kings 2:1–15; Sirach 48:9). This second example is the one Luke invokes. While the language of the shorter text of Luke 24:51 is restrained – 'he withdrew from them' – the originality of the longer text – 'and he was carried up into heaven' – is not a precondition for understanding the text as referring to an ascent. For Luke signalled his understanding well in advance with a heavily Elijah-conditioned story of Jesus in which the narrator speaks of how 'the days drew near for him to be taken up' (9:51, cf. 2 Kings 2:9, 11). By invoking the Elijah story Luke took further his transformation of the resurrection of Jesus as a physicalised experience: the Jesus who ascends like Elijah has been made into a man like Elijah. But then we are left with the notion that we could well have done without, for all that many a painter and stained glass creator has revelled in it, the notion of an upward movement to a heaven 'up there' by a flesh-and-blood human being.

THE END OF IT ALL: A MEAL AND A MISSION

The Jesus of Luke has constantly used meals to set the tone for his mission. At those meals he has sometimes been the host, sometimes a guest. At all times the persons who have shared the meals have been important, their presence sending a loud message about Jesus, and indeed about the God by whom Jesus is sent (cf. 10:16). The reader of this Gospel is hardly surprised that meals should be so very prominent in its final chapter. In the triptych of scenes which forms this chapter, the defining moments of both the second and the third occur in the setting of meals. Both have to do with the interpretation of Jesus himself – first, a 'knowledge' (v. 35) which demonstrates *that* he is risen, and second, a demonstration of *how* he is risen (v. 39). But both also have to do with the impact of his risen-ness on those who eat together, in the one case without him and in the other case with him.

Within the Emmaus story the narrator has no interest in *how* the two travellers came to recognise Jesus: all the interest is concentrated on *when* it happened. 'Their eyes were opened' must surely be a so-called 'divine passive' – in which case, at that exact moment they were caught up in a process of divine disclosure. Who do they represent, this pair of otherwise unknown followers of Jesus whose ordinary meal becomes extraordinary as a moment of encounter with resurrection life?

Answer: anyone and everyone. These two are not the 'top brass' of early Christian leadership.

In the hands of Luke the issue of leadership status becomes more important. The women, as we have seen, are viewed as quite distinct from the male group, which is variously described as 'the eleven and all the rest' and 'the apostles' (vv. 9, 10). The story of Peter's visit to the tomb (v. 12) is superimposed on the story of the women's visit, evidently in preparation for the superimposition of the report of the appearance to Peter on the story of the Emmaus travellers. It is not accurate to speak of the apostolic group's having been in continuous session through the day of Easter (so, Dillon 1978: 53), for the joyful announcement that 'the Lord has risen indeed, and he has appeared to Simon' (v. 34) presumes that the appearance which he saw was seen by him alone and not by the group as a whole. For them it is enough to depend upon something that they have not experienced. That serves only to reinforce the supremacy of Peter. The terms of the announcement alert us to Luke's use of an early tradition – thus, the use of the name Simon, and the primacy of his experience (cf. 1 Corinthians 15:5: 'he appeared to Cephas, then to the twelve') – but it is a tradition that Luke has made his own and made definitive (i) by inserting the word 'truly' (ὄντως, cf. Luke 23:47), and especially (ii) by making sure that the report, and therefore the reality, of what happened to Peter has priority over what happened in Emmaus. The combination of the two Peter-dominated verses (vv. 12, 34) serves to make the Easter story the story of the arrival of Peter at resurrection faith. Those who also arrive by different means at the same goal – the women (let's not forget them!) and the Emmaus duo – are for Luke of rather less significance than the ecclesiastical heavyweights. Thus emerges a picture of the community with Peter at the centre, the other ten of the eleven in a circle around him, a wider male group consisting of 'the others', and finally the women. For the devotees of ecclesiastical structure and of authority-type strata it's neat and clear; for those who would prefer a theologically-informed gender-blindness it's not a pretty picture. It is, of course, the picture concerning which Luke forewarned his readers when in a subtle LukeR modification of the call of the apostles (Luke 6:12–16 diff. Mark 3:13–19) he separated out from 'his disciples' the twelve, of whom Peter alone was renamed and thus given the highest status, and had them named 'apostles'. In similar vein, the so-called ministering women are positioned by Luke as the counterparts of 'his disciples' (8:1–3), the outer group distinct from the inner group of twelve centred on Jesus.

This hierarchy-structured view of the 'resurrection people' is, from a sociological perspective, in some tension with Luke's employment of a quite different view of the resurrection witnesses as prophetic. They are told to speak in the name of Jesus in the tones of John the baptist and prophet, they have a model in the prophetic Jesus, they are promised an endowment with Spirit by the one whose departure is modelled on that of Elijah – all of that puts them in the sphere of 'charisma' and the role of the 'prophet', to use the language of Max Weber. But the heavy emphasis on structure and hierarchy takes Luke, and doubtless his own contemporary community, firmly into the sphere of the 'routinisation of charisma' and the role of the 'priest'.

So much for mission, but what of the meals? The final meal of Jesus and his chosen circle is not confined to the twelve – the Emmaus travellers are there, and so are 'their companions' (vv. 33, 36). That final meal is not eucharistic, and it is not hosted by Jesus. But as a meal in which Jesus participates, and as an event in a sequence which has seen reminders being issued of what was said and done 'while he was still in Galilee' (v. 6) or 'while I was still with you' (v. 44), this meal could not but evoke memories of so many other meals. Most especially must this have been so since the persons involved in this meal were about to be sent out in the name of Jesus to announce 'repentance and the forgiveness of sins', and that is exactly what one meal after another during Jesus' 'past' had been about.

First, Luke takes pains to clarify that Levi, not Jesus, was the host at the great meal which followed his entry to discipleship; he also delays a reference to 'sinners' in the story so they are equated with tax-collectors rather than being a separate and distinct group; he also modifies Jesus' clarification of what turns out to be his overall strategy: 'I have not come to call the righteous but sinners *to repentance*'. Thus this story (Luke 5:27–32 diff. Mark 2:13–17) anticipates the story of Zacchaeus, which we have already considered, and is the first of two episodes making the same points in the same way.

Second, it may or may not have been the Marcan story of the anointing of Jesus (Mark 14:3–9) that Luke redacted and inserted, together with the note about the ministering women, at the junction between Q material and the Marcan parable of the sower (Luke 7:36–50; 8:1–3). The woman is not a guest at the meal to which Jesus is invited, but that meal is the setting for 'table talk' (Smith 1987: 614) about basic principles which she illustrates and Jesus underlines. The story is shot through with irony: (i) the host thinks that Jesus' prophet-hood is called into question by his not knowing that the woman is a prostitute, whereas in fact Jesus' prophet-hood is demonstrated precisely by means of such knowledge; (ii) the letting down of the woman's hair, normally a matter of shame and dishonour (*m. Baba Kamma* 8:6), is a means of her being honoured through the honouring of Jesus. It would be possible to remove from the tradition the parable about the two debtors and the concluding words of Jesus to the woman, which align the story with other stories like the healings of the paralytic, the haemorrhaging woman, the lepers and the blind man of Jericho, but the presence of these elements makes the story an epitome of Jesus' whole work (7:48–50, cf. 5:20–1; 8:48; 17:19; 18:42). And this whole story serves to highlight Jesus' commitment to a strategy of barrier-breaking forgiveness.

Third, the Lucan version of the mission charge (Luke 10:4–7) gives prominence to the peace-effecting strategy of accepting hospitality in the name of the gospel of the kingdom from those who are 'sons of peace' and who thus come within the terms of Isaiah 52:7. Each of those sent by Jesus becomes 'the messenger who announces peace, who brings good news, who announces salvation, who says . . . "Your God reigns" '. Each of them, sent out in a state of poverty, accepts hospitality as someone who travels in the cause of that kingdom. That is, the provision of hospitality is an anticipation of that great intervention of God which is announced in the gospel and which addresses the problems of conflict and of poverty.

Fourth, the poor are the invited guests in Jesus' teaching parable of the great supper (Luke 14:15–24/Matthew 22:1–10). In achieving that result Luke has probably carried out a major remodelling of the parable (Reiser 1997: 241–5). (i) The 'poor, crippled, lame and blind' are the persons he has already listed in Luke 14:13, and they can scarcely have been the *second* group of invitees in a parable designed to reflect the strategy of the mission of the historical Jesus. (ii) The original parable was probably about an appeal to all Israel, and envisaged only the substitution of gentiles for those Jews who set aside the original invitation – a scheme well attested in other authentic sayings material, cf. Matthew 8:11–12/Luke 13:28–9; Matthew 12:41–2/Luke 11: 31–2. (iii) The two-phase strategy implemented after the original guests have declined has one stage too many: the artificiality would fall away if, say, Luke 14:21b–23a were assigned to LukeR. But, artificial though the expansion of the parable may be, it reveals the mind of Luke. In his view, Jesus' fellowship meals, which foreshadow the eschatological banquet which God will host, have an all-inclusive guest list. The only people who are not present are those who deliberately decide that they have better things to do – good things, honourable things, sensible things, but at the end of the day disastrously distracting things.

Finally, each of the trio of parables which rebut, but also

exploit, the criticism that 'this fellow welcomes sinners and eats with them' (Luke 15:2) has a significant prehistory. In the case of the parable of the lost sheep, the party to which the shepherd calls his friends and relatives to celebrate the finding of a single lost sheep may seem a little excessive! Can the Jesus of Luke really appeal to what anyone would do in the circumstances – 'Which of you who . . .?' (Luke 15:4) – and suppose that anyone and everyone would lay on such a party on such a pretext? Hardly. So the meal is probably an extra element, inserted in order to insist that the true character of gospel-informed meals is exhibited in the guests, and the gospel-effected bonding which those meals achieve is a sight which brings heavenly joy. As for the parable of the prodigal son, or, as it should be called, the parable of the compassionate father, it has been convincingly shown (Holgate 1999) to fit into the Greco-Roman discussion of the ideal of liberality (represented by the father), as over against the vices of prodigality and meanness (represented by the two sons), and as such a unit of material to give no undue emphasis to the celebratory meal with roast beef on the menu, and with music and dancing setting the tone. But in the context where Luke sets the parable, the meal arguably cannot be em-phasised enough. It is the common thread which holds all three parables in Luke 15 together and rounds off the reply to the opponents' criticism. And what makes the parable special for our study is that the father's final soundbite (vv. 24, 32) equates recovery with resurrection. It could have been said of all the persons who were drawn into Jesus' festive meal strategy, but it was said with a depth of emotion in the case of the younger son, 'This son of mine was dead and is alive again; he was lost and is found!' In essence he was typical of those to whom the prophet of Nazareth aligned his mission, and he was typical of those to whom the prophetic successors of Jesus were required to align theirs. In a phrase, he was one of the resurrection people.

In surveying the final chapter of Luke's Gospel we may from time to time feel some reservation about what he has written, and indeed the presuppositions that lie behind it all. The evangelist's partially incoherent and sometimes unprogressive presentation of the risen Jesus should not, however, discolour for us the tapestry he has woven so skilfully. He was a conservative soul, heavily into ecclesiastical authority structures, traditional in his treatment of gender issues, not always instinctively in tune with the potential for innovation that the gospel of the resurrection made available to reflective Christians. But there remains in his narrative quite enough to draw from us some sympathy with George Bernard Shaw's tribute: 'It is Luke's Jesus who has won our hearts.' If we endorse the tribute, as I believe we should, we have at the same time to recognise that there was more remaining to be done after Luke laid down his pen. He saw some, but certainly not all, of what was and is involved in being 'resurrection people'.

Chapter Four

∞∞∞∞∞∞∞∞∞∞∞∞∞∞∞

THE TEXT AS WINDOW AND THE
COMMUNITY AS CHRIST:
LOOKING AND LISTENING WITH
JOHN

INTRODUCTION

In one of the most haunting passages of his great novel, *Jude the Obscure*, Thomas Hardy took his readers to a small and depressing room in the university city of Christminster. The house in which that room was set was prevented by the silent, black and windowless walls of Sarcophagus College from being touched by the light of either the moon by night or the sun by day. In that room of shadows, temporary lodging for a pregnant woman and her three tiny children, there took place the deaths of the three, explained by one of the shortest and saddest of suicide notes ever written: 'Done because we are too meny'. In the hours that followed the three tragedies, while Jude and Sue, his partner, waited for the coroner's inquest in that bleak and cheerless room, the religious life of Christminster could be heard proceeding as if nothing had happened. The organist of the nearby college chapel practised the anthem, 'Truly God is loving unto Israel', and two religious persons had an argument outside in the street. To Sue in her distress they must be talking about her and Jude: 'We are made a spectacle unto the world, and to angels, and to men!' To Jude, the truth was different, and worse:

'No – they are not talking of us. They are two clergymen of different views, arguing about the eastward position. Good God – the eastward position, and all creation groaning!' (Hardy 1987: 351–6)

That sense that, one way or another, a human drama is set on a cosmic stage, and that the ultimate context of a human story only becomes visible at the frontier between life and death, pervades the story of Jesus in the Gospel of John (4G): Thomas Hardy chose to echo the apostle Paul in pursuing that theme and in the process exposing the flaws of introspective religiosity, but the same cosmic perspective, the same sense that one person's story is creation's story, is of course characteristic of the fourth evangelist. And his story of Jesus has probably affected Christian history more profoundly than any of the other Gospels, even Matthew.

Many of the themes, many of the people, who appear in the resurrection narratives of the 4G are familiar to readers of the Synoptic Gospels. Here as there, they are taken to an open tomb, lacking a body but containing angels. Here as there, they meet an appearing Jesus, a Jesus who overcomes the perplexity of Mary Magdalene and dispels the uncertainty of the disciples. And so one could go on . . . But in the case of the 4G, there is a very particular question to be asked about the two chapters in which those familiar stories are set: Are they included simply in deference to tradition, given the breathtakingly bold decision of the evangelist to turn the crucifixion into exaltation and glorification, the ascent of the Son of Man to where he was before? In other words, do John 20 and 21 really belong?

To pose the question is necessary. In so doing we very properly defer to some of the finest of recent interpreters of the Fourth Gospel, who have rightly seen the essential Johannine pattern (or myth) as the story of the one who descends and ascends, one whose crucifixion is not so much the ultimate humiliation conditioned by an agonised sense of personal abandonment – the sort of thing that Mark conveyed with such consummate skill – as the final triumph coloured by a sense of completion and achievement (Ashton 1991: 485–90, cf. Käsemann 1968: 4–8). But to answer the question it is only necessary to ask how well the 4G would read if nothing followed the traditions of the piercing of Jesus' side and the subsequent burial – or, perhaps we should say, if nothing followed the triumphant cry, 'It is finished', as the spirit of Jesus was handed over to God. If Jesus insists more than once that he has the authority and the innate power not only to lay down his life but also to take it back again and to raise himself (thus, 2:19; 10:17–18), can the story really end without an account which reveals his having done so? If it were simply a matter of Jesus' being received into the divine presence, and maybe revealed as being there like the vindicated righteous servant of God in Wisdom 2–5, would not the anticipations of resurrection in the stories of the Temple cleansing and the triumphal entry (2:22; 12:16) require some narrative fulfilment? If some at least of the promises of a future return to the disciples 'in a little while' (14:19) are to be understood as the return of the risen one, must not his story include that return? And if Peter, participating in Jesus like the rest of the disciples by virtue of his being washed (13:8–10), is isolated from them in his abandonment and denial of Jesus, must he not be rehabilitated, at least as a member of that disciple group? So if the descent-cum-ascent myth does not require a resurrection sequel, the narrative with which that myth is fused certainly does. We cannot make sense of the 4G without the story of the resurrection people. John 20 and 21 really do belong.

A PERSPECTIVE ON THE FOURTH GOSPEL

In order to try and do justice to those two final chapters in this Gospel it is necessary to spend rather more time than was the case with the Synoptic Gospels in trying to discern the world in which it was set.

As has so often been observed, the Jesus of the 4G is a *strikingly* different figure from Jesus of Nazareth. From his lips we only rarely hear about 'the kingdom of God' (3:3, 5); the most famous of his parables are absent; and the majority of his disputes with legal experts are no longer on the agenda. Instead he has just one all-absorbing preoccupation – himself! This topic – himself – is the cause of a violent rupture within the Jewish community, the sort of rupture that would have been unthinkable in the lifetime of the historical Jesus. 'The Jews had already agreed that anyone who confessed Jesus to be the Messiah would be put out of the synagogue' (9:22; cf. 12:42; 16:2). The effect of this is at least in part to turn the story of Jesus into the story of a believing but beleaguered Christian community – a community whose members have been transformed from Christian Jews into Jewish Christians (Martyn 1979). Their story echoes through what may sound like the story of Jesus. Or, to change the metaphor, his story is a window through which we may peer and discern their story. In effect, he and they are much of the time interchangeable.

If the 'story of Jesus' is at least in part the story of a community which had, against its will, experienced a painful severance, then we should be on the alert for two different sorts of evidence within the Johannine text.

First, there may be features typical of a separated religious group which has been forced into becoming, sociologically speaking, a sect. Among those can be listed, as has classically been observed, a beginning in circumstances of protest; a rejection of the norms assumed by the parent body; membership not by birth but by conscious decision; an egalitarian approach to membership and leadership; the development of specially intense, warm and loving relationships among members; and a demand for unreserved commitment from each individual (Scroggs 1999: 69–91). To these might be added still more typical sectarian tendencies, epitomised by such terms as denunciation, antithesis and reinterpretation (Watson 1986: 43–5): a swingeing and

undifferentiated writing off of the opposition; a sense of alienation, shown in sharp polarisations (in/out, light/darkness,
truth/error, and the like); an insistence that the definitive
traditions belong to, and are more truly respected by, the off-
spring than the parent body. One might also add recourse to
predestination to explain how the experience of God has come
to be confined to so small a group.

Second, there may be evidence of internal splits, which
develop in time within the new group: splits involving some
members who go to extremes which are more than the 'mod-
erate' mainstream members can take, and perhaps splits involving
some who regret their decision to identify with the expelled
ones and opt in time to go back and rejoin those who had done
the expelling.

THE GOSPEL OF JOHN: PROCESS AND PRODUCT

There is a very particular question to be asked about the two
chapters with which the 4G ends. How is our understanding of
them extended and enriched by a sense of how the Gospel
evolved, an alertness to the production process as well as the
product? The answer will emerge if we begin with the fact that
the 4G as we have it is a very dislocated document.

First, it keeps treating events as past when in fact they are still
future. Thus, John the Baptist looks back in 1:15, 'This is he of
whom I *said* . . .', to something he said later in 1:30; and Mary
of Bethany is introduced in 11:2 as 'the one who anointed the
Lord with perfume and wiped his feet with her hair' which she
only did in 12:1–8. In similar vein, things are presumed not to
have happened, when in fact they have. Thus, the brothers of
Jesus presume in 7:3–4 that he has not performed miracles in
Judea, but that is exactly what he was doing in 2:23–5, and
exactly what stirred the Jerusalem-based Nicodemus to the
modest but not inconsiderable inference that 'you are a teacher

who has come from God, for no one can do these signs that you do apart from the presence of God' (3:2).

Second, sometimes things ought to be close to one another, but something in between separates them. Thus, there is a heated argument in 7:21–4 about 'one work', which has exasperated opponents. We quickly recognise that the 'one work' is the healing of the paralytic in 5:1–9 – but in between there is a lot of coming and going as a result of another miracle, the feeding of the crowds in 6:1–15.

Third, sometimes we think an episode is ending – and then it goes on! Jesus' last words to the disciples come to an end in 14:31: 'Rise, let us go.' But there follows some more teaching in 15–16, plus a prayer in 17 which, being much more horizontal than vertical in direction, is in fact yet more teaching. We also think the Gospel as a whole is ending in 20:30–1, 'Now Jesus did many other signs in the presence of his disciples . . . But these are written . . .' – and indeed it ought to, but it certainly doesn't, for there before our eyes is chapter 21!

All these signs of a complicated production process are, in my view, more or less readily explained by the hypothesis that there was a relatively short first edition of the 4G which was then expanded to form a considerably longer second edition (Lindars 1972: 46–54; Ashton 1991: 76–90). Let's call them 4G^1 and 4G^2. That conclusion, if correct, will be a real boon for interpreters of John. Once we allow the text to be a window on the experience of a community that believed in Jesus, two editions of that text will enable us to track that experience and to see how life moved on for the (mostly) Jewish Christians who had once been Christian Jews.

It is worth looking in a little more detail at some of the dislocations mentioned above to check how the 4G^1/4G^2 hypothesis actually works.

As we have seen, 'I performed one work, and all of you are astonished' introduces a defence of Jesus' healing of a paralytic on a sabbath (7:21–4, cf. 5:1–16). Even when allowance is made for retrospective comments on an earlier miracle (thus, 10:19–21, picking up on 9:1–34), there is so much material between the event and the defence, including miracle material, that some way of bringing the two nearer to one another seems highly desirable. In short, to assign chapter 6 to 4G² is an attractive proposition. But that still does not solve the problem posed by the conversation between Jesus and his brothers in 7:1–10. Their attempt to persuade him to go to Jerusalem and perform acts of power there (7:3–4) has some internal 'hiccups' which suggest the expansion of an earlier and briefer story (Ashton 1993: 331). More importantly for our purpose, it has obvious similarities with the Cana wedding tradition: the Galilean setting, a rare appearance by members of Jesus' family, their recognition of him as a miracle worker, their pressing him to use that power, serious tension between him and both his mother (2:4) and his brothers (7:5), his resistance grounded in the thought of his special time (ὥρα, 2:4; καιρός, 7:6), and his eventual compliance with their suggestion. But what about the sequence? The conversation presupposes that hitherto Jesus has been at work exclusively in Galilee – contrary to the reports of signs in general (2:23–5) and the specific healing of the paralytic in Jerusalem (5:1–9)! It looks then as if 7:1–10 – whether the present or an earlier version of the tradition – ought at least to precede 5:1–9. And we note in this connection that even in 4G² the conversation with the brothers occurs very shortly before the debate about that healing (7:21–4). It would make sense if in 4G¹ the conversation with the brothers were set nearer to the encounter with his mother, rounding off the Galilean phase, and building a bridge to the Jerusalem phase which the healing of the paralytic inaugurates. Whether this is possible depends on what can be done about the material which is framed by movement to (2:13), and then from (4:3, 43–5), the capital city.

This essentially Jerusalem-focused complex is in rough terms a unity. (i) The prospect of a different system of worship ('destroy this temple . . . he spoke of the temple of his body') in 2:19–21 is picked up in the 'neither in Jerusalem nor on Gerizim' speech in 4:20-4. (ii) The performance of signs in 2:23-5 forms the essential basis of the conversation with Nicodemus and therefore of the whole succeeding narrative, which itself probably grew by stages into a carefully structured whole (Ashton 1993: 374-7). (iii) The scepticism encountered by Jesus in 3:11 (contrast 2:23) is picked up and assessed in 4:43-5 as the regular reaction to a prophet in his home town (πατρίς) – now no longer Nazareth (cf. 1:45-6) but Jerusalem, the heart of the nation, where 'he came to what was his own, and his own people did not accept him'. (iv) Jesus' prophetic insight and superhuman knowledge of humankind in 2:25 is in use again in 4:16-19, provoking the Samaritan woman to draw the same conclusion about a prophetic Jesus as Nicodemus had done in 3:2.

This unified section is controlled by that most aggressive and theologically loaded of confrontations between Jesus and 'the Jews' in 2:13-22. Within it the trio of Temple cleansing, request for a sign, and Temple destruction saying reminds us of the same trio in the same order in Mark 11:15-17, 27-33; 14:58, following the 'triumphal' entry in Mark 11:1-11. The author of the 4G shows that he himself recognises an intimate connection between entry and cleansing, for only in 2:17, 22 and 12:16 do we read that 'the disciples remembered' after the resurrection and discerned a connection between a scriptural passage and a word or action of Jesus. We gain the strong impression that 2:13-22 belonged originally next to the triumphal entry in 12:12-16, and that it has been supplanted as the original cause of the proceedings against Jesus by the Lazarus episode (Lindars 1972: 378-82). Our impression is greatly strengthened by the evidence, already mentioned, that the reference to Mary in 11:2, and therefore the whole Mary-Martha-Lazarus story which follows, presupposes the anointing in 12:1-8 rather than vice versa, and owes its present position to editorial work at the 4G² stage.

It seems therefore that in 4G¹ there was a Galilean phase, framed by two miracles, and concluding with a conversation between Jesus and his brothers; then a Jerusalem phase, itself also framed by two miracles involving a paralytic and a blind man, with a final confrontation between Jesus and the authorities stemming from the closely connected entry into Jerusalem and Temple cleansing. Then for $4G^2$ the tradition of the Temple cleansing was transposed, after having attached to it the material in 2:23–4:45; the tradition of the miracle of the loaves, together with all associated material, was inserted (6:1–71); the conversation between Jesus and his brothers (7:1–10) was relocated immediately afterwards; all the Lazarus material (11:1–45; 12: 9–11, 17–18) was inserted; and finally, as already noted, 15–17 made an appearance for the first time.

We have already noted the significance of 'Now Jesus did many other signs in the presence of his disciples . . .', which reads like the ending of a whole document. One of the most widely agreed conclusions drawn by Johannine specialists is that in 20:30–1 the evangelist does indeed finish his work. But then there is more, notably another sign (21:1–14) and the personal rehabilitation of Peter (21:15–23), rounded off with what reads suspiciously like another ending, ' . . . there are also many other things that Jesus did . . .' (21:25). While some regard 21 as a later appendix, a sort of $4G^3$, and others take it to be an addition at the time of $4G^2$, it is at least clear that it did not figure in $4G^1$. In fact, we shall see later that the links between this chapter and material added at the $4G^2$ stage are so strong – notably the eucharistic feeding (6:11/21:13; cf. 6:31–58), and the appeal to the testifying disciple (19:35/21:24) – as well as links with $4G^1$ material – the beloved disciple complexes – that we can almost certainly say the same of $4G^3$ as was once famously said in another connection, 'We have no need of this hypothesis!'

For our recovery of the 4G production process it now remains simply to travel from the end of the Gospel to the beginning – and what a beginning! A careful reading of the prologue in John 1 brings to light the presence of two competing first lines: 'In the beginning was the Word . . .' and 'There was a man sent from God . . .' All the references to John the Baptist, verses 6–8, 15, serve only to interrupt the smoothness of the flow and to introduce alien considerations. Their presence is widely recognised as redactional. With the likely removal of verse 8, which repeats the definition of John's role as witness, and is most emphatic that he could not himself be identified as the light (vv. 4b, 5, where, in any case, light is probably used in a different sense), it is possible to see verses 6–7 as not only leading directly into verse 19, 'And this is the testimony of John . . .', but also (as it happens) matching the way in which other biblical books begin – thus, 1 Samuel 1:1; Job 1:1; Susanna 1:1. What is left after the removal of verses 6–8, 15 is itself arguably in part pre-Johannine tradition and in part JohnR. Given the redactional tendency towards repetition (cf. v. 8), it is likely that verse 2, 'He was in the beginning with God', is an insertion designed in typical Johannine mode to stress pre-existence. More crucially, if the climactic declaration in verse 14, 'And the Word became flesh', is to achieve maximum impact it must be the first statement of incarnation. That requires two conditions to be met. (i) Nothing in verses 1–5 should be incarnational, which is indeed the case: life, says verse 4 with a conscious side glance at Genesis 2:7, was brought into being by the creative Word and must be understood as light, the common human endowment with wisdom, and it is that common human endowment which, according to verse 5, continues unquenched. So the shining of the unquenched light is not the continuing influence of an incarnate person, but rather something that is innate in humankind. (ii) All of verses 9–13 should be attributed to the evangelist, which it is very easy to do. The theme is the rejection of the incarnate Word by the Jewish people, apart (that is) from a believing community whose membership is defined not by physical descent but by belief/baptism. Theologically the redaction here matches in language and in content the thrust of the John 3 passage, inserted at the time of the production of $4G^2$. With verse 17 providing a fine ending for what we can now call the pre-Johannine poem, boldly identifying the previously unidentified Word as none other than Jesus Christ, and with verse 18 detracting somewhat from it by introducing the sort of anti-Mosaic polemic that also appears in John 3:13 (Ashton 1993: 348–56), it is not difficult to assemble a multi-part solution to the problem of the dislocations in 1:1–18: first, a relic of the beginning of 4G¹ (vv. 6–7); second, JohnR material (vv. 2, 8, 9–13, 15, 18); third, a pre-Johannine poem (vv. 1, 3–5, 14, 16–17). On this showing the pre-Johannine poem would have looked like this:

> ¹In the beginning was the Word, and the Word was with God, and the Word was God. ³All things came into being through him, and without him nothing came into being which did come into being. ⁴In him was life, and the life was the light of humankind. ⁵The light shines in the darkness, and the darkness has not overcome it.
>
> ¹⁴And the Word became flesh, and we have seen his glory, the glory as of the Father's only Son, full of grace and truth. ¹⁶For of his fullness we have all received, grace upon grace. ¹⁷The law indeed was given through Moses; grace and truth came through Jesus Christ.

This will be of some importance when we come to assess John 20: the insistence on physical realism, the sense of alienation from 'the Jews', and the conviction that the Genesis 2:7 experience of in-breathing is known not simply in the universal human endowment with wisdom but in the community's particular endowment with the Spirit. The discussion of all these themes is, as we shall see, initiated in John 1 and concluded in John 20.

So far we have seen that when the text of the 4G is allowed to be a window on the experience of a community that believed in Jesus, two editions of that text may be expected to document how life moved on for the (mostly) Jewish Christians who had once been Christian Jews. In following up the idea of two

Resurrection People

successive editions, it would be tempting to suppose that we could simply read off the community's earlier situation from $4G^1$ and its later situation from $4G^2$. Would that it were so easy! More realistically, the text encourages us (i) to see episodes in the $4G^1$ material as either already reflecting successive stages in the community's experience or as having been edited further for $4G^2$, and also (ii) to see blocks of material which were inserted at that later time recording as well as extending the sort of argument and emphasis which characterised earlier stages in the arguments between Christians and their opponents. On reflection, neither of these two observations is surprising: the evangelist was not interested in preserving inviolate as exhibits in some theological museum the artefacts of past arguments, nor is it likely that in any setting of ferocious ideological conflict, such as the one his community faced, those patterns of past argument would have no continuing part to play. Two examples of this sort, which will prove significant when we take up the task of interpreting the resurrection traditions later on, are worth considering. They concern the paralytic and the blind man.

The famous story of the healing of the blind man in John 9 describes the miracle itself (vv. 1–7), and then breaks up into a series of four episodes (vv. 8–12, 13–17, 18–23, 24–34). All but the first of the four episodes take place in some location where an official investigation and judgement by those in authority takes place: 'they brought [him] to the Pharisees . . . they called the parents . . . for a second time they called the man who had been born blind . . . they drove him out' (vv. 13, 18, 24, 34). The thread common to all four is the 'how?' question. But in first dealing with the identification of the man who sees as the man born blind, and then second arguing the status of the healer – a sinner *in spite of* being a miracle worker, or a prophet *because of* being an unprecedented miracle worker? – the four episodes relate to one another in an a-b-a-b sequence. That neat scheme is in a certain sense marred by what happens in the episode involving the parents, verses 18–23, which only goes to show the evangelist's creative handling and development of tradition. (i) Verses 22–3 are alien to their context: the healer is here defined as 'the Messiah' rather than as elsewhere as prophetic, and nothing said previously in chapter 9 even hints at such an idea. (ii) The investigating persons are uniquely defined as 'the Jews' in verses 18, 22, rather than as elsewhere in John 9:1–34 as the Pharisees. The narrative would read more smoothly if verses 22–3 were not there at all, and if the personnel in verse 18 were the Pharisees, in short if the dislocating material were regarded as redactional.

The story effectively ends in verse 34 with the expulsion of the blind man – 'they drove him out' – an expulsion which, incidentally, is not in the same league as the drastic and formal expulsion of which verse 22 speaks. Moreover, this expulsion is accompanied by a comment on his having been born in sin, which creates an *inclusio* with Jesus' own response to the disciples' initial opening up of that very possibility (vv. 2–3). This means that the narrative of the final encounter between Jesus and the blind man, with some Pharisees in earshot (vv. 35–41), is an unoriginal postscript designed to promote a considerably more advanced christology, itself in no way prepared for in the original narrative – Jesus the judging Son of Man.

What is interesting about this two-stage narrative development is that the first stage, which everyone accepts as having figured in 4G[1], records a conflict whose life setting can be dated prior to the formal synagogue ban. The duly constituted authorities, the 'disciples (and interpreters) of Moses', receive and sift evidence. For them the ambiguity of Jesus' case arises from the sabbath issue: first, Jesus' conduct threatens the identity of Israel, distinguished as it is by the sabbath observance (cf. 1 Maccabees 1:43; 2 Maccabees 8:27; *Jubilees* 2:17–19), so that his actions place him on a par with gentiles; second, a miracle is itself in any case a highly ambiguous phenomenon, as earlier Johannine allusions to Deuteronomy 13:1–5 confirm (cf. 7:12, 'He is deceiving the crowd'; 7:47, 'Surely you have not been deceived, too, have you?'); third, a genuine difference of opinion can be maintained within the community of Israel, as 10:19–21 will subsequently confirm. If this is true of the first stage, what of the second? At this stage the Pharisees have become 'the Jews', Jesus has become not only the Messiah, in recognition of which role his disciples are expelled from the synagogue, but also and more importantly the Son of Man, in which role he judges those who have carried out the expulsion.

From the blind man in John 9 we turn to the paralytic in John 5. With the two miracle stories forming an *inclusio* framing the Jerusalem phase of revelation, this one also grew with the expansion of 4G^1 into 4G^2.

The correspondences between the two stories deserve to be listed: (i) they do both occur in Jerusalem; (ii) the timing on the sabbath is introduced retrospectively; (iii) the issue of the sinfulness of the healed person is introduced; (iv) after performing the healing Jesus disappears; (v) Jesus' conduct causes offence. Alongside the correspondences there are, however, several significant non-correspondences: (i) the healed person this time *is* a sinner, whereas the blind person was not; (ii) the healed person breaches the sabbath conventions, whereas the formerly blind man does not; (iii) the paralytic neither identifies with nor acknowledges confessionally the status of the healer, and is therefore precluded from being a type of Christian discipleship – indeed one might ask whether he is not a type of those who have indeed benefited from Christian acts of healing but remained distanced from the Christian Jews; consequently, (iv) the spotlight falls on Jesus, and Jesus alone, and the authorities take action against him, and him alone; (v) the action is nothing short of an attempt to kill him; (vi) the authorities are throughout described as 'the Jews' and never as the Pharisees.

In order to take proper account of these two sets of correspondences and non-correspondences, we need to hear the heavy hint dropped by that small section 7:21–4 which allowed us to detach chapter 6 and assign it to 4G^2. In 7:21–4 the argument is not christological in any way at all: it belongs within the parameters of the community whose leaders' attachment to Moses is recognised, and whose style of argument is respected. In other words, 7:21–4 points to an underlying story whose general tenor is exactly like that of the underlying story in John 9. How much of John 5, we may ask, could be set inside just such a context? The answer is: none of 5:17–18, 19–29, but most, if not all, of 5:31–47 (cf. Neyrey 1988: 9–25). In 5:31–47 the witness of the Baptist is invoked – and had not the Jews in Jerusalem subjected him to sustained interrogation in 1:19–28? – and shared respect for Moses is a platform for argument about credentials, specifically with miracles in mind. The tone may be partisan and polemical, but the substance does not necessarily propel the Christian position beyond the limits recognised by the community of Israel. But in 5:17–18, 19–29 it is altogether different: the equality of Father and Son is explored in terms of the two great functions of creation and judgement (Ashton 1991: 137–40), and when, as the text puts it, 'the Jews were seeking all the more to kill him, because he was not only breaking the sabbath, but was also calling God his own Father, thereby making himself equal with God', the interpretation of Jesus' status which was fatal for him and correspondingly fatal for his community was brought to light. In other words, 5:17–29 is evidence which dovetails with the evidence of 9:22–3: when Jesus teeters on the edge of assassination, his community hovers on the brink of expulsion. A further dovetailing can also be observed: as we have seen, the spotlight falls on Jesus the judging Son of Man in the added section 9:35–41, and on whom does the spotlight fall when 5:19–29 explores the ultimate significance of Jesus' Sonship? Answer: Jesus the judging Son of Man (5:27).

There is no reason to suppose that 4G[1] lacked either 5:17–18, 19–29 or 9:22–3, 35–41. If that is right, then the earliest edition of the Gospel preserved the sort of argument which was going on prior to the schism, as well as documenting the cause célèbre which precipitated that schism.

It will be of some considerable importance when we reach the Johannine resurrection narratives to recognise where the Synoptic Gospels fit – or do not fit – into the world of the Johannine Christians and their evangelist. As a matter of fact, there is plenty of evidence in and around the Johannine stories we have already brought into play that the evangelist was not simply drawing on material which the Synoptic writers used but, more precisely, drawing upon their own finished work. This can be seen in three examples: the healing of the officer's son, the sequence beginning with the miracle of the loaves, and the controversy following the good shepherd discourse.

The story of the healing of the officer's son (4:46–54) has clearly grown in the Johannine telling. Virtually everyone who is anyone in Johannine studies agrees that verse 48 is unoriginal: 'Unless you [plural] see signs and wonders you will not believe.' The officer has made no such stipulation, and a plural address to a singular person indicates that the real audience is a community, a community which demands evidence of the sort which defined the prophet like Moses, the performer par excellence of signs and wonders, as a host of texts from Deuteronomy 34:10–12 onward demonstrates (cf. Exodus 7:3, 9; 11:9–10; Nehemiah 9:10; Psalms 78:43; 105:27; 135:9; Jeremiah 32:20–1; Wisdom 10:16; Baruch 2:11). Once verse 48 is, as it were, removed, the repetition of the officer's request from verse 47 in verse 49 also has to go. Moreover, since the first believing by the officer in verse 50b is in some competition with, and indeed detracts from, the climactic second believing in verse 53, it appears that it also may have to go. The second believing response is dependent upon the report of the timing of the boy's recovery, a report which only has to be made because of the significant distance separating Cana (where Jesus and the officer meet) and Capernaum (where the family home is situated), a separation which is plainly introduced by the evangelist in view of verse 46a: 'Then he came again to Cana in Galilee where he had changed the water into wine.' Given the journey which has to take place between the two places, Cana and Capernaum, it is the timing which convinces the officer that a miracle has indeed occurred, that is, that the recovery is not just natural but an achievement of Jesus. His checking out of the minutiae brings him to faith, faith which he has therefore *not* exhibited previously. In so checking he follows the same scrutinising process as we saw in operation in chapter 9. Small wonder then that he turns out to be a representative figure, standing for Jewish community members who will not believe unless they see signs and wonders. But, and this is important within the evangelist's apologetic, *he does believe*! In a community divided over the case of Jesus, he ends up on the side of the angels.

It appears that JohnR in this story is very extensive indeed. The underlying story of the healing of an officer's critically ill son from a distance is, of course, familiar from Matthew 8:5–13/ Luke 7:1–10. There is nothing in John's version which appears to be earlier than Matthean/Lucan data, and which could therefore stem from pre-Synoptic tradition. To the contrary, a small and not very prominent detail can be added as further support for direct dependence on Matthew (cf. Neirynck 1991a: 685). 'Yesterday at one in the afternoon *the fever left him*,' said the officer's slaves (v. 52). Fever had not been mentioned among the details of the boy's condition (v. 46b), nor was it mentioned in either of the two Synoptic versions of the incident. More than that, sick people very rarely suffer from fever in the Gospels – elsewhere only Peter's mother-in-law, of whom it is said that 'the fever left her' (Matthew 8:15/Mark 1:31/Luke 4:38–9). This being so, and since the evangelist Matthew juxtaposed in his 8:5–13, 14–15 sequence the Marcan story of Peter's mother-in-law and the Q story of the officer's son, we can infer that the latter caught the fever from the former by Matthean redaction! And if the 4G is influenced by Matthean redaction, John knew Matthew.

If John knew the Synoptic version of the tradition, he knew that it began with Jesus' entering Capernaum (see Matthew 8:5/ Luke 7:1), and it is a reminiscence of this detail which he retains in his 2:12a: 'After this he went down to Capernaum with his mother, his brothers, and his disciples . . .'. If, as we have argued, 4G¹ began Jesus' public mission with the wedding in Cana and the healing of the officer's son, it is a reminiscence of this detail which we find in his 4:54: 'this was the second sign that Jesus did after coming from Judea to Galilee', for all that he can only add this statement after imposing redactionally the Judea-Galilee scheme, that is, when introducing 2:13–4:45 at the stage of producing 4G². But what emerges from the literary investigation as theologically very significant is a trio of points: first, funda-mental to the evangelist's thought is the intimate link he sees and wishes to underline between the two miracles, both of which he locates in Cana; second, the Cana complex follows on from an introductory scene which highlights the figure of Nathanael, who is known in Johannine circles to come from Cana (cf. 21:2); and third, the complex of ideas associated with 4:48 will inform the interpretation of the 'seeing . . . believing' nexus in John 20.

The whole chapter which begins with the miracle of the loaves is, as we have already inferred, a new feature of 4G². In it we have a sequence which matches in a quite remarkable way the Marcan sequence. That sequence was itself constructed by Mark himself and adopted later on by Matthew: a feeding miracle (6:1–15, cf. Mark 6:30–44; 8:1–10), the walking on the water (vv. 16–21, cf. Mark 6:45–52), the refusal of a sign (vv. 22–30, cf. Mark 8:11–13), a discourse about bread (vv. 31–59, cf. Mark 8:14–21), and Peter's confession (vv. 60–71, cf. Mark 8:27–33). The natural – can one not say necessary? – inference from the correspondence between the 4G and Mark/Matthew is that the former depended directly on one or both of the latter.

Once again, there will be some theological spin-off from the literary decision when we reach the stage of interpreting John 21.

Johannine redaction in chapter 6 has introduced rich eucharistic reflection which 21:13 will recall, as well as a change of emphasis in the presentation of Peter which is not without relevance to 21:15–21.

The essential thrust of our results thus far is that in 4G^1 the public mission of Jesus began with two signs in Galilee and was followed by several episodes in Jerusalem. The bridge between the Galilee and Jerusalem phases was provided by the conversation between Jesus and his brothers (material underlying 7:1–10), and the Jerusalem phase itself was set in the frame of two extensively corresponding signs involving the paralytic (chapter 5) and the blind man (chapter 9). It is now possible to extend the series of John 5/9 correspondences and at the same time to note still further evidence of dependence on the Synoptic Gospels.

The story of the healing of the blind man (as we have seen, essentially 9:1–21, 24–34) receives an appendix in which Jesus as judging Son of Man draws forth faith from the blind man and pronounces judgement on the Pharisees (9:35–9, 40–1). Not long after, there is a further episode which, while it records a negative dismissal of Jesus because of the words just spoken in the shepherd discourse of 10:1–18, also brings the healing of the blind man back into view as defining evidence of Jesus' status: 'These are not the sayings of a demon-possessed person. A demon cannot open the eyes of blind people, can he?' (10:19–21). The effect is to clamp the shepherd discourse firmly to the issue of the blind man's healing. As the story develops on from there, a further piece of shepherd/sheep argument appears (10:26–9), the effect of which is also to attach the section in which 10:26–9 is set firmly to the main shepherd/sheep material, and therefore to the story of the blind man. The overall section, 10:22–42, is held together in two ways.

First, there is the especially intense sequence of references to 'works' (vv. 25, 32, 33, 37, 38). This also takes us back to John 9, where an initial conversation between Jesus and his disciples is about whether sinning by the blind man himself or by his parents was responsible for his predicament. That conversation is in a sense ended wholly satisfactorily, but there is added to it a saying which would be a more or less proverbial truism if it ran, 'We must work ... while it is day; night comes, when no one can work' (9:3-4). What takes the saying far beyond the realm of proverb is the phrase 'the works of him who sent me'. This is exactly the language of John 10:36 about the one sent by God, who performs works in his Father's name which are, according to 10:37, effectively the works of God himself.

Second, there is in 10:24-5, 36 a building upon a common Synoptic base. In Luke 22:67-8, 70 the Marcan interrogation of Jesus by the high priest has been changed from ' "Are you the Messiah, the Son of the Blessed?" ... "I am" ' (14:61-2) to ' "If you are the Messiah, tell us." ... "If I tell you, you will not believe; and if I question you, you will not answer." ... "Are you, then, the Son of God?" ... "You say that I am".' This is precisely what we encounter in a rewritten and characteristically Johannine form in the John 10 concluding exchange between Jesus and his adversaries. It is worth pausing over this final episode to draw two important conclusions from that part of the exchange which is an argument, rather than a mere reaffirmation that the miracles reveal the truth about Jesus and his relationship to the Father. (i) The charge against Jesus is 'blasphemy, because you, though only a human being, are making yourself God' (10:33). This is *exactly* the formulation of the charge against Jesus in John 5:18, where again he was reflecting on how his 'works' are the works of the Father. This serves to reinforce the correspondence between John 5 and John 9: in both there is an expansion of the tradition, and one which takes place along the same lines. (ii) The argumentation in John 10:34-6, using Psalm 82:6, has produced much disagreement as Johannine specialists have debated the identity of 'the gods to whom the word of God came' (10:35): are they human, superhuman, angelic, or whatever? Various proposals have been ventured, but any one of them fails if its proponent does not keep one eye fixed on the essential question which is being disputed: is it, or is it not, possible to describe as divine someone whose humanity is the agreed starting point? Jesus' argument is that it *is* possible, and indeed *shown* to be possible, by a text in 'your law'. Just as 7:21–4 worked within Mosaic parameters to defend an action of Jesus, so too 10:34–6 works within Mosaic parameters to defend a personal claim of Jesus. Even when the text is drawn from 'your [*sic*] law', the speaker is not in practice separating himself from the law. That is, even when voicing the claims that brought Jesus to the brink of execution, *or* when voicing the claims that brought the Christian Jews to the point of expulsion, the attempt is being made to stake out a position in such traditional Jewish terms as would persuade those who specialised in legal argument. This is a community which, intellectually and spiritually, continues to think and to speak from within the tradition. One might put it this way: the community's self-consciousness remains Israelite, it is not – as some notable interpreters of the 4G have urged – gentile.

RESURRECTION PEOPLE: MARY MAGDALENE

The first of the Johannine resurrection people is Mary Magdalene. Her function in the Johannine narrative can be viewed from several angles: the effects of the John/Synoptics relationship, her standing as a woman, and her representative function within the community.

As the Gospel tradition developed Mary Magdalene experienced a distinct shift of function. At the pre-Marcan stage she was, as we have seen, the prime witness to the empty tomb, and the prime recipient of the angel's explanation of that emptiness. At the Marcan stage she became in addition the recipient of the angelic message to the disciple group. In Luke she was back where she had been in the pre-Marcan situation: no message for the disciples was passed to her, though she and her colleagues did represent the whole Galilean audience of the teaching of Jesus. In Matthew she became the witness to the actual opening of the tomb, and more importantly the first to meet the risen Jesus. In John her function in relation to the tomb is cut back: she sees it is open and empty, and she sees an angelic presence within it, but no explanation is provided, and therefore even after her exchange with the angels she persists with a natural explanation of its emptiness. All the weight is placed, therefore, on the encounter with Jesus.

The encounter with Jesus is almost certainly written up by the evangelist as a revision of what he read in at least two of the Synoptic Gospels. To begin, there is no compelling evidence of any non-Marcan tradition at the point where Luke changes one angel into two (Luke 24:4 diff. Mark 16:5). John, who does not need more than one angel to achieve his purpose in 20:11–13, is acquainted with the idea of two angels, and is therefore indebted to LukeR. More significant is his debt to MattR, which becomes most visible in connection with the message Mary receives from the risen Jesus. (i) As we saw earlier, the message originated in the Matthean adoption of what came into being through MarkR: Matthew picked up from Mark – and did so not once but twice – the message about a journey to Galilee. That was the way, the only way, that the message came to include the journey motif. Of course, the Johannine message is couched in characteristically Johannine terms – a journey from earth to heaven, not from Jerusalem to Galilee – but the sheer fact that it is there at all in the 4G, especially when it is not necessary preparation for a subsequent meeting with the disciples, points to John's dependence on MattR. (ii) The intended recipients of the message are 'my brothers' – a unique term for disciples in the 4G apart from 4G^2 usage in 21:23, but one imported by MattR into his version of the Jesus/Mary encounter in Matthew 28:10. Doubtless that expresses his view of the disciple group as a new family of brothers of Jesus (cf. Matthew 12:46–50; 23:8). (iii)

Without the message in Matthew 28:9–10 there is no significant content left to provide the basis for an independent tradition, and there are no features of John's narrative which are earlier than what can be read in Matthew, and which might therefore attest earlier independent tradition.

John's use of the Synoptics serves to highlight the drastic changes he made to their versions of the traditions. Mary came not to anoint (that task had been completed by Joseph of Arimathea and Nicodemus, 19:39–40) but only to grieve: the issue is stark and simple (cf. the 'crying' in grief and mourning envisaged in two blocks which were introduced in 4G^2: 11:31, 33; 16:20). The account of her first visit in 20:1–2 is not without dislocation: there is no preparation for her coming to the tomb in terms of prior observation of the burial itself (contrast Mark 15:47); the inference of a theft is drawn from the tomb's openness alone; and she speaks in the plural (v. 2, contrast v. 13) when she alone has been there. The account of her second visit includes no reference to her return to the tomb, and has two angels whose function is only to ask, in preparation for Jesus' asking the same question, 'Why are you weeping?' The repetition of both the incorrect inference from the tomb's openness (vv. 2, 13, 15) and the question (vv. 13, 15) serves to shift all the attention towards the meeting with Jesus, indeed to shift it decisively further than was the case in Matthew.

How far is it significant that Mary Magdalene, the person who has that first meeting with Jesus, is a woman? Before answering that question it will perhaps be helpful to assemble evidence of the very special status of her experience, at least as far as the evangelist presented it. The form he gave to the 'Mary Magdalene complex' (20:1–18) points to a certain distinctness: verses 1–2, 18 form an *inclusio*, detailing at start and finish her coming from the tomb to the disciples with a message about the Lord: 'They have taken away the Lord . . . I have seen the Lord.' To that formal distinctness corresponds a certain distinctness of content: 4G^2 would speak of three appearances of the Lord, that is, to the disciples minus Thomas (vv. 19–23), the disciples including Thomas (vv. 24–8), and the seven disciples by the lake (21:1–14). Mary's experience was not included in the list: it had something special about it, it stood alone. The specialness can also be seen in the setting aside of tangible evidence, whereas the subsequent encounters with the disciples are dominated by it: 'he showed them his hands and his side' (v. 20a. cf. vv. 25, 27). Put in another way, Mary is the only one who is brought to recognise the risen one, not by sight or touch nor even by the sound of his voice (for he speaks in v. 15a) but by his naming her personally (v. 16a). To this very special feature we shall return. And even more specialness can be detected: the message to the 'brothers' is about the ascent to the Father, which is therefore presupposed as having occurred before 'seeing the Lord' takes place again (v. 18, cf. vv. 20, 25). Only to Mary comes the reminder of that ascent which would again figure in crucial sayings in $4G^2$ (cf. 3:13; 6:62).

All these considerations suggest that the quite special significance of what happened to Mary was clear in the mind of the evangelist when producing both $4G^1$ and $4G^2$. But was any *gender* significance involved? In $4G^1$ this is not excluded but there is no real evidence. But in $4G^2$ there are straws in the wind, straws which suggest a developing culture or atmosphere within the Johannine community.

First, the reader of John 20 could not forget – was certainly intended not to forget – what had been read earlier in John 4. The Samaritan woman comes to faith and goes on to act as a mediating messenger, as a result of which a community has direct experience of Jesus and itself comes to faith. Her story, and that of her community, could be told without the interlude in which Jesus gives the disciples private instruction on strategy (4:31–8). That private instruction in no way required that 'the disciples [should have been] astonished that he was speaking with a woman' (4:27). But the presence of the unrequired statement serves only to emphasise that for the evangelist a point of wider relevance needed to be made. It was important for readers of the Gospel to understand that Jesus – no less – had set aside the traditional and instinctive tendency of men to devalue women.

Second, the reader of John 20 in $4G^2$ could not forget what had been read earlier in John 11. This chapter, almost certainly the result of very heavy editorial activity on the part of the evangelist, is marked by a striking transformation in the image of Martha. In $4G^1$ she had been much the same old Martha as in Luke 10:38–42: the first of the two sisters to be mentioned (and therefore probably the elder), the *chef de cuisine* busy with the serving who had no claim to fame for sitting at, or anointing, the feet of Jesus – therefore *not* the one given special honour by the story (Luke 10:39–42; John 12:3–8). But in John 11 almost everything is different. Both the sisters say to Jesus, 'If you had been here, my brother would not have died' (vv. 21, 32), but whereas there is very strikingly no conversational follow-up at all between Jesus and Mary, the essence of Johannine faith is covered in the conversation between Jesus and Martha (vv. 22–7). In assenting to a christological confession which includes and at the same time transcends Jewish apocalyptic expectations (vv. 24–7), Martha becomes a representative figure: she believes and speaks as the Johannine community believes and speaks (cf. 20:30–1). From one end of the 4G to the other there is no one – not even Peter (6:69) – no one other than Nathanael (1:49: 'Rabbi! You are the Son of God! You are the King of Israel!') who comes within range of Martha's formal and detailed statement of faith, 'I believe that you are the Messiah, the Son of God, the one coming into the world.'

Third, we come back to Mary Magdalene. She too is a representative figure. The second person plural formulation in the message to the brothers (20:17) points to a reality which is not confined to the immediate recipients of that message: ' . . . your Father . . . your God', but to a whole community which is being addressed through a specially chosen and representative woman. That she stands for that whole community is evident also from the correspondence between Jesus' calling her by name and his calling all his sheep by name in his role as the good and true shepherd (John 10:3, 4): 'Jesus said to her, "Mary!" She turned and said to him in Hebrew, "Rabbouni!" (which means Teacher).' To do justice to that allusion, it is appropriate to pause briefly over the good shepherd material.

The discourse in John 10, while working throughout within the parameters of sheep/shepherd imagery, is dislocated. That again points to stages in its development, and a weaving into a single tapestry of several different themes: (i) Jesus is presented as the good shepherd, the one whose voice is recognised by Mary-type believers. His being 'good' sets him over against other persons, other shepherds, who turn out to be the Pharisees, i.e. the leaders and teachers of the synagogue community which has expelled its Christian members. Mary is therefore representative of those who believe, i.e. all the Johannine Christians. (ii) Jesus is presented as the door, the sole means of entry to the sheepfold, which is therefore the sphere of safety and salvation. Mary therefore belongs among those who acknowledge that (contrary to what the synagogue community thinks) there is only *one* person who is 'the way, the truth and the life', and through whom *alone* people come to the Father. In affirming that a breakaway group is the exclusive sphere of salvation, the 4G speaks for a sectarian group, of which Mary is a representative member. (iii) The love of the shepherd is presented as showing itself in a death which will extend the scope of the true flock to include 'other sheep'. Who, we may ask, are they? Almost certainly, in $4G^1$ the God-fearing gentiles, typified by those who already recognise the God of Israel by coming to Jerusalem to worship at the festival (12:20), and then in $4G^2$ the Samaritans as well, typified by those who recognise Jesus as the saviour of the world (4:1–42).

It is important to note that while the second and the third of these themes are doubtless present as subdued sub-themes, it is the first which is given prominence by Jesus' calling Mary by name. Her response, couched in Hebrew and therefore making her very consciously a representative of the *Jewish* Christians within the community, might seem rather low-powered, 'Teacher'. But actually it is extremely high-powered: it is a confessional statement whereby she acknowledges and commits herself to the whole corpus of revelation that the Son has brought from the Father. In this she, just *one*, just one *woman*, speaks for *all*, the whole community of faith.

RESURRECTION PEOPLE: THE 'BELOVED DISCIPLE'

The 'beloved disciple' (BD) never ceases to mystify and yet to fascinate readers of the 4G. Can we work out who he is? Is he a real person who lived a human life and played a leading role in early Christianity, or is he a paper figure, dreamed up artificially by the evangelist? Does it matter anyway? If we have trouble deciding who he is and where he came from, can we do better in working out what he is there in the narrative – and perhaps in the community – to do? Such questions make the BD nothing short of a delight for the devotees of detective investigation!

In order to get on his track we need to begin in what may seem an unlikely context, the story of how two pairs of disciples not only followed Jesus but also acclaimed him with high-powered christological titles (1:35–50).

The Johannine story of how these disciples attached themselves to Jesus is quite clearly derived from the Synoptic traditions of the call of the two pairs of disciples (Mark 1:16–20/Matthew 4:18–22) and the confession of Peter at Caesarea Philippi (Mark 8:27–33/Matthew 16:13–23/Luke 9:18–22). Of the three Synoptic versions of the latter tradition it is Matthew's which seems to be the basis for John's version, for the evangelist is aware of distinctive MattR features. (i) Nathanael acclaims Jesus as *Son of God* as well as King of Israel (v. 49; cf. Matthew 16:16 diff. Mark 8:29). (ii) Acclamations *of* Jesus (vv. 41, 45, 49) are joined with acclamations *by* Jesus (vv. 42, 47): Simon Peter is to be renamed Cephas/Peter (cf. Matthew 16:16, 17–19 diff. Mark 8:29), while Nathanael is hailed as a truly representative Israelite.

Using Matthew, then, the fourth evangelist embarks on a rewriting process, involving some important alterations. Not the least important is the partial changing of the identity of the two pairs of disciples. Moreover, instead of all four being called on an equal footing, there is a sequence in each case whereby one of the pair brings the other into contact with Jesus. Thus Andrew brings Peter, and Philip brings Nathanael. The Andrew/Philip pairing will reappear, once in $4G^1$ at the very sensitive point where they act as intermediaries to bring gentiles into contact with the freshly acclaimed King of Israel (12:12, 20–3), and then again in $4G^2$ as conversation partners with Jesus prior to the feeding of the five thousand (6:5–9). The Peter/Nathanael pairing, whether or not it appears later, is arresting at this point: although they are both brought to Jesus, they are not treated equally, and of the two there is no doubt that Nathanael is the more dominant. Four considerations suggest this conclusion.

First, the great confession of Jesus is voiced, not by Peter, who as a matter of fact says nothing, but initially by Andrew and then in a specially intense form by Nathanael, 'Rabbi, you are the Son of God! You are the King of Israel!' (vv. 41, 49).

Second, the encounter with Nathanael is the high peak and climax of the initial sequence of events. It is given an atmosphere of formality by the use of a 'disclosure formula' (v. 47) – 'seeing . . . he said . . . behold . . .' (cf. de Goedt 1962) – which is used on only one other occasion, and that a highly significant one, with Jesus as the subject of the verbs: the episode involving the crucified Jesus, his mother and the BD (19:26–7). These two episodes form an *inclusio* for a story which begins here and ends at the cross once the status of the BD has been clarified (19:28–30).

Third, no attempt is made to develop the community significance of Peter's new name, whereas Nathanael is very plainly a representative community person: he is hailed as 'truly an Israelite' (v. 47). In 4G² this will be made even clearer, in that he is addressed in the plural and placed in the same position as the patriarch Jacob (v. 51). By virtue of his being described by Jesus as 'truly an Israelite', and also because of his acknowledging Jesus as 'the King of Israel', Nathanael is set very firmly in the context of conversation within the Jewish community, with shared religious convictions about the people's relationship to God to the fore: gentiles, who tended to use the term Jews to describe from outside (as it were) that nation and its religious practice are simply not 'on screen' here (cf. Tomson 1986). Nathanael, we can say therefore, represents indirectly the success of the mission of the Baptist, the intention of which was 'that [Jesus] might be revealed to Israel' (v. 31), and a prize exhibit of the movement which was designed to swell the ranks of the believing Christian Jews within the pre-schism religious community.

Fourth, it is not Peter but Nathanael who is promised an experience of revelation, the ultimate disclosure of the truth about Jesus (v. 50). Following on from that, although 4G¹ did not specify it, it was known in Johannine circles that Nathanael came from Cana (cf. 21:2). Now of the four disciples named in John 1, three come from Bethsaida (v. 44) and Nathanael is the only one whose home town is not stated. But once we know, then it is impressive that the two introductory signs performed by Jesus in this Gospel are both set by the evangelist in Nathanael's home town (2:1, 11; 4:46). That means, as the reader observes Jesus at work in those two episodes, the recollection is all the while kept fresh that Jesus had said to Nathanael and to him alone, 'You will see greater things than these' (v. 50). All these aspects of the Nathanael episode in the Jesus story need to be borne in mind as we wend our way through the series of explicit BD stories.

In John 13:23–6 the BD has been imposed on the Synoptic tradition about the traitor (Mark 14:17–21). Peter, too, emerges from the anonymity of the collective group of disciples to press for clarification of the traitor's identity. But he cannot gain this information except through the BD, who is positioned 'in the bosom of Jesus' (13:23, 25): that language points to the BD as having been placed by Jesus on his immediate right in the position of highest honour at the meal (cf. Smith 1987: 626), certainly higher than that assigned to Peter. That same language would be used in 4G^2 to describe all that the evangelist understood concerning the intimate relationship between the Father and the Son: 'The only Son, who is in the bosom of the Father, he has made him known' (1:18). That means that there is a chain of revelation stretching from Father to Son, from Son to BD, and from BD to other disciples. Peter's importance is recognised by his being introduced by name, but at the same time his dependence upon the super-important figure of the BD is conveyed by the latter's unique closeness to Jesus and his role in the revelation process. He is both representative – for *all* disciples are loved by Jesus (13:1) – and impressively distinct.

In John 19:25–7 the BD makes his next substantial appearance (he is probably 'the other disciple' of 18:15–17, but that lacks substance and does not need to be discussed here). Uniquely among the BD passages, this one does not involve Peter, and the pair who occupy centre stage are the BD and Mary. Once again the Synoptic Gospels, known and used by this evangelist, provide a useful yardstick.

In the 4G the women are positioned *near* the cross, not some distance from it, and they are introduced into the story before Jesus dies, not afterwards (v. 25, by contrast with Matthew 27:55; Mark 15:40; Luke 23:49). Almost as an afterthought – though we know better – when the list of those present might be thought complete (v. 25), the BD is suddenly mentioned: 'Jesus saw his mother and the disciple whom he loved . . .' (v. 26). His presence permits the crucially important words of Jesus to be spoken, words which are set within the disclosure formula 'seeing . . . he said . . . behold . . .' (vv. 26–7: cf. de Goedt 1962:

142–50). That they are crucially important is further underlined by their setting. Two small incidents take place in fulfilment of scripture after the crucifixion and the argument about the *titulus* (vv. 16b–22). The first is the allocation of Jesus' clothing, in fulfilment of Psalm 22:18 (vv. 23–4, developing Matthew 27:35; Mark 15:24; Luke 23:34). The second is the tortured cry of thirst and the response of the bystanders, in fulfilment of Psalm 22:15; 69:21 (vv. 28–30, developing Matthew 27:48; Mark 15:36; Luke 23:36). The words spoken to Mary and the BD (vv. 25–7) are framed by the two incidents fulfilling scripture, thus certainly highlighting what Jesus says, but the relationship between the three episodes is more subtle than that. The evangelist uses a 'both [the soldiers' action] . . . and [the words to Mary and the BD]' formulation to unite the first two, and begins the third by saying that 'after *this* [singular] Jesus, knowing that all things had *already* been completed' (v. 28). So the words spoken to Mary and the BD are the sine qua non of Jesus' dying. So, and only so, it becomes possible for the dying Jesus to make the triumphant last cry, 'It is finished'.

The meaning of those words, 'Behold your son . . . Behold your mother', is critically important and illuminated by a parallel. When at the moment of his death, the loyalist hero Mattathias set about establishing the succession to himself he bypassed his eldest son John, committed military responsibility to the third son Judas, and gave primacy to the second son Simeon, 'Here is your brother Simeon who, I know, is wise in counsel: always listen to him; *he shall be your father.*' The use of family metaphor in 1 Maccabees 2:65 in such a way as to transcend natural family definitions, and all for the purpose of securing the succession, establishing a sapiential role, and safeguarding the community, provides precedent for the use of family metaphor in John 19: 26–7. The designated successor to Jesus is announced in his last words to his mother and the BD.

His mother and the BD – yes indeed, not Mary Magdalene and the BD! Mary Magdalene has been displaced to third/fourth position in deference to the kinship ties represented by mother and aunt. Mary Magdalene would soon emerge as the model disciple, the model member of the community all of whose members can be seen for the first time as 'brothers', that is persons bonded to the common Father (20:17). Thus has family language been reorganised. But does the new family include the old, or the bond of the Spirit include fleshly kinship? Not until the cross, it seems, for the mother and the brothers of Jesus, who are treated equally by him (2:1–11; 7:1–9), accept him as one who performs signs and yet remain in the category of unbelief (cf. 7:5). An initial refusal to perform signs at the bidding of either mother or brothers because the hour – emphatically his hour (ὥρα/καιρός) – has not yet come, has to be subsumed within the multiplicity of sayings which equate that hour with the hour of his glorification. And it is in that hour, which must be the hour of belief and knowledge, that the deliberate distancing of Jesus from his mother (2:4) is replaced by the closest association possible – which happens now to be with the BD! So, no, the relationship of spirit/Spirit does not exclude the relationship of flesh, for all that it transcends it. But, yes, it is the BD who now personally represents that higher order to Mary.

His mother and the BD – yes indeed, not his mother and Peter! Peter was locally available (20:2), but at the cross he is nowhere to be seen. Doubtless his dissociation of himself from Jesus is a serious, maybe fatal, disqualification (18:15–18, 25–7). However that may be, the absence of Peter and the presence of the BD at the cross are both heavily significant. Both followed Jesus (18:15), one stayed constant, the other denied. The following of the second was not a true following, for all that true following would occur later (13:36–8). Given the transparency of the Johannine text, the message could scarcely be clearer.

In John 20:3–10 the BD appears alongside Peter, now once more described as a 'disciple' in spite of what happened in the high priest's courtyard. Internal evidence suggests that this is a rewritten version of Luke 24:12, with the BD superimposed upon it. The double preposition in verse 2, 'she ran therefore and came *to* Simon Peter and *to* the other disciple whom Jesus loved', suggests this; the singular/plural confusion in verse 3, 'then Peter and the other disciple went out [singular], and they went to the tomb', tends only to confirm it. Then there is the curious doubling up of the very exact description of the wrappings, visible outside as well as inside the tomb (vv. 5–7), and the even more curious pattern of the BD's movements, arriving first, having a look but not going in, waiting for Peter so that he may go in first, and then following him into the tomb (vv. 4b, 5b, 6, 8a). Most curious of all, one might say, is the response to what is seen there: a lack of understanding, which is then explained, and leads to the lowest of low-key endings: 'Then the disciples returned to their homes.' But that response is only curious when juxtaposed with the information that the BD 'saw and believed' (v. 8b). The solution to the problem posed by all these curiosities is fairly clear: the BD has been imposed, not altogether skilfully, on an earlier tradition of a visit by Peter to the tomb, according to which he saw the cloths that had been wrapped around Jesus' body but did not on that basis reach a position of belief. As far as the evangelist's intention is concerned, the specialness of Peter is respected – he it is to whom Mary Magdalene comes primarily; he it is who first enters the tomb – but the extra-specialness of the BD is carefully affirmed – he it is who is the first witness of the wrappings, and above all, he it is who sees and believes, whereas Peter only sees. In short, there is only one prototypical resurrection believer, and only one person to whom the evangelist and his community look back to provide legitimation of their own resurrection belief. And that one person is not Peter!

In John 21:1–14, and its sequel 21:15–23, to which we shall return, the BD appears again in the company of Peter. It is extremely likely that Luke has provided the foundation traditions for John 21 (cf. Luke 5:1–12; 24:13–35, 36–43: see Neirynck

1991: 601–16), and that again the BD is a secondary development in the story which dominates the chapter, the fish miracle. For here again there are dislocations for which his presence is ultimately responsible.

First, although Jesus is on the shore approximately 100 metres away from the disciples, he knows about the failure of their fishing expedition (vv. 5, 8). It would have been more realistic for him to know this if he had been in the boat with them, but then it would not have been possible for him to be recognised – by the BD, of course! – or to prepare and provide that sacramental meal which is the ultimate concern of the story (vv. 9, 12a, 13).

Second, the disciples in general do not recognise Jesus (v. 4b) – notwithstanding what happened according to 20:19–29! Their failure to recognise him is in tension with their ready acceptance of his instructions, backed by his supernatural awareness that this will bring success (v. 6). The evidence concerning his identity, which was manifestly available to all, produced a recognition by just one – surprise, surprise, the BD! – and Peter responds to that recognition which he owes to another. It is said, rather oddly, that 'he heard' it (v. 7b), which serves only to draw more attention to his dependence on the BD who told him.

Third, the chain of events started by the BD's recognition, 'It is the Lord' (v. 7a), involves a fair degree of complication, one might even say confusion. If he had not recognised Jesus and told Peter – but not apparently the other five disciples – Peter would not have made his unilateral rush to shore to meet Jesus (v. 7b), and would not in consequence have been separated from the rest as they brought the catch ashore (v. 8). This would not have necessitated his response to an instruction from Jesus to the disciples to bring the fish ashore (vv. 10–11), odd in itself since (i) we would have assumed from verse 8 that the catch had already been brought ashore, and (ii) the fish brought ashore remain separate from the fish which Jesus has prepared (v. 13).

Finally, the statement that none of the disciples dared to ask

---

him, 'Who are you?' because they knew it was the Lord (v. 12b) is artificially placed within a sequence which moves smoothly from Jesus as preparer of the fire, the cooked fish and the bread (v. 9), to his invitation to the disciples to share that food (v. 12) and his distribution of the food as a eucharistic meal (v. 13).

How may we explain these dislocations or, as one might put it, this tangle of several threads? To the evangelist each of the threads is vitally important. The first is the underlying story of a miraculous catch of fish, brought about by instructions from a Jesus who has supernatural knowledge. The second is the eucharistic celebration, within which the other five are brought to experience and share the recognition of the risen Jesus. The third is the Peter/BD interaction, kept separate from the experience of the other five disciples. In presenting this interaction the evangelist is careful to establish the primacy of the BD as a resurrection believer and the dependence of Peter upon him.

How, one has to ask, does 21:15–22 add to all this? Essentially, it completes hitherto unfinished business in relation to Peter and his rehabilitation. His specialness had been implied in $4G^1$: singled out to be a leader by virtue of his being brought to Jesus and renamed in 1:40–2, and then after a long silence singled out in 13:6–9 to be a representative figure (note the plural in 13:10–11) experiencing that baptism, the mysterious meaning of which will become clear in the light of the passion. Still within $4G^1$, and shortly after that, disaster is foreshadowed in 13:36–7 and realised in 18:15–18, 25–7. Even after his denial, the fact that he still counted as a disciple had been implicit in 20:2, but in 20:8–10 he had not been enlisted as one who 'saw and believed'. In 20:19–23 he was doubtless among the twelve who saw the Lord, but he is subsumed in the larger group and, one might say, his own agenda is not addressed. In 21:15–22 it is.

(i) The address 'Simon, son of John' (used only in 1:42 and 21:15–17) takes him back to the beginning, indeed before the beginning when he was renamed, brought under new ownership, as it were, and enlisted as a follower. Jesus accepts with heavy irony Peter's dissociation of himself from the disciple group. (ii) The threefold questioning deliberately evokes 18:15–18, 25–7. As some might put it, he revisits the trauma. (iii) The wording of the questioning, 'Do you love me (more than these)?' deliberately recalls Peter's singling out of himself as a uniquely faithful follower in 13:37–8. In that same exchange it is laid down that there will be (in Jesus' view) a following to be undertaken later, and Peter's view that in his own case following shows itself in the laying down of his life for Jesus is picked up in what is said in 21:18–19 about following and the prospect of martyrdom. (iv) The wording 'Do you love me . . .?' points straight back to John 10 and the fundamental principles of authentic leadership: the true leader acts out the example of that love and knowledge which are effected in the laying down of life for others (10:13–15). (v) In the same vein, the commission, 'Feed my lambs/sheep' (21:15–17) spells out in positive terms the leadership role which Peter is to exercise. We do not, contrary to the view of some interpreters, have here a movement by Johannine Christianity to 'cosy up' at a later stage to the so-called Great Church, represented allegedly by Peter. No, in 21:1–14 we have exactly the same portrayal of the Peter/BD relationship as in the earlier BD passages; in 21:15–19 we have a completion of the line of thought which is already implicit in the Peter passages in $4G^1$; in 21:20–2 the uniqueness of the Jesus/BD relationship is reasserted, for the BD is partly defined by having been given an answer to a question about the future action of one of the disciples (v. 20, cf. 13:23–6), but when Peter asks a question about the future action of the most important disciple of all, he gets no answer at all (vv. 21–2).

In conclusion, the BD passages in the 4G convey a powerful message about a person who is, first, a representative figure; second, a person upon whom the Johannine community depends for the revelation that defines its theological and religious position, and to whom it looks for legitimation; third, a person who is superior to Peter, for all that the latter's special position is always respected. That was exactly the message which the early narrative in the 4G conveyed concerning Nathanael. He represented the community, as the prototype Christian Jew who came to Jesus, acclaiming him as the Son of God and King of Israel, and being in his turn formally acclaimed as 'truly an Israelite'. He was the person in whose home town of Cana the key introductory signs exhibiting the glory of Jesus took place. He was the person who was paired with Peter and yet, notwithstanding the key position of the latter, overshadowed him. The Nathanael pattern and the BD pattern are so extraordinarily comparable, that an equation between the two is almost irresistible! And if we run with that equation we can see how the 4G, in spite of its conspicuous and often negative treatment of 'the Jews', remains constant in its preoccupation with 'Israel'. The figure of the BD/Nathanael is testimony to its instinctive longing to continue to talk *within* the Israelite community about the person to whom the sacred scriptures of that community bear witness.

RESURRECTION PEOPLE: THE DISCIPLES

Again and again throughout the 4G the evangelist draws on the resources of the wisdom tradition to present Jesus as Wisdom in person. Again and again the 4G also draws on the pattern of the angelophany traditions: Jesus descends and ascends, he appears in human shape, he is subordinate to God and yet in a certain sense equivalent to God, and all the while he discloses God. It is this angelic model which comes most readily to mind when Jesus says to Mary Magdalene, 'I have not yet ascended to the Father. . . . I am ascending to my Father and your Father, to your God and my God' (20:17). One has only to recall the angel Raphael's announcement to Tobit and Tobiah at the end of an extended narrative, also in a recognition scene, 'See, I am ascending to him who sent me' (Tobit 12:20). In the context of such angelic recognition scenes it is normal, even mandatory, that there should be an acknowledgement of the God whom the angelic figure serves and has revealed (cf. Tobit 12:6–7, 17–18, 20, 22). This is probably the thrust of the reference to the Father who is said to be – and here we encounter one of the most severely subordinationist formulae in the 4G – 'my Father and your Father, my God and your God'. The acknowledgement that the God and Father of Jesus is the God and Father of the community is not only a recognition that what has taken place in and through Jesus is indeed a revelation of God. To the implicit acknowledgement *by the community* there is added an implicit acknowledgement *of the community*. That God is confirmed as their Father serves to distinguish them from those who claim 'one Father, God himself', and who have been icily dismissed, 'If God were your Father, you would love me, for I came from God and now I am here' (8:41–2). Sonship is exclusively reserved for those who receive the divine emissary and who through baptism enter into a relationship which transcends human bonds (1:11–13; 3:3–8). In the glow of Easter the resurrection people can for the first time be designated 'brothers'.

The literary evidence we uncovered earlier on throws a flood of light on this situation. It points to the conclusion that sustained editorial work at the 4G^2 stage was designed to promote the ideas of the new and separated Christian community as a new family – sons in relation to God, and brothers in relation to one another – and a new temple. If this is correct, it means that the evangelist's timing of his first reference to the disciples as brothers of Jesus was strategically impeccable and theologically resonant.

First, when the present form of the prologue was attached at the 4G^2 stage, a new understanding of what it means to be 'the children of God' was introduced redactionally: it was for those 'who believed in his name' and experienced a birth which was – here the language becomes very loaded – 'not of blood, or of the will of the flesh or of the will of man, but of God' (1:12–13). Here the status which the members of the Jewish community thought was theirs, is now being taken away from them and given to others whose faith-decision was a second birth. This adds up to being 're-socialised', crossing a boundary into a new and distinct community. The use of language which in a Christian context could only evoke baptism enables the reader to discern the sacramental boundary-marker which defines the new community.

Second, and still working with what happened at the $4G^2$ stage of the literary process, when the Temple material was moved to its present position in 2:13–22, it provided the control for the Nicodemus and Samaritan woman episodes which were (as we have seen) inserted at the same time. (i) The presentation of the heavenly birth by water-and-Spirit is plainly intended to amplify what was said in 1:12–13 about a new and transcendent birth. (ii) The section of the conversation with the Samaritan woman devoted to temple worship is something of an interruption: the transition from her acknowledgement of Jesus as a prophet on the basis of his reference to her sexually permissive past, to 'Our ancestors worshipped on this mountain . . .' is abrupt and a distraction away from the only item which not only impresses the woman but also provides a thread of continuity and forms the sole content of her testimony: 'Come and see a man who told me everything I have ever done . . . He told me everything I have ever done' (vv. 16–19, 29, 39). It looks as if verses 20–4 are an editorially inserted section. But that section devoted to temple worship is all about the new order – 'the hour is coming and now is' – which is quite unmistakably the resurrection order: talk elsewhere of 'the hour [which] is coming and now is' is resurrection talk (cf. 5:25, 28), and talk in the Temple cleansing incident of the present order of temple worship being replaced by a new order is talk about an order which is, paradoxically, inaugurated by the dead-raising Jesus and embodied in the risen Jesus (2:19–22).

The community addressed through Mary continues to come into focus in the story of how the one who had already ascended subsequently appeared (20:19–23, 24–9). The material shows signs of having been expanded, and the process of theological enquiry has therefore to reckon once again with more than one stage.

The tradition-historical evidence is as follows: (i) The repeated greeting, 'Peace be with you' (vv. 19, 21) gives the meeting two starts, and the disciples' gladness would be better provoked by the sheer fact of seeing him than by the offering of hands and side as evidence (v. 20a). This suggests that in verses 19–20 secondary redaction can be detected in 'and said, "Peace be with you". After he had said this, he showed them his hands and his side', the removal of which leaves a straightforward and smooth sequence. (ii) The Thomas incident which follows in verses 24–9 depends on verse 20a, but is itself in tension with some elements of verses 1–18: the concession to the demand for sight and touch in verses 25, 27 is ill at ease with the prohibition of touch in verse 17, and the negative perspective on seeing and believing in verse 29 cannot but cast a certain shadow over the BD's seeing and believing in verse 8. (iii) The consequence of assigning verses 20a, 24–9 to redaction is that the same must be done to 19:31–7. That is in itself entirely unproblematic: 19:35 links with 21:24, which was not in 4G¹; the time-note in 19:42 referring to 'the day of Preparation' is made redundant by the earlier time-note in 19:31 saying the same thing; the two requests to Pilate for permission to remove Jesus' body in verses 31, 38 compete with one another, especially since one would have inferred from verses 31b–2 that the first request had been granted; and the crucifixion narrative reads more smoothly in a sequence which juxtaposes verse 30 and verse 38.

The concluding scene in 4G¹ consisted therefore of an appearance of Jesus in circumstances of secrecy and fear, bringing joy to the disciples, and a sequence of sayings involving, first, the gift of peace and a commission; and, second, the in-breathing with the Holy Spirit and an authorisation in respect of the forgiveness and retention of sins. The 4G¹ text, with 4G² additions italicised, ran as follows:

> ¹⁹When it was evening on that day, the first day of the week, and the doors of the house where the disciples had met were locked for fear of the Jews, Jesus came and stood among them *and said, 'Peace be with you.'* ²⁰ᵃ*After he said this, he showed them his hands and his side.* ²⁰ᵇThen the disciples rejoiced when they saw the Lord. ²¹Jesus said to them, 'Peace be with you. As the Father has sent me, so I send you.' ²²When he had said this, he breathed on them and said to them, 'Receive the Holy Spirit. ²³If you forgive the sins of any, they are forgiven them; if you retain the sins of any, they are retained.'

This story, the final incident in the 4G¹ narrative, holds together several of the themes which have come to the fore in the body of the Gospel, themes which have been opened up in the earlier part of this presentation. Not the least striking is the Christians versus Jews scenario.

The picture of a small frightened group of followers of Jesus, gathered together on a Sunday evening, acutely conscious of their exposure to threats from 'the Jews', is doubtless a transparent representation of what life was like in the Johannine community. The resurrection of Jesus, brought firmly to mind by the time of meeting, was the cornerstone of their faith. The first day of the week was a working day, but the evening was a time when work was finished and they could meet to celebrate the presence of the one in whom they believed. That belief was strenuously resisted by those with whom most of them had not long before been joined by shared participation in the richness of the life of Israel, 'the Jews'.

That loaded term, 'the Jews': it is important to recall how varied usage of the two terms 'the Jews' and 'Israel' reflects different socio-religious perspectives. A comprehensive review of Jewish literature (Tomson 1986) over centuries reveals that the first term expresses a *non*-Jewish perspective and includes an awareness of the Jews in the wider community of nations, while the second term expresses an *inner*-Jewish perspective, with writer and readers sharing a strong covenantal and salvation-historical consciousness. When a writer uses both terms in a single document, his or her personal position (inner-Jewish or non-Jewish) will determine which sections of the document are simply, as it were, part of the story, and which sections are direct communication with the reader. And having said that, one cannot but recall as well that the Johannine use of the term 'the Jews' has given rise to serious misgivings in the minds of Christian interpreters of the 4G, as well as fierce criticism from Jewish partners in Jewish-Christian dialogue. The dialogue must not, however, be the tail that wags the dog, nor must the misuse of the Gospel of John by those whose perspectives and purposes are worlds apart from those of the evangelist prevent us from recognising the careful nuancing which characterises his use of both terms 'the Jews' and 'Israel'.

First, the term 'the Jews' does represent negatively the non-Christian community which has expelled the Christian Jews. The developing narrative in John 9 painted a picture of 'the Jews' carrying out that expulsion: in superimposing 'the Jews' on 'the Pharisees' (cf. 9:18, 22–3) the evangelist absorbed the idea of a scrutinising leadership group which had been engaged in checking out, as was wholly appropriate, the credentials of Jesus. As the leadership group they could be seen both as representative of the *whole* community and also as that *part* of the community divided by Jesus (Ashton 1991: 151–9). Their own ultimately negative decision about Jesus brought John 9, where the Pharisees were conspicuously present, into line with John 5, where they were conspicuously absent.

Second, we have repeatedly seen within the debates about Jesus evidence of – can we say? – an inner-Jewish instinct on both sides of the argument. Thus, while the arguments are drawn from 'your' law they remain arguments which genuinely attempt to justify the Christian position in Mosaic terms.

Third, even after the recrimination between two alienated groups had become acute and vitriolic at the $4G^2$ stage, 4:1–42 could show how the term 'Jew' could be introduced by a non-Jew (4:9) but picked up by the Jewish conversation partner in a resoundingly salvation-historical statement (4:22). While the *language* of 'salvation is from the Jews' may be an accommodation to a non-Jewish hearer, the *thought* is plainly that 'salvation is from Israel'.

Fourth, while instances of the term 'the Jews' massively outnumber instances of the term 'Israel' we should shun statistical hypnosis. The Israel-references are, as it were, 'quality references': John the Baptist, whose witness directly determines the introductory phase in 1:6–7, 19–35, and whose influence pervades the Jerusalem phase of Jesus' own mission in 5:33–6 and 10:40–2, has one and only one intention – revelation to *Israel* (1:31). Nathanael, the representative community figure, the new Jacob (1:47), acclaims Jesus as Son of God, and in so doing incorporates the role of 'King of *Israel*' (1:49): through the BD his influence pervades the passion narrative. As the Jerusalem period covered by chapters 5, 7–10 comes to an end and the passion period begins, the crowd's acclamation of Jesus as 'the King of *Israel*', scripture's portrayal of him as Zion's king (12:12–15), not only reiterates what has been said before but affirms what the resurrection will confirm (12:16).

Fifth, while the community of the 4G has almost certainly attracted members from outside Israel – the 'other sheep', including Samaritans (4:39–42) and God-fearing gentiles (12:20–3) – and has therefore to provide clarification of festivals 'of the Jews' and translation of non-Greek terms (1:41; 20:16), these explanations are provided, as it were, from *within* the continuity of salvation-history rather than from outside it. Therefore the fact that an expulsion from the community of 'the Jews' has occurred should not be taken as an endorsement of that expulsion on the part of those expelled: they believe that in the conflict between the two presently separated bodies they are the ones – better, Jesus is the one – in whom the continuity of God's salvation-historical dealings with the world and with Israel can be recognised. With 5:39–47 in mind we can conclude that as resurrection people they experience that life towards which the writings of Moses pointed.

Returning to the appearance of Jesus to the beleaguered disciple group, we note that he comes as the one who has ascended to the Father. In $4G^1$, it is in line with the transcendence of his existence that he should 'come' to a group sheltering behind locked doors (20:19). That understanding of his existence was in line with that of most other resurrection appearance traditions, in the Gospels most notably on Luke's road to Emmaus (24:13–35) and Matthew's mountain in Galilee (28:16–20). For $4G^2$, however, this was not adequate, any more than it had been when Luke wrote his 24:36–43. The extreme physical realism of the existence of the risen Jesus, relying on the extreme physical realism of the damage done to him in his dying moments (20:20a, 24–7, cf. 19:31–7), opens a window on the debates which came to engulf the Johannine Christians. They had moved on. In the debate with fellow-Jews they had perforce to defend the attribution of God-language to one whose manhood was tacit and unquestioned (see above on 5:17–18; 10:33–6). That was the 'external' bone of contention. But 'internally' that high-powered christology was taken further, and the full humanity of the transcendent divine one, it seems, came into question. Some Christians became more Johannine than John.

So a new preface had to be provided for the 4G – thus, accompanied by some JohnR assertions, the poem about the Word, which drew upon the resources of the Wisdom and angelic models, but which went further than any other Wisdom or angelic text had ever gone before and affirmed that 'the Word became flesh'. And a new epilogue had also to be provided to form an *inclusio* with the prologue, in order to declare that Jesus was indeed God (20:28, cf. 1:1), and to ensure that the risen Jesus was no longer understood by analogy with the angels. In his incarnation, yes, and no less in his resurrection, his unqualified physicality had to be affirmed. One can only say that in making this affirmation the Johannine Christians, like Luke before them, fashioned for themselves a bed of nails.

This interpretation of the Thomas incident connects the Johannine expansion to the 'internal' development of the community. But the theological texture of the community can be perceived by 'insiders' and also by those who are on the boundary between 'outside' and 'inside' territory. In this case Thomas, as one of the twelve who have been defined previously in $4G^2$ as persons chosen by Jesus (6:67, 70), seems to symbolise those who are 'in'. Yet we know from the career of another of the twelve (6:71; 13:18–19, 21–30) that to be 'in' is not necessarily a permanent state, and therefore if seeing and believing are now focused on Jesus as risen it is necessary once again to stand on the boundary with those who are, paradoxically, 'on the outside looking in'. His demand, 'Unless I see . . . I will not believe', points to this situation by the precision with which it recalls what was said to the representative non-Christian Jew, 'Unless you see signs and wonders you will not believe' (4:48), the person who was brought to faith by material proof that Jesus' word was confirmed. It is belief in the resurrection – resurrection as understood in extremely physical terms – which constitutes the boundary between Christians and non-Christian Jews.

What the risen Jesus says to the disciples is on any showing crucial. Although more would follow in $4G^2$, the Jesus of $4G^1$ has no more to do or say. What he says has two parts, each with its own introduction.

In the first part, the gift of peace and the commissioning both function within the continuity of the Gospel to renew what was said in the $4G^1$ shorter version of the farewell discourse. This is not surprising, since the function of a farewell discourse is to lay down the guidelines which control time after the speaker's departure. In the preamble to the first farewell discourse there had been two 'interruptions', both indicative of major perspectives on what would follow. The first was the 'sending' saying (13:20), a Johannine recycling of that Synoptic saying which perhaps epitomises more than any other the mission of the historical Jesus (cf. Matthew 10:42/Luke 10:16), and here diverting the discussion of the betrayer (13:18–19, 21–30). The second is the allegedly new, though actually old, command to love other members of the community (13:34–5), a saying reflecting the typical atmosphere of a sectarian community, and here interrupting the discussion of where Jesus is going (13:33, 36–8). After the preamble there follows the discourse, framed by the encouragement that the disciples' hearts should not be troubled (14:1, 27). The peace to which the discourse refers is a peace informed by the belief that the one who goes away will come back (14:28). In the story of Jesus that coming back is told by the resurrection narrative – in the story of the Johannine Christians which becomes visible through the window of the resurrection narrative. The community enjoys security and peace through its joyful experience of the unseen presence of the risen Jesus.

In the second part, prefaced with the distinctive introduction, 'When he had said this he breathed on them and said to them . . .' (v. 22), the risen Jesus gives the Holy Spirit and lays down the community position on forgiveness and retention of sins. Doubtless this 'in-breathing' means that the risen Jesus is the one upon whom all life depends (cf. Genesis 2:7; Wisdom 15:11), the one 'in whom was life, the light of all people' (1:3–4), the one through whom the destiny of humankind can be reached, the one who has not only experienced resurrection but now imparts it (cf. Ezekiel 37:10). Doubtless also this gift of the Holy Spirit is understood by the evangelist, writing his 4G[1], as the activation of that baptism with the Holy Spirit that John the Baptist has envisaged, the fulfilment of Jesus' own promises, given publicly at the Feast of Tabernacles (7:37–9) and privately in the farewell discourse (14:17, 26). There were no other references to the Holy Spirit in 4G[1]. The evangelist caused the mission of John to be absorbed into a revelatory scheme: the identity of the future baptiser had first to be revealed to him (1:32), and then his own baptism became the means of revelation to others (1:33). Nothing was left of a 'baptism of repentance for the forgiveness of sins' (Mark 1:4). It can scarcely be coincidental that the one and only Johannine reference to the forgiveness of sins should occur alongside the saying about the reception of the Spirit, and moreover that it should involve a substitution of forgiveness/retention for the binding/loosing language of Matthew 16:19, 18:18. No longer are we dealing with discipline within the church: now it is baptismal entry into the community, entry which takes place not by birth but by voluntary association. That characteristically sectarian development brings to bear on the sacrament of baptism a powerful sense that the body which is being entered is the community of the resurrection.

That community self-understanding, and the sectarian reflex associated with it, are reinforced by the Johannine treatment, rare in itself, of the topic of sin. Within the continuity of the narrative overall, and in the setting of miracle in particular, the relationship between sin and ill health has twice been addressed (5:14; 9:2–3, 34): it is possible that this could come into play again as the community exercises the authority conferred by the risen Jesus in 20:23. After all, the promise had been given of post-resurrection works identical with, or even greater than, those of the pre-resurrection Jesus (14:12). Equally important, however, is the fact that the only other occasions when the topic of sin is treated occur in confrontations with opponents or defecting followers of Jesus (8:21, 24, 34; 9:41). From this it becomes clear that belief in the risen Jesus, freedom from sins, and faithfulness to the community are inextricably bound together. Given the characteristic concern of a sectarian community to define its identity by clear boundaries, and also to retain a relentless hold upon its members, the final saying of Jesus in 20:23 could not but function to reassure those who were 'in' of the rich significance of their baptism, and to warn those who were in danger of slipping 'out' that they would cross the line out of the community of the resurrection into the sphere where 'sins remain'.

Baptism, then, is the implicit theme with which $4G^1$ came to an end. For $4G^2$, the joyful celebration of the eucharist was the great climax. Already in $4G^1$ there had been unmistakable eucharistic as well as baptismal overtones in the John 13 story of the final supper: the eating of the bread of Jesus (v. 18). Not the least striking feature of that story is the prominence given to Judas (vv. 18–19, 21–30). But in that narrative, while Peter represents all the baptised, and the BD represents all those who are loved, Judas represents none but himself. In $4G^2$, however, this would change.

As already observed, John 6 made its appearance only at the $4G^2$ stage. It involved a rewriting of material in Matthew/Mark. Peter's confession was still the end-term in the sequence of events, and characteristic features of the Matthew/Mark versions of that tradition can still be observed: (i) an acknowledgement of Jesus' status (ii) in direct speech (iii) by Peter, who (iv) speaks for the whole disciple group (v) in a setting overshadowed by the thought of death, while (vi) the presence of the devil (vii) in the life of a disciple (viii) is acknowledged by Jesus. What can also be observed is the evangelist's remodelling of Peter's confession and his provision of a revised context for it. In verses 31–58 Jesus had delivered a sermon on the text of Exodus 16:4, 15, and had caused both consternation among 'the Jews' and a split among the disciples (Borgen 1963). His speaking of himself in extremely strong and realistic terms as God's gift in word and sacrament had proved more than some of the disciples could take. The immediately following question from Jesus, 'Do you also wish to go away?' (v. 67) enabled Peter's answer to be the confession of those who stayed faithful and loyal to Jesus. This thought can be followed up.

First, Jesus had spoken about some disciples who

(paradoxically) did not believe (v. 64), and he appealed to the idea of predestination in evaluating them (v. 65, cf. v. 44). That involved a quotation of the main argument he had used to counter criticism from 'the Jews' (vv. 41–2). To appeal to predestination is yet another sectarian reflex. So the faithful loyalists, whom Peter represents, have the problem that some of their own number defect and go back to where they have come from.

Second, the Johannine version does not have the devil speaking through Peter: instead he is at work in Judas (v. 70) and in those former Christian Jews who, having become Jewish Christians, now go back to the synagogue community. To associate one's religious opponents not only with Judas Iscariot but also with Satan exhibits another typically sectarian tendency to divide the world into two sharply polarised zones – 'a way of assuring the members of the writer's own sect that they are really on the winning side' (Ashton 1993: 212) – you are either 'in', enjoying light, possessing truth, belonging to God's elect, or you are 'out', groping in darkness, beset by falsehood, excluded from the (small) circle of God's people . . .

Third, the cause of the offence is obvious: the deepest possible repugnance was caused to Jews and to some disciples by talk of Jesus as not only the giver but also, in the form of 'flesh', the divine gift. These disciples are represented by Judas. He was said in 13:18 to be the one eating (τρώγων) the bread of Jesus, and that rare word, introduced redactionally into the quotation of Psalm 41:9, 'The one who ate my bread has lifted his heel against me', is used again here in 6:54, 56, 58. Those who find what Jesus is now saying repugnant are repeating the pattern of the one who shared Jesus' bread before defecting and disappearing into the darkness. If we once again allow the Johannine text to be transparent, it must mean that sometime after the initial severance of Christian Jews from the synagogue their new community was itself torn by dispute. Some of its members, whose reflexes remained through and through Jewish, objected most strongly to the direction in which eucharistic reflection was moving.

From the skilful and subtle editorial work which is on display in chapter 6 we can move first to chapter 15, the beginning of the expansion of the farewell discourse. Using eucharistic imagery the evangelist returned to the theme that effective sacramental life depends on being cleansed at the deepest level by the word of Jesus: Judas was a tragic example of how, without that cleansing, one may participate in baptism and eucharist and still be 'thrown away' (v. 6) or 'lost' (cf. 17:12). To remain in Jesus, which is the sine qua non for safety, is simply a coded way of insisting on the need to remain in the Johannine community. And then we can move finally to chapter 21, where the representative group of seven disciples relives the experience of 6:11, 'Jesus took the loaves, and when he had given thanks, he distributed them . . . so also the fish . . .'. What has changed in 21:13 when 'he came and took the bread and gave it to them, and did the same with the fish'? Why, nothing, except that he is risen and they are renewed. He and they, sharing the meal, are resurrection people.

Chapter Five

JESUS AND THE RESURRECTION PEOPLE

INTRODUCTION

Long before the educational world of the UK echoed to the sound of 'the national curriculum', the 'numeracy hour' and the 'literacy hour', a teacher with a mouth 'wide, thin and hard set', a voice 'inflexible, dry and dictatorial', and a head whose very shape suggested that it 'had scarcely warehouse-room for the facts stored inside', laid down his uncompromising pedagogical law: 'In this life,' he said, 'we want nothing but Facts, Sir; nothing but Facts! Plant nothing else, and root out everything else. You can only form the minds of reasoning animals upon Facts: nothing else will ever be of service to them.' Thus spoke that paragon of educational liberalism, Mr Thomas Gradgrind. And thus began Charles Dickens' story of *Hard Times*.

The resurrection narratives which round off four extended stories of the earthly Jesus have emerged from our studies as part of a process of growth and development, and they are richly varied. They are as varied as the communities which treasured them and the theologies of the evangelists who exploited them. But sooner or later contemporary readers are bound to ask whether there are facts of human experience which gave rise to them, facts for which they may dare to search. And surely they are right: we must dare, we cannot but search. As Alfred Lord

Tennyson might have written, 'tis better to have searched and failed, than never to have searched at all.

Three questions, incorporating that search, form the agenda of this our final study. They are partly historical and partly theological. First, what can be known of that post-death happening which was labelled 'resurrection'? Second, what did (or could) the mission of the historical Jesus contribute to the post-resurrection reflection and experience of those who were pulled back from the precipice of despair by the conviction that he had been raised from the dead? Third, what is the legacy to contemporary Christianity of the resurrection of Jesus, the Gospel narratives which bear witness to it, and indeed the richly varying early Christian communities which were sustained by it?

There is, however, a question behind the questions, and that is the question of God. Unless we opt for the view that everything started in the inner psyche of this or that leading figure in early Christianity, a view which current discussion of the resurrection of Jesus compels us to take seriously (Lüdemann 1994; Wedderburn 1999), all talk of resurrection is ultimately God-talk, and indeed God-talk which is prepared to take the double risk of believing in God and understanding his/her relation to the world in a particular way. If there was any such thing as a 'post-death happening' of the sort that appears to underlie the testimony of the evangelists and those upon whom they depended, God, and *a certain sort of interventionist God*, would appear to be a necessary premise. If the mission of the historical Jesus is to contribute anything at all to post-resurrection reflection, it must at the very least take seriously the idea of his speaking and acting with such *an immediate and specially personal sense of God* as would enable him to be classified as a prophet. And if the contemporary Christian community is to live in the light and life of the resurrection, it too has *to believe in God* – probably a good deal more, certainly not less.

A specialist discussion of the grounds for belief in God belongs outside the range of this book and its writer. As a modus operandi, therefore, the work of others has to be presumed, and most notably the understanding of God which has recently been renewed specifically in the setting of a discussion of the resurrection of Jesus. For our study we need to have in place, as it were, 'a being essentially omnipotent, omniscient and perfectly free'; a being whose existence is supported by 'the evidence of the existence of a complex physical universe, the (almost invariable) conformity of material bodies to natural laws, the evolution of animals and humans (souls connected to bodies), the providential ordering of the world in various ways, and the widespread phenomenon of religious experience (in the form of people seeming to be aware of the presence of God)'; a being 'who might be expected to intervene occasionally in the natural order' and who might, therefore, on the basis of supporting historical evidence be thought to have done so (Swinburne 1998: 198, 202). On that basis we will proceed to discuss the three main agenda items already listed.

THE MIND OF THE MOVEMENT

The one unassailable fact with which we may begin our search is that the term 'resurrection' was used in the earliest days following the death of Jesus by persons who had been at the heart of the movement he led. Now 'resurrection' had been a single theme with many variations during the two hundred years before Jesus – variations born of different circumstances, different intellectual approaches, different social strata, different strategies of portrayal, some more poetic and artistically impressionistic than others (Nickelsburg 1972). A single systematic scheme is just not forthcoming, and to look for one is to ask for the impossible. That way lies nothing but confusion and frustration. What we can say, however, is that those who belonged to the Jesus movement (i) belonged to a certain stratum of society, and (ii) they had listened to Jesus.

Their convictions about Jesus would probably have conformed to the view of resurrection which the careful preservation of bones in Jewish ossuaries presupposes, that is, the view that the person is somehow identified with his or her bones, and that those bones will form the basis of the future resurrection/restoration of the person to earthly existence (Harvey 1994: 71). That scheme stretched back as far as Maccabean times when the restoration of mutilated limbs was a vital part of God's vindication of faithful martyrs, as a classic text like 2 Maccabees 7 attests (Nickelsburg 1972: 95). Such a text confirms that 'resurrection was the preserve of the disenfranchised classes of people who could not abide foreign domination', when 'the palpability of bodily resurrection was a quintessentially nationalist, Hebrew idea, organizing national liberation from the Syrian Greeks' (Segal 1998: 99, 102). Whereas the immortality of the soul came into Jewish thinking via Hellenistic intellectual activity in society's higher echelons, and was unrelated to the painful theological and personal challenge of the martyrdom of faithful loyalists, ideas of bodily resurrection were, as it were, a home-grown response to the human tragedy of martyrdom: it was not life renewed in some form or other, but life restored in a very familiar form. Two centuries further on, the followers of Jesus did not come from the higher echelons of society, and Jesus himself could not be viewed by them as anything other than a martyr.

As for what those who listened to Jesus would have picked up concerning the resurrection idea, there are four traditions which are worth checking out: the report that Jesus was a resurrected version of John the Baptist (Mark 6:14–16; 8:27–9), the parable of the rich man and Lazarus (Luke 16:19–31), the celebratory meal of the gentiles with the patriarchs (Matthew 8:11–12/Luke 13:28–9), and the debate with the Sadducees about future resurrection (Mark 12:18–27).

In the first of these four traditions, Mark sets out three popular estimates of Jesus – 'John the baptizer raised from the dead . . . Elijah . . . a prophet, like one of the prophets of old'. He does so more fully in 6:14–16 than in 8:28, but this list of inadequate or wrong estimates would not have survived in early Christian circles as a useful tradition without being balanced by the 'correct' estimate voiced by Peter in 8:29: 'You are the Messiah.' The discussion must therefore focus on Mark 8:27–9. This tradition is, however, very likely to be a Marcan construct: the notion of Jesus' identity as a matter of mystery and speculation is part and parcel of the messianic secret scheme, and part of the presentation of Jesus as a heavenly being transcending all human categories: as such it is typically Marcan (cf. 1:34; 4:41; 6:2). So is the notion of Peter as the leading figure and mouthpiece of the disciple group (cf. 1:16; 5:37; 9:2–6). So is the use of christological one-liners (1:24; 3:11; 14:61; 15:2). So is the attachment of the term 'messiah' to someone whose activities in history had not been messianic, and whose likely messianic expectations were focused on the future (Mark 10:35–7, 40; 11:7–11a; Matthew 19:28/Luke 22:30) rather than the present. As for the artificial notion that John the Baptist, an independent prophet spearheading a mission of renewal for Israel (Matthew 3:7–12/Luke 3:7–9, 16–17; Matthew 11:12–13/Luke 16:16), was the source of 'the powers at work in [Jesus]', it hardly deserves to be taken seriously. John had not been a miracle worker, and in any case the transmission of a prophet's powers to his successor does not provoke the use of 'resurrection' language, cf. the case of Elijah/Elisha (2 Kings 2:1–15, especially vv. 9, 15). So the alleged reaction of Antipas and others to the activity of Jesus is likely not to be historical. It therefore gives no ground for the suggestion that Jewish thinking about resurrection was so flexible that it could even include reincarnation (thus, Harvey 1994: 69), nor for the idea that a person could be said to have been raised, notwithstanding the presence of his body in a tomb. If the latter position is to be defended, it will need a more convincing witness than the unhistorical Antipas of Mark. As for the understanding of resurrection that was current inside the Jesus movement, this first tradition gives us no clue.

The parable of the rich man and Lazarus (Luke 16:19–31) turns out to be a better investment. It belongs to a family of stories (Bauckham 1991), and family resemblances can be seen from beginning to end: (i) the postmortem reversal of the experience of rich and poor in this world; (ii) the unbridgeable separation of those in torment and those in bliss; (iii) the disclosure to the living of the fate of the dead; (iv) the expectation of the return of a recently dead person. The parable is therefore a unity, and the urge to locate an original ending after the first or even the second exchange between the rich man and Abraham (vv. 26, 28) should be firmly resisted. The point of the total parable is Abraham's insistence – twice, in vv. 27–9, 30–1 – that there will be no return by a recently deceased person, and that Moses and the prophets set out everything that needs to be known about the reversal of the conditions of the rich qua rich, and the poor qua poor. 'The point is no more than the law and the prophets say – and that no more than the law and the prophets say is required' (Bauckham 1991: 245). The world of the text is from start to finish the non-Christian Jewish world, the world of popular folklore, the world of fundamental, black-and-white perceptions of divine justice, the world of the historical Jesus.

The text ends with a punchline that is usually translated, 'If they do not listen to Moses and the prophets, neither will they be convinced even if someone rises from the dead.' But there is manuscript uncertainty here – should the reading be 'rises' (ἀναστῇ), 'is raised' (ἐγερθῇ), or 'goes' (ἀπελθῇ)? The balance must surely tip in favour of ἀπελθῇ, since (i) it is easier to imagine an alteration of 'goes' to 'rises' or 'is raised' by a copyist reflecting on and artificially superimposing Jewish rejection of the message of the resurrection of Jesus, than vice versa; (ii) the proposed journey by Lazarus to the brothers of the rich man has been defined in verses 27–30 without using resurrection language, and indeed resurrection language, which belongs properly to an eschatological context, would not be appropriate. That being so, the contribution of the parable to our reflections is twofold: (i) it shows Abraham as belonging to the shadowy and non-earthly world of the pre-resurrection dead; and (ii) it shows that the traditional idea of a recently deceased person making a temporary appearance, whether as a ghost or in a dream, to earthly human beings, and being heard by them as well as seen, does not in itself generate or justify the use of resurrection language about that person. This suggests that when members of the Jesus movement found themselves using resurrection language they would not have done so on the basis of an 'appearance' of Jesus like that envisaged for Lazarus in this parable.

From the parable we move to the tradition of the celebratory meal. A Q tradition (Matthew 8:11–12/Luke 13:28–9), its original wording has almost certainly been preserved exactly by Matthew (rightly, Reiser 1997: 230–3):

> [11]Many will come from east and west, and will recline at table with Abraham and Isaac and Jacob in the kingdom of God, [12]while the sons of the kingdom will be thrown out where there will be weeping and gnashing of teeth.

This saying – 'intolerably impudent . . . provocative proclamation' (Reiser 1997: 239) – is designed not as a promise to gentiles but as a warning to Jewish people. It is just about as securely authentic as any saying in the Gospels, given (i) its bold and almost intolerable claim that gentiles would be included in the great eschatological banquet at the expense of Jews, and (ii) its agreement in every significant detail – hence multiple attestation – with the woes on Galilean towns in Matthew 11:21–3/Luke 10:13–15, and the warnings to 'this generation' in Matthew 12:41–2/Luke 11:31–2.

Its boldness as a judgement saying is all the more striking for its use of traditional motifs: (i) the connection with the patriarchs; (ii) the convergence of gentiles on Zion when God has established his kingship there (Isaiah 2:2–4; 49:22–3; 66:23–4;

Tobit 13:11); (iii) their participation in the eschatological banquet there (Isaiah 25:6); (iv) the proximity of Zion and the valley of Hinnom, where following the judgement the dead bodies of rebels against God would be visibly and horrifically subject to unquenchable fire (Isaiah 66:24); and (v) the weeping of those so judged (Judith 16:17). Traditional the saying may be, but it stands on its head the standard expectation of full Jewish participation in the great Event which is to come, and stands critically opposed to the tendency of rabbinic interpreters, drawing on Psalm 23:5 and Isaiah 65:13 (Reiser 1997: 234–5) to claim that following the judgement Jewish persons would participate while gentiles would experience shame and exclusion. It also presumes two crucial ideas, namely repentance and resurrection: (i) repentance, because while the criteria of inclusion and exclusion are not spelt out here they do come to the surface in the related sayings about the prosecution witnesses in the final judgement, the queen of the south who listened to wisdom and the men of Nineveh who repented (Reiser 1997: 207); and (ii) resurrection, because the patriarchs are now at the heart of 'the kingdom of God', the new post-judgement and post-resurrection order of earthly life centred on Zion. Abraham, Isaac and Jacob had been buried in known tombs (Genesis 49:29–32), and doubtless had since then existed in the shadowy world of the dead envisaged by the parable of the rich man and Lazarus, but now they have been returned by God to an existence that is not only earthly but also bodily. Whether a divine miracle has brought their dead bodies to life and removed them from their tombs is not made clear, but their existence has to be such that on an earthly plane they, the formerly dead, can live and share an ultimate experience of God with persons presently living.

From this saying we turn to yet another tradition in which the patriarchs play a central role. The issue in the debate between Jesus and the Sadducees about resurrection (Mark 12:18–27) is quite explicit: *future* resurrection – 'whose wife *will* [the woman who ran through seven husbands] be?' (v. 23). That *future* resurrection is defined initially as similar to heavenly angelic existence – boringly asexual existence! – in which new marriages are not initiated – barely tolerable existence! – and earthly marriages are no longer relevant – mega-disappointing existence! Doubtless the word 'like' (ὡς) should be taken seriously: resurrection existence is similar to, but not identical with, that of angels in heaven. That is, those who have been raised are not straightforwardly angelic, nor are they themselves in heaven. Since entry to this new existence is for the *future*, it again follows that the dead are presently in some sort of waiting state, cf. Luke 16: 19–31. Jesus' initial answer to the question set (vv. 24–5) does not therefore encourage the idea that, when their great moment arrives, the dead will be transported to heaven without their bodies being involved, or even that they will be transported to heaven with their bodies transformed. It fits more naturally with the restoration-cum-transformation of bodies for a new earthly existence.

The second part of Jesus' answer (vv. 26–7) has sometimes been set aside as a secondary attachment – 'a piece of scholastic elaboration' (Perkins 1984: 74) – but it is rather more likely to be a deliberate complement to what has gone before. Jesus first replies within the terms of the satirical question, and then moves on to confront the presupposition of that question. What was a satirical question coming from Sadducees (vv. 19–23) could easily have been a serious question asked by Pharisees, so the anti-resurrection position of those who actually do ask it (v. 18) needs to be answered, as indeed it is (vv. 26–7). The appeal to that Mosaic corpus of scripture which the Sadducees recognise is anticipated in the reference to 'knowing the scriptures' (v. 24), which would be redundant if the final pronouncement (v. 25) were alone needed. The concluding answer, when it comes, sounds like a *tour de force*: God is the God of the patriarchs, and God is the God of the living, ergo the patriarchs will experience resurrection. The notion of resurrection here probably matches that of *Testament of Judah* 25:1, 'And after these things Abraham and Isaac and Jacob will rise to life, and I and my brothers will be chiefs of our tribes in Israel (ἐν Ἰσραήλ)' and of *Testament of Benjamin* 10:6, 'Then you will see Enoch, Noah and Shem and Abraham and Isaac and Jacob rising on the right hand in gladness; then we also will rise each one over our tribe'. If so, it is clear that earthly, not heavenly, existence is in view (cf. Enoch, who has already been in heaven, Genesis 5:24!). The only change envisaged by Jesus for the new messianic era of a restored and reconstituted Israel (cf. Nickelsburg 1972: 34–5) is the substitution, according to another authentic tradition (Matthew 19:28/Luke 22:30), of the twelve disciples of Jesus for the twelve sons of Jacob!

From the three traditions which are authentic we are able to gain a flavour of resurrection thinking within the Jesus movement. In accordance with the through-and-through Jewish context of that movement, resurrection belongs to an *earthly* setting, presupposes the final divine judgement, and almost certainly involves the removal of bodies from tombs. The experience of seeing and hearing a recently deceased person who has returned from the postmortem world to this world would definitely not count as resurrection. Nor would some internal experience, explicable in depth-psychological terms, generate talk of resurrection. This enables us to conclude that within the Jesus movement the appearances *would* not demonstrate the resurrection of Jesus, just as the absence of his body from the tomb *could* not and – as the Gospel traditions always affirm, convincingly – *did* not verify resurrection faith.

THE TOMB: OCCUPIED OR EMPTY?

The empty tomb tradition has been in the eye of the historical-critical storm for literally centuries. Much controversy, no consensus here! Plainly the force of the evidence is not compelling.

With that in mind, it may be worth recalling the probable content of the pre-Marcan version of the tradition:

> [2(1)]Very early on the first day of the week Mary Magdalene, and Mary the mother of James the younger and Joses, and Salome went to the tomb. [4a]And when they looked up they saw that the stone had been rolled away. [5]As they entered the tomb they saw a young man, dressed in a white robe, sitting on the right side; and they were alarmed. [6]But he said to them, 'Do not be alarmed; you are looking for Jesus of Nazareth, who was crucified. He has been raised; he is not here. Look, there is the place where they laid him.' [8a]So they went out and fled from the tomb, for fear and trembling had seized them.

The Marcan story has long been the target of four historical reservations. First, there is the delayed anointing of the body, not only improbable in hot Middle Eastern circumstances where decomposition would set in fast, but also unnecessary if the burial process had – does Mark 15:46 suggest this? – been completed. Second, there is the conversation of the women en route to the tomb: their travelling on without having worked out how they might gain access to the tomb 'betrays a more than tolerable degree of thoughtlessness' (Campenhausen 1966: 24)! Third, there is the appearance of an angel, in itself more a pointer to a literary genre than an historical reality. Fourth, there is the silence of the women, an extraordinary reaction to so overwhelming an experience, and probably a telltale indication that the story of the empty tomb was a later development outside the ken of the very earliest Christian community. These four points recur with varied nuances in works by those who doubt (Evans 1970: 75–9) and by those who affirm (Campenhausen 1966: 23–6) the historicity of the empty tomb, therefore they do not in themselves carry all before them or finally decide the issue. To the four must now be added a fifth critical argument, namely that the location of the tomb in which Jesus was allegedly buried hastily and without honour by an agent of the Jewish authorities, Joseph of Arimathea, himself neither friend nor foe of Jesus, was in fact unknown to the followers of Jesus (Lüdemann 1994: 39–45; Wedderburn 1999: 61–5).

On the basis of the source-critical enquiry whose results are set out in the proposed pre-Marcan tradition, the decisiveness of the five reservations is seriously reduced. For the first, the second, and the fourth of the objections simply do not apply at all to the pre-Marcan version: the material giving rise to those problems owes its presence in Mark 16:1–8 to MarkR. So only the third, the involvement of the angel, and the fifth, the location of the tomb, remain for consideration.

Most modern readers would probably agree that the involvement of the angel is unhistorical. But while the *story* as a whole is shaped according to the classical scheme of an angelic appearance story, the *introduction* to that story (vv. 2, 4a) is not dependent upon the scheme, and could in principle attest an historical reality upon which that scheme was superimposed. Just as the introduction to the pre-Matthean tradition in Matthew 1:18–25 arguably preserved an historical reality (the scarcely invented memory of the premarital pregnancy of the engaged mother of Jesus), and at the same time had an angelic dream-appearance superimposed upon it, so too here. By analogy, therefore, the decision about historicity may in effect hinge on the introduction to the pre-Marcan tradition:

> [2(1)]Very early on the first day of the week Mary Magdalene, and Mary the mother of James the younger and Joses, and Salome went to the tomb. [4a]And when they looked up they saw that the stone had been rolled away.

The discussion of the tomb must take off from conventional burial procedure. Rabbinic texts speak of laying out, washing and anointing the corpse, binding the chin, closing the eyes (*m. Shabbath* 23:5), and the provision of burial cloths, the last mentioned being 'by reason of the honour due to it' (*m.*

Sanhedrin 6:5). Mark 15:46 mentions only the last detail; Mark 16:1 presumes that anointing did not occur prior to the wrapping up of the body, and in this may be supported by Mark 14:8, 'She has anointed my body beforehand for its burial.' Rabbinic texts and Mark therefore combine to suggest an economical but honourable burial. Working again with Marcan data, Joseph of Arimathea probably is regarded as representative of the authorities – 'a respected council member [βουλευτής]', cf. the συμβούλιον of the authorities, 3:6; 15:1 – and not a close associate of Jesus. (i) It is unlikely that Pilate would have released the body of Jesus to a member of the movement of a messianic claimant, cf. Mark 15:26. (ii) Mark carefully distances the women disciples from the person carrying out the burial (Brown 1994: 1218). On the other hand, (iii) that Joseph should *also* (ὅς καὶ αὐτός) have been looking for the kingdom of God means more than his praying the *kaddish* prayer that God would 'establish his kingdom in your lifetime and in your days and in the lifetime of all the house of Israel ever speedily and at a near time': it places him close to the enquiring scribe who is entirely in agreement with Jesus and is 'not far from the kingdom of God' (Mark 12:34), and in the setting of the Gospel of Mark it implies that he looked for the kingdom of God as proclaimed by Jesus (*contra* Brown 1994: 1216). The trend in post-Marcan versions of the tradition of Joseph's involvement unquestionably brings him closer and closer to discipleship, but the trend was not created *ex nihilo*.

What should we make of Acts 13:29, 'when they had carried out everything that had been written about him, they took him down from the tree and laid him in a tomb', from which a hostile and dishonourable burial by the authorities is inferred, and John 19:31, from which an initiative by the Jewish authorities to bury Jesus is again inferred? (i) Speeches in Acts are *Lucan* speeches, and Acts 13:29 must therefore match the LukeR handling of the Marcan burial narrative. Such revisions as Luke introduces there serve simply to strengthen the character reference for Joseph, to distance him from the judicial action of his colleagues, and to reinforce the honour shown to Jesus in his burial: the tomb was one 'where no one had ever been laid' (Luke 23:53). One significant detail in Acts 13:29 is the deliberate description of the cross as 'the tree' (cf. Acts 5:30; 10:39), a clear hint of Deuteronomy 21:23 and therefore of respect for the requirement that 'his corpse must not remain all night upon the tree', a hint which again draws out, but does not go beyond, the implication of the Marcan narrative. (ii) As for the Johannine evidence, it invites the same assessment as the Lucan evidence. Both are drawing out the implications of what Mark had written.

The burial narrative contains no Christian motifs and may even be a Marcan construction preparing for the MarkR revised version of the story of the women's visit to the tomb. That would make the depiction of Joseph all the more noteworthy. The precision of his personal name and origin, and the fact that as a 'respected councillor' he swims against the tide of generalising Marcan denunciation of the Jewish authorities (cf. 14:55, 64), suggest a genuine reminiscence on Mark's part. If so, one might add, it is extremely difficult to believe that the recollection of his name would persist in connection with something he had done, while at the same time the location where he had done it remained unknown. It is easier to associate a known agent of burial with a known place of burial, and therefore to be open to the possibility that there was indeed a specific tomb available for visiting shortly after Jesus' death. If so, while the presumption that the tomb of Jesus was known and available to be visited *might* be erroneous (Lüdemann 1994: 39–45), and it is theoretically conceivable that 'Jesus' body had been thrown into a common grave or more precisely a criminal's grave' (Wedderburn 1999: 62), the Marcan tradition scarcely turns remote possibility into real probability. And if so, the fifth objection to the pre-Marcan tradition fails.

At this point the named trio of women comes into the

---

reckoning. In line with patriarchal instincts, Mary the mother of James the younger and Joses is defined with reference to male relatives, who must be well enough known to those who receive the tradition; moreover, one of those sons, James the younger, is distinguished from some other James – presumably James the elder/greater – who is also presumed known to the recipients of the tradition. The other two women, Mary Magdalene and Salome, have no male reference attached, and must be presumed to be single women (or conceivably widowed or even divorced), and known as such. Even the place of origin of the first of them – Magdala on the western edge of the Sea of Galilee – is known. Now the grouping of the named women suggests a role might be assigned to them as guarantors of something (cf. Deuteronomy 19:15), witnesses in spite of the handicap of their being female, witnesses notwithstanding the well-documented tendency to treat the testimony of men as preferable and certainly more persuasive. While it is important not to overstate this handicap – and it is certainly true that some rabbinic texts do envisage a woman's giving testimony in certain circumstances (Witherington 1984: 9–10) – it remains true that the tendency is equally well documented in those texts. They receive strong support from Josephus, even if his patronising and sexist theorising grates on modern ears:

> 'Put no trust in a single witness, but let there be three or at least two, whose evidence shall be accredited by their past lives. From women let no evidence be accepted, because of the levity and temerity of their sex; neither let slaves bear witness, since whether from cupidity or fear it is like that they will not attest the truth.' (*Antiquities* 4:219)

The tendency to classify people into men, women, slaves and gentiles – on a descending scale in respect of status – is a point of agreement between him and the rabbis (cf. *m. Nazir* 9:1), and must reflect an established position. So, to return to the pre-Marcan tradition, would anyone wishing to tell a convincing story have assigned the role of witnesses to a group of women? The instinct which caused Luke to superimpose a checking visit to the tomb by Peter because the adequacy of the women is doubted, is exactly the instinct which would have kept the women out of any story created *ex nihilo* – and yet they are here! Not just here, but as a threesome described with such careful attention to detail that they cannot but be taken seriously as witnesses.

Could they, in the earlier stages of the process of the development of traditions, have been witnesses to something other than the evidence of the tomb? In principle it is possible that they were the first to have an experience of 'seeing Jesus', and that this was transferred to a tomb tradition as well as being ignored in the 1 Corinthians 15:3–7 tradition for reasons connected with ecclesiastical validation. The only positive evidence to which advocates of such a proposal can appeal is the story in Matthew 28:9–10/John 20:11–18, and the case has already been made for viewing that tradition as no more than a MattR remodelling of material found in Mark 16:1–8. It seems that if the involvement of a trio of women in 'resurrection happenings' is to be taken seriously, it must be in connection with the tomb.

The pre-Gospel tradition of the women's discovery of the emptiness of the known tomb of Jesus therefore seems to rest on a sound foundation. Its role in the process which led members of the Jesus movement to use resurrection language now needs to be defined.

One possible reconstruction of events has Jesus' dedicated followers, taking seriously the authority of his prophetic mission and the charisma which made him ring true for them, being unable to think of his death without simultaneously registering a belief that he had been exalted to heaven (cf. Philippians 2:6–11), and then, having discovered the empty tomb, feeling impelled to shift their definition of what had happened from exaltation to resurrection (Harvey 1994: 72–5). There are, however, two problems with this scheme. (i) It would be a mistake to suppose that exaltation language was used *in early Christianity* without resurrection's being presupposed, and exaltation by itself and without resurrection would not have distinguished Jesus from the revered patriarchs or the many honoured martyrs of Israel. (ii) For his followers, just as much as for anyone else, an empty tomb was interpretable as a desecration and a robbery. When the Gospels without any equivocation affirm that the followers of Jesus regarded an open and empty tomb as suspicious, they should be believed. And the combination of an exaltation belief and an empty tomb would not have amounted to resurrection, at least not in the terms indicated by the authentic Jesus traditions which sustained those followers of Jesus. Something more which impinged in the world of human sense-perception was needed.

At the same time as the empty tomb was too precarious a datum to be the immediate cause of resurrection faith, it is probably true that it was a sine qua non of that faith – not sufficient but still necessary. If we use as a yardstick the parable of the rich man and Lazarus, the appearance of someone who had recently died and been buried would not by itself suffice as the immediate cause of such faith. If we use as a second yardstick the saying about (resurrected) patriarchs and gentiles joining in a celebratory meal in the kingdom of God in Zion, the case of Jesus seems to require a combination of an empty tomb and a very special sort of appearance, that is, some sort of existence which is comparable even if not identical with the existence of human persons in the world. If we use as yet another yardstick what was said in the debate with the Sadducees, the case of Jesus seems to require an existence which is like but also unlike that of angels, and capable of being set in an earthly context. The critical factor in the case of Jesus seems therefore to be *the sort of existence he exhibited when seen* by his close associates after the discovery that his body was gone from the tomb.

Within the Gospel narratives whose pre-history we examined, there were, apart from the empty tomb narrative, just three underlying traditions which remained for further discussion. They concerned (i) an *appearance to a group of disciples*, a story to which MarkR alludes and which, in view of Matthew/Luke agreements, also stems from non-Marcan tradition available to both the later evangelists, from whom the 4G in turn derived it; (ii) an *appearance to Simon*, preserved only by Luke in a quotation of a joyful exclamation by others; (iii) *an appearance to two Emmaus-bound travellers*, arguably preserved in a pre-Lucan narrative tradition. All other appearance traditions turned out to be secondary growths.

To those Gospel traditions, which have a claim to stem from earlier material, can be added Paul's first-hand evidence as well as the earlier material he quotes in 1 Corinthians 15:3–7, a tradition whose history itself needs scrutiny.

On the level of the letter to Corinth two parts of Paul's argument make clear that no attempt is being made to 'prove' the resurrection. (i) There is verse 6: 'he appeared to more than five hundred brothers at one time, most of whom are still alive, though some have died.' Had Paul been trying to 'prove' the resurrection, such a 'proof' would have been better served by saying 'some of whom have died, but most are still alive', that is, they remain available to act as witnesses. Instead, he is trying to underline the agreed Christian position that belonging to the community of the resurrection does not prevent death, and that participation in the general resurrection, as affirmed by apocalyptic, is still a matter for the future. (ii) There are verses 12–19, in which the fundamental reality to which Paul appeals is again belief in the general resurrection of the dead. Logically, this is the sole starting point: without the general resurrection of the dead ($\dot{\alpha}\nu\dot{\alpha}\sigma\tau\alpha\sigma\iota\varsigma$ $\nu\epsilon\kappa\rho\hat{\omega}\nu$) as the premise, it would not be possible to make the definitive Christian claim that the specific person Christ had been raised from the dead. Paul does not at this point move from the specific, Christ, to the general, but rather from the general to the specific. His readers are simply reminded that it is of the essence of the Christian faith, *their* Christian faith, that they should stay where they started, that is, with the unprovable conviction of Jewish apocalyptic that dead persons will be raised.

Paul presents his own experience as equivalent to, but not necessarily identical with, that of the persons listed in verses 5–7. The recurrent defining verb, 'he appeared [ὤφθη]', is used in biblical tradition to cover a range of experiences: (i) divine and angelic epiphanies (Genesis 12:7; 17:1), sometimes presented as conscious encounters and sometimes at night and/or in dreams (Genesis 31:13; 1 Kings 3:5; Daniel 8:1), sometimes to individuals and at other times to more than one person (Numbers 20:6; Tobit 12:22), usually to favoured persons but sometimes to an opponent (2 Maccabees 3:24–39), sometimes in the form of a cloud or 'the glory of the Lord' appearing to an assembled community (Exodus 16:10; Leviticus 9:4, 23; Numbers 14:10), usually without physicality but sometimes with terrifying tangibility (2 Maccabees 3:25); (ii) human 'appearances' of specific persons in a particular place, e.g. the two prostitutes before Solomon (1 Kings 3:16) or a prophet in Israel (1 Kings 18:15; 1 Maccabees 9:27); (iii) metaphorical appearances, for example, a storm (2 Samuel 22:11) or the invisible intellectual presence of Wisdom who 'appeared on earth and lived with humankind' (Baruch 3:22, 37). Given the flexibility and adaptability of the usage, it is necessary to allow for the possibility that the experiences of Paul and of the persons listed were not precisely identical – internal or external to one who sees, firmly physical or not in the case of the one who is seen – but fall within a *range* covered by the chosen verb. In respect of physicality, the flow of the argument in 1 Corinthians suggests that the risen-ness of Jesus is for Paul a manifestation of that future general state of risen-ness, and that the latter involves personal continuity but a transformation tantamount to replacement of the old flesh/body/ glory existence. That may well be the best way of understanding 'resurrection'. In respect of the internal/external question, matters are more complicated, and we shall return to them.

The much-used material which is a sine qua non for the investigation of what may have happened, is set out in 1 Corinthians 15:3–7:

> ^{3b}Christ died | for our sins | in accordance with the scriptures;
> ^{4a}he was buried;
> ^{4b}he has been raised | on the third day | in accordance with the scriptures;
> ^{5a}he appeared
>> ^{5b}to Cephas, then to the twelve;
>> ⁷to James, then to all the apostles.

The arguments for a pre-Pauline 'formula' are well enough known (Theissen 1998: 487): (i) Paul's own claim that 'I *handed on* to you . . . what I had first *received*', reinforced by his later comment that it sums up what 'they', i.e. the named persons who lead the Jerusalem community, proclaim; (ii) the three-phrase parallelism between verses 3b, 4b; (iii) the un-Pauline way of referring to both sins and scripture – not 'for sin' but 'for our sins', and not 'as it was written' or even 'as the scripture says' but 'according to the scriptures'; (iv) the reference to 'the twelve', unparalleled elsewhere in Paul, and the notion of a closed apostolic group – '*all* the apostles' – which leaves no room for the additional figure, determinedly assertive of his own apostolic status, Paul himself!

Should we speak of just one 'formula'? The carefully constructed parallelism in verses 3b, 4b could be matched by a further parallelism between the single-word statements in verses 4a, 5a that 'he was buried . . . he appeared [ἐτάφη . . . ὤφθη]'. But 'he appeared' belongs with the four-part list of those to whom he appeared (vv. 5b, 7), which itself has a two-line parallelism – first an individual, Cephas or James, and then a group

---

of status-possessing persons headed by that named individual, 'the twelve' and 'all the apostles'. It therefore disturbs the apparent parallelism between verses 4a, 5a. That awareness of Christian community status which gives verses 5ab, 7 something of a validating function is discrepant with the function of verses 3b–4. This is both christological and community-soteriological in perspective: (i) the ὑπέρ-formula, 'for our sins', makes Messiah's death an event which draws the community into its influence; (ii) the rare reference to burial, while it could be designed to affirm the reality of death, or the completion of the death process (cf. Luke 16:22) – but why should either be necessary, and especially within a primitive intra-community confession? – is more likely to reflect a baptismal use of burial language (cf. Romans 6:4; Colossians 2:12); (iii) the use of the perfect tense in 'he has been raised [ἐγήγερται]' conveys a sense that the community lives in the permanent and ongoing reality of resurrection.

Consequently, there appears to be an underlying tradition, whose sub-text is the community's saving experience of Christ's death and resurrection (vv. 3b–4), and then quite distinct from that tradition some additional material listing appearances (vv. 5ab, 7). In respect of the additional material we have available to us two options: *either* it existed quite separately and independently of the salvation-formula *or* it was a later growth, a graft attached to the salvation-formula. Since the parallelism in verses 5b, 7 can hardly be a coincidence, and more likely stems from imitation, perhaps reflecting a shift of power and status within the Jerusalem leadership, the same process of growth may well account for verse 5ab. In that case, though we cannot do more than make an educated guess, there may have been three stages in the development of the pre-Pauline formula: a salvation-formula, consisting of verses 3b–4b first of all; then an extension to impose ecclesiastical status concerns, and producing verses 3b–5b at the second stage; then a further extension to reflect

and validate a shift in personnel and function within the leadership, and producing verses 3b–5b, 7 at the third stage.

The cluster of references to alleged sightings of Jesus brings
us up against the acute difficulty of handling from the perspective
of the historian all claims to visionary experiences. No small
part of the difficulty is defining what is meant in the first place!
Three possibilities have recently been reviewed (Davis 1998:
126–47). The first, which is scarcely a runner, is 'subjective
vision' or 'hallucination', put forward with sincerity but
grounded in nothing accessible to anyone else (Davis 1998:
127). This has been proposed, especially in connection with the
'appearance' to Peter, but it does not fit easily with the community dimension, specifically the well-attested 'appearance' to
a *group* of persons. The second is 'normal vision', in accordance
with which processes of perception work regularly, and the
object seen is material. 'Normal vision' would, so it is suggested,
mean that 'a camera could have taken a snapshot of the risen
Jesus' (Davis 1998: 128, 147). This is a runner which may work
quite well with some of the appearance traditions, but less well
with others. Hesitation would probably be provoked by (i) the
use of the angelic model at the earliest stage of the history of
the traditions of the appearances to the group and the Emmaus
travellers; (ii) the evidence of a scaling up of physicality in *later*
strata of the Gospels; and (iii) the fluctuation in the report of
whether what was visible or audible to Paul was visible or audible
to his fellow-travellers (Acts 9:7; 22:9; cf. Daniel 10:7). The third
runner, 'objective vision', involves a claim made with sincerity,
centred on a vision which is not accessible to anyone else, and
involves a 'visualising' which comes about because 'the person
who has the objective vision has been enabled by God to see
the real and objective presence of the thing; the see-er has an
ability to see it that others lack'. As to the hypothetical camera,
it 'would have detected nothing, or at least nothing recognisable'
(Davis 1998: 127).

Given that what the followers of Jesus 'saw' provoked them

into using 'resurrection' language, the first option is unattractive, and the traditions in their earliest forms belong somewhere between the second and the third options. The discussion is vexed and vexing, and it is difficult to be precise. One has a sense of the danger of imposing the categories of the present human order of existence upon a reality which is by definition set in a higher order of existence. But perhaps, with due caution, the following points may take the discussion of the appearance experiences forward.

First, we have the experience of Peter. This is doubly attested in pre-Lucan and pre-Pauline tradition. The historicity of the experience is seldom doubted, but the interpretation of it more controversial. A depth-psychological interpretation (Lüdemann 1994: 84–100) has presently to be considered if its content and its influence are to be judged accurately.

The depth-psychological interpretation of what happened to Peter centres on the mourner's sense of forgiveness and liberation from guilt. It understands 'he appeared to Cephas/Simon' as the coming to Peter of Jesus' word of forgiveness 'as something living, as an encounter with the whole Jesus himself, in an image' (Lüdemann 1994: 97). Here the historical Jesus becomes a primary influence. Now, to address the supporting arguments, it is certainly true that the distinct and historical tradition of Peter's denial and dissociation of himself from Jesus (Mark 14:66–72) requires a context for its preservation and use, and the obvious context is indeed a 'before and after' narrative sequence involving denying/seeing Jesus. The seeing would then provide a context in which the denial might safely be recorded and remembered in Christian circles, by confirming that it had been reversed and repaired. It may well be that the recollection of this traditional connection occasionally colours a Gospel tradition – for example, (i) the LukeR remodelling of the call of the disciples (Luke 5:1–11 diff. Mark 1:16–20) so that it concentrates on Peter, quotes him as saying, 'Go away from me, Lord, for I am a sinful man!', and records a call to mission which is timed 'from

Resurrection People

now on' (Lüdemann 1994: 86–7); (ii) the 'sifting' of Peter by Satan (Luke 22:31–2), which is presumed to have taken place, and is the subject of a prayer by Jesus that his faith may not fail, that is, that his commitment may not utterly collapse, and that after repentance/forgiveness (καὶ σύ ποτε ἐπιστρέψας, cf. Mark 4:12; Luke 17:4; Acts 3:19) he may have a responsible community role. If, as the argument suggests, a bereaved person's mourning process is liable to be impeded by three factors – 'a sudden death; an ambivalent attitude to the dead person associated with guilt feelings; and a dependent relationship' (Lüdemann 1994: 99) – then Peter certainly qualifies. Immersed in deep grief and despair, shocked by the pitiless suddenness of it all, keenly aware of his own recent defection, and cast adrift in a situation where following Jesus had involved abandonment of all the normal human support systems, he meets all the requirements. In a condition of being overwhelmed by grief, his seeing Jesus might well be formally similar to 'reports by mourners, which occasionally also contain the element of the image of the presence of a beloved person who has died' (Lüdemann 1994: 97), and it might indeed address therapeutically his trauma. But – and here is the nub – in addressing it, did the grief induce the seeing? Was it a matter of freeing him *to* grieve, and of mourning being 'enormously helped . . . by a vision' (Lüdemann 1994: 100), or rather of being freed *from* mourning and grief? And would a vision which enabled him to go on mourning healthily serve at the same time to install him as leader of the continuing community, for all that he would serve as a prime example of that forgiveness on which the mission of Jesus had been centred? Would such an experience – theoretically possible as it is – have called for the use of the language of resurrection by that community? Would there be any substantial continuity between resurrection language, supposing for a moment that it might have been used to describe the person whom Peter 'saw' in this way, and resurrection thinking as expressed in the authentic Jesus traditions we have considered? It must surely be extremely doubtful. Something less easily located on the boundary between the conscious and the unconscious in Peter, something more external and directly accessible to others, something more 'earthy' and realistic, would seem to be needed.

This brings us, second, to the question of the influence of Peter's experience. Here we notice a difference between 'the Lord is risen indeed, and has appeared to Simon' (Luke 24:34) and 'he appeared to Cephas, and then to the twelve ...' (1 Corinthians 15:5). The pre-Lucan tradition points to belief in the resurrection by those who have not seen Jesus for themselves, but are content to rely on Simon; the pre-Pauline tradition envisages others as actually having seen him. Here we must take account of several factors. (i) The group appearance – hinted at by Mark, narrated in the tradition used by both Matthew and Luke, and included in both second and third stages of the evolution of the pre-Pauline tradition – is in fact the best attested of all the appearances, and cannot easily be set aside as dependent. Invariably associated with a missionary role – doubtless originally that of continuing as 'the twelve' with the mission of Jesus to Israel, now led by Peter (cf. Galatians 2:8), before the wider universalising vocation took hold – the appearance to the group is a central feature of early Christian resurrection claims. (ii) Paul in his handling of his earlier tradition presents himself as knowing in detail what happened to key Jerusalem personnel in the years before his Damascus road experience, that is, knowing where the appearance to the 500 should be set in the sequence, knowing about the deaths of the minority of them and the survival of the majority, and thus drawing upon the close contact that he had occasionally had with Jerusalem personnel (Galatians 1:18–2:10). The idea of an 'infectious' appearance experience of Peter, like the idea of an exclusively 'internal' experience, gets into difficulty in view of Paul's first-hand evidence.

From here we turn, third, to the experience of James, which is arguably due for rescue from neglect. Like his mother, his brothers, and his sisters, the historical James was evidently part of a dysfunctional family, part of the fabric of disaffection vis-à-vis the prophetic eldest son. That is a recollection which remains, as it were, swimming against the tide of the tendency to bathe the family of Jesus in the warm glow of respect and appreciation. Such a tendency almost certainly projects their post-resurrection position on to their pre-resurrection past, which was not like that at all. For James to become an integral part of the earliest community at a very early stage of its life (cf. Galatians 1:19), and moreover to become later the leading pillar-type witness (cf. Galatians 2:9), even during the period of Peter's presence within that community, is a development which requires some explanation. How could a community which *ab initio* saw its leaders validated by visions of the resurrected Jesus (thus, 1 Corinthians 15:5b, 7) allow those leaders to slip to a position below someone who could appeal to no such visionary experience? It would be almost impossible to explain. But such an explanation is rendered unnecessary by the evidence of the pre-Pauline tradition, 'he appeared to James'. And the appearance to James was therefore not one which could work from an already existing sympathy or commitment. In that respect it was not dissimilar to what happened later to Paul.

The claimed appearance to Paul is our fourth datum. Once again, as in the case of Peter, a depth-psychological interpretation (Lüdemann 1994: 79–84) has to be considered. This time the key element is Paul's pre-Christian combination of two things: (i) internal conflict, ignored in Philippians 3:4–11 but attested by Romans 7:13–25, the latter being an autobiographical report of 'a genuine conflict . . . not too far removed from the Damascus event'; (ii) external persecution of the Christian community: 'behind Paul's vehemently rejecting, aggressive attitude to Christians there was an inner build-up in his person of the kind that numerous works of depth psychology have ascertained in other cases to be the basic motivation for aggressive behaviour'. Certain elements of early Christian preaching attracted him unconsciously, but were projected onto the Christians and then attacked 'out of fear of his unconscious strivings'. Those aspects of the Christian position which simultaneously generated attraction and attack were, so runs the argument, 'the proclamation of the crucified Messiah, the criticism of the Temple and – closely connected with this – the *de facto* disregard of the Torah which came about in social dealings with Gentiles (Gentile Christians) as a consequence of Jesus' "gospel of love", from the time of the Hellenists around Stephen onwards'. That doubt-suppressing fanaticism was 'formally released in a vision of Christ'. 'What he had desired unconsciously had become reality in a person.'

Some parts of this case are distinctly stronger than others. (i) If the conflict between Paul the Pharisee and some Christians is to be connected with the historical Jesus, its roots can arguably be located in the sociological antithesis of prophet versus priest (cf. Weber, in Gill 1987: 36–45). In that context the historical Jesus mounted a sweeping critique of the alleged Pharisaic neglect of basic covenantal commitments like 'justice and mercy and faithfulness' (Matthew 23:23), a critique which probably gave meaning to the so-called cleansing of the Temple (Mark 11:17) and was directed more widely than at Pharisees alone. The 'criticism of the temple' was not a matter of principle, rather a sign of judgement on an unresponsive people. Given the serious difficulty of establishing that the Hellenists of Acts 6–7 went further than this, and given that the Hebrews had (if Acts 1–5 is to be believed) certainly not done so, the above interpretation of the causes célèbres which enraged Paul perhaps needs modification. (ii) It is hard to believe that any wing of the Jerusalem community was disregarding the Torah in social dealings with gentile Christians. Where, one might ask, is the evidence? It looks much more like a problem that was placed on the early Christian agenda by later happenings in Antioch, reinforced by the Pauline mission to the gentiles. (iii) Romans 7:13–25 does indeed provide some illumination, and Philippians 3 should not (*pace* Wedderburn 1999: 268) be seen as 'the Achilles' heel of [this] account'. The self-confidence of the latter is at variance with the whole of the argument of Romans, and not just with 7:13–25. Thus, the thrust of Romans 1:18–3:31 is that Jews, without exception, are subject to that indictment of idolatrous rebellion against God (1:23, cf. Psalm 106:20) which they are accustomed to level at gentiles. There is no space within the territory mapped by Romans for an exceptional and wholly law-keeping Jewish person, whether the pre-Christian Paul or anyone else. As for the autobiographical passage in the body of the letter, Paul there develops a defence of the Torah: it is neither to be equated with Sin (7:7–12) nor to be seen as the cause of death (7:13–25), for all that it is part of, and not a solution to, the Sin-death problem. Adamic man in a Mosaic context is caught up in an unwinnable conflict between one alliance, human flesh and Sin, and another alliance, the human mind and the Torah. The victory which the second alliance achieves, according to 4 Maccabees 2, is unachievable, according to Paul. From that conflict, which is the dilemma of humankind in a Torah-defined, and therefore Jewish, context, Paul can hardly be dissociating himself. His argument would be punctured by the existence of any Adamic person in the sphere of Moses who did not experience the conflict. He is, in that sense, writing autobiographically, though it is *an inclusive autobiography*. In his view, the solution to the problem of how any Jewish person whose autobiography this is can be successfully Torah-observant is to be found in the gift of the Spirit, the identifying hallmark of life within the one person who embodies the new universal humanity, Christ himself. To introduce the vision of the risen one, which was exclusive to Paul and a few others, is to treat Romans 7:13–25 as *an exclusive autobiography*. That being so, this passage probably does not give us an angle on the vision of Christ. (iv) If we are left with the proclamation of the crucified Messiah as the target of the pre-Christian Paul's wrath, we have to ask what there was here that would exert the unconscious attraction which underlay the conscious attacks. The issue here seems to be more theological than psychological, an issue which an external rather than an internal stimulus would perhaps be more likely to resolve.

The accounts in Acts 9, 22 and 26 of what happened to Paul, and the tradition upon which all three accounts are based, share some defining features with the narrative of what happened to Heliodorus in 2 Maccabees 3: an opponent of a religious community, who is hell-bent on attacking what is central to that community's religious position, receiving at a spot close to the target of his hostile action an epiphany involving bright light, throwing him to the ground in a state of considerable physical distress, and bringing about an acknowledgement of the intervention of God in the epiphany: 'He bore testimony to all concerning the deeds of the supreme God, which he had seen with his own eyes' (2 Maccabees 3:36). While we cannot read the Heliodorus episode as more than a story, we can read as first-hand testimony the Pauline account which would ultimately generate those reports in Acts. Maybe this is where we can gain a perspective on what Paul had in mind when, after listing known and checkable appearances, he declared that 'he appeared also to me'.

FROM JESUS TO THE RESURRECTION PEOPLE — THEN AND NOW

For those who were originally caught up in the dynamic of Jesus' resurrection it was essential that the person whom God had raised was emphatically the person they had known and seen and heard. That means *continuity* and some theological investment in the historical Jesus. At the same time, the resurrection did inaugurate something new. That means development beyond, perhaps even *discontinuity* with, the historical Jesus. Both continuity and discontinuity can be detected in the schemes which the four evangelists construct in their resurrection narratives. And both continuity and discontinuity must be involved in interactive engagement with one another in any attempt in any era, including our own, if the Christian community is to do justice to itself as the community of the resurrection. To allow the resurrection to quench all interest, historical and theological, in the historical Jesus is not only to fly in the face of a deep-seated human instinct but also to forget that the resurrection was itself a statement about the historical Jesus. It may have been, indeed was, more: it certainly was not less. In the view of Christians everywhere and always, it was an emphatic and incontrovertible 'yes' from the God who had sent him, and as such a compelling rebuttal of the tragic 'no' from his opponents. But equally, to allow the historical Jesus so to dominate Christian reflection that the dynamism of resurrection life, its intoxicating newness, its in-built imperative for change, are marginalised is neither right nor realistic. Apart from anything else, there were aspects of the mission of the historical Jesus which *could* not, and indeed *should* not, be transplanted into any post-resurrection setting.

As we move to the conclusion of our studies of the resurrection narratives, our task is therefore to position ourselves in relation to some of the issues with which the evangelists struggled, issues on which the historical Jesus may have touched. In doing so, we need a sense of the *overall* character of his mission, before turning to matters of detail.

The historical Jesus *might* have been essentially a teacher in the wisdom tradition, but if so his mission would have needed no divine endorsement, for wisdom teaching is part of the common stock of human reflection, poses no threat, envisages no crisis to come. Posing no threat, such a Jesus would scarcely have attracted the interest, let alone the intervention, of the authorities. What happened on Friday 14 Nisan in the year 30 CE would be one of the most impenetrable mysteries of history. But Jesus was *not* essentially a teacher in the wisdom tradition: in spite of incorporating wisdom speech within his overall

---

message, he at times subverted the wisdom approach, and has to be classified as a prophet.

It is plain, it is clear, it is unmistakable that his profile is an aggregation of typical prophetic features. The profile itself, and the evidence for Jesus' conformity to it, can be discerned as follows: (i) The prophet has an intense sense of closeness to God, sometimes involving dreams and ecstatic experiences, which private contact with the divine gives authorisation and content to public pronouncements: Jesus' sense of intimacy with God can be seen in ecstatic experiences (Mark 1:10–11; 3:21; Luke 10:17–20) and in the prayer reviewing his mission in the round (Matthew 11:25–6/Luke 10:21). (ii) The prophet is an individual figure, standing outside, and often in tension with, systems and institutions, and therefore depending for recognition on 'ringing true' and carrying conviction for a given audience – thus 'charisma': Jesus' characteristic authority, not acquired through authorisation by any contemporary group, but expressing his prophetic sense of God, and perhaps not unrelated to his recognition of the prophetic mission of John the Baptist (Matthew 11:7–9, 11a/Luke 7:24–6, 28a), is widely and convincingly attested. (iii) The prophet is a person who may, as it were, share his charisma with his closest associates: Jesus' followers were committed to the same mission, made the same sacrifices, embraced the same insecurity, and announced the same message (Mark 1:16–20; Matthew 8:19–22/Luke 9:57–60; Luke 10:3–12). (iv) The prophet is not a community-forming person, though in time she or he may become the focus of a community as the 'routinisation of charisma' sets in: Jesus worked for the renewal of Israel and had no interest in founding a sect or party within the nation, and certainly not in separating from the community of the Jewish people. (iv) The prophet is a person who typically recalls an audience to old and fundamental realities rather than revealing new ones: Jesus' charge that the Pharisees have neglected the great concerns of 'justice/judgement, mercy and faithfulness' (Matthew 23:23/Luke 11:42) is projected in numerous debates on specific issues. (v) The prophet has an interest in the future, though normally a short-term future, so that announcements of doom or comfort engage with the present situation and do so with direct immediacy: here in a nutshell is Jesus' announcement of the near kingdom (Mark 1:15). (vi) A prophet is no mere purveyor of words but someone who may, by virtue of the dynamism of the word, combine act with speech: Jesus' acts of power belong here, as do the celebratory gestures of inclusiveness in the fellowship meals, but perhaps most important of all is the climactic event in his mission which very probably led directly to the authorities' intervention against him, namely, the 'cleansing' of the Temple (Mark 11:15–17).

If a contemporary resurrection-conditioned Christian community is to include any contribution at all from the historical Jesus, it must therefore learn to live with him as a prophet. No prophet, no Jesus! And the difficulty of living with a prophet is not just the problem of taking seriously the charisma when the tide of 'routinisation of charisma' is flowing so strongly. That sociological problem is certainly substantial. But even more substantial is, for example, learning to live permanently *under judgement* – for the kingship theme at the heart of the prophetic message is by definition a judgement theme – or learning to keep *the big issues* in focus – for the deep-seated human tendency seems to be the remodelling of the concept of obedience to God in terms of increasingly pedantic preoccupation with minutiae – or, as a corollary of the last point, resisting the urge to treat prophetic *demands* as if they were laws. The centre of gravity of the mission of the definitively prophetic Jesus was, this must be repeated, neither in the sphere of wisdom speech nor in the province of legal debate and decision. Human beings have wisdom in their bones, and they feel safe with the neat and precise definitions of obedience provided by law. But the prophetic Jesus issues a call to liberated insecurity and to unprotected responsibility.

Let us examine first the event which holds within itself the meaning of the whole mission, namely the cleansing of the Temple (Mark 11:15–17). There is widespread agreement that this event is likely to have caused the final dénouement in Jesus' career – and very little agreement as to its meaning! But if it was indeed the proximate cause of the action against Jesus which led ultimately to his death, then the resurrection could not be less than an assertion that Jesus' speech and actions on this occasion did indeed reflect the mind of God, and that those who resisted him stood under judgement. Here we certainly have to reckon with resurrection-endorsed continuity.

The tradition, recorded only in Mark, must have been meaningful and relevant to an early Christian community to be preserved. It is difficult to suppose that a bare narrative reporting of Jesus' actions (vv. 15–16) would have established that meaning and relevance. The tradition is therefore likely to have included, 'Is it not written, "My house shall be called a house of prayer for all nations"? But you have made it a den of robbers' (v. 17 = Isaiah 56:7 + Jeremiah 7:11). The action itself should be interpreted in the light of these passages. That the action, with its accompanying word, is authentic – could so drastic and perplexing an incident be a Christian creation? – is reinforced by the remarkable overlap with the judgement saying of Jesus which we have already examined, 'Many shall come from east and west and recline at table with Abraham, Isaac and Jacob in the kingdom of God, but the sons of the kingdom shall be expelled outside' (Matthew 8:11–12/Luke 13:28–9). Shared features include (i) a two-line antithetical saying, with the emphasis placed on the second line; (ii) the notion of the movement of the nations towards the central point in God's dealings with humankind; (iii) an expulsion of Jewish persons, notwithstanding the overall context of covenant affirmation. As far as the Temple incident is concerned, covenant obligations are polemically reasserted in an overall context where indifference to those obligations is allegedly making the sacrifices unacceptable (cf. Jeremiah 6:20; 14:11). Jesus' action is not an attempted coup, nor an attack on the status of the Jewish people, nor an ethically grounded protest against profiteering, nor a criticism of the use of the Court of the Gentiles for trade rather than prayer, nor an action inherently symbolising destruction, nor a critique of the Temple (which is still 'my house') and its cult as such, but a gesture of interruption and interference with the worship system (cf. also v. 16), a sign that the worshippers are neglectful of the covenant and unresponsive to the summons of the kingdom. While not in itself indicating either the destruction of, or the withdrawal of the divine presence from, the Temple (cf. Mark 13:2; Matthew 23:37–8/Luke 13:34–5a), it could be viewed as complementary to both themes – in short, a typically prophetic word/action combination conveying a message of judgement on community/city/temple when the warning appeal of God for renewal has fallen on deaf ears. The appeal, which makes the choice of Jeremiah 7:11 apposite, is the appeal of a Jeremiah-like prophet for repentance, justice, social compassion, and worship grounded in moral and religious integrity.

To live in the light of resurrection is to live under the influence of the Temple incident. To live in the light of resurrection is therefore to sit under judgement, not to stand in judgement, and to take seriously the criteria of acceptable worship – to see the great imperatives on 'the big screen' and not to seek security in the system, however divinely authorised, however hallowed by history, however meticulously executed. That is the enduring meaning of the message at the heart of the mission of the historical Jesus.

Talk of mission, and of Jesus' deep conviction of having been sent (Luke 10:16), brings us to a topic which was also at the very heart of the existence of the post-resurrection Christians, the resurrection people whom we have seen represented in the final chapters of the Gospels. It is a topic which embraces several sub-topics, notably the gentiles, the poor, and the sinners.

The four evangelists used their resurrection narratives as a means of handling the question of mission, with its corollary for them of Jews and gentiles coming together as Christians. Standing, all of them, on the other side of the mission of Paul, they position themselves in varied ways in relation to his achievement and legacy. The lordship of the risen Jesus, according to Paul, established that the people of God could not be equated straightforwardly with the Jewish people. The outcome of the Pauline controversies over this issue was to prove decisive for the survival and development of Christianity – but not everyone, certainly not Matthew, saw it that way. We for our part may ask what happens when we retreat from the evangelists, and even from Paul, back to the historical Jesus, and then come forward again.

As a prophet committed to the renewal of Israel, Jesus' horizon was limited. The saying, 'I was sent only to the lost sheep of the house of Israel' (Matthew 15:24; cf. 10:6) is unlikely to be an authentic saying, being more probably derived from the narrative statement that 'Jesus had compassion on [a great crowd] because they were like sheep without a shepherd' (Mark 6:34/Matthew 9:36). Nevertheless it expresses accurately Jesus' guiding principle. It also expresses his keen sense of continuity with the patriarchs (Matthew 8:11/Luke 13:28), which informed not only his hope for the future but also his bringing healing and social inclusion to those who were sick and/or sinful (Luke 13:16; 19:9). The quest for renewal led, as far as we can judge, to a strategic decision to concentrate on those who for whatever reason were marginalised, or who risked being treated as such. In the first case, it was the sinners; in the second, the poor. The righteousness of 'the righteous' could be assumed (cf. Mark 2:17), the security of the sheep who had not strayed taken for granted (Matthew 18:12–14/Luke 15:3–7), the conformity of the obedient acknowledged, even if a little sadly in view of their joyless criticism of Jesus' riskier and more adventurous strategy (Luke 15:25–32). But in the two, quite separate, cases of the poor and the sinners, the prophet for *the whole of Israel* would not be deterred, and a striking combination of word and sign gave dynamism to his programme.

In the case of the poor, it was made very plain that the message of the kingdom was for them above all. When 'The kingdom of God has come near to you' (Mark 1:15; Matthew 10:7/Luke 10:9) was unpacked, it turned out to be 'Blessed are the poor, the mourners, the hungry, for theirs is (i.e. will be) the future kingdom of God, and the comfort and food which God will provide'. Multiple attestation of this theme puts the matter beyond uncertainty. But the word of the kingdom was conveyed not just in substance but also in sign, not just in message but also in mode and manner. The mission of the disciples, doubtless designed to be a replica and extension of Jesus' own mission, had to be carried out by those who carried neither money nor bag, neither sandals nor staff (Matthew 10:9–10/Luke 10:4). (i) Lack of a staff, and thus of the means of support and self-defence, was something which later transmitters of the tradition found one requirement too many (Mark 6:8). But it was a gesture expressing the message whose hallmark was 'peace' (Luke 10:6, cf. Isaiah 52:7). (ii) Lack of money meant voluntary and visible poverty – the sort of thing which made the disciples eligible to glean the corn on the outer edges of the fields (Mark 2:23–4), or burdened them with anxiety about the supply of food and clothing (Matthew 6:25–33/Luke 12:22–31). Thus, those who announced God's kingship as the solution to the problem of poverty also identified with those to whom the announcement was made. Likewise, (iii) the lack of the bag, itself the conventional means of carrying food (cf. Judith 10:5; 13:10), implied voluntary dependence on others, and even vulnerability to shame and dishonour – what the rabbis called 'a life which is no life'. For the disciples of Jesus, that spelt out identification with the hungry. Finally, (iv) the lack of sandals, an idea which later transmitters of the tradition again found more than they could take (Mark 6:9), and which ancient texts show to involve the lack of a quite basic necessity, as well as openness to insult and shame – this looks like an identification with the barefoot walking of the mourner (cf. Deuteronomy 25:9–10; Isaiah 20:2–3).

So these missionaries of Jesus exhibited visually, not the solution which the gospel affirmed but the problem with which it engaged. If this prophetic 'word and sign' combination has anything to contribute to the continuity which persists into the post-resurrection world, where might that contribution be? Perhaps towards a solution to the extraordinary schizophrenia exhibited in some Christian communities who, with some justice, pride themselves on their support for the Jubilee 2000 campaign and the cancellation of the debt of the poorest nations, but at the same time spend scarce resources on themselves. Take, as one small example, lavish vestments for those responsible for worship. At the time of writing, distinguished clergy are going on record in the media with the claim that rich vestments are a manifestation of 'the mystery of the gospel' and 'a way of recovering the splendour of medieval Christianity'. But the missionaries of Jesus exhibited visually the *problem* which the gospel of the kingdom addressed, their *identification* with those who had the problem, and their *indifference* to the honour and shame assumptions of their society. When a poor person enters a place of Christian worship, and finds that those who lead the worship have opted *into* rather than *out of* the world of riches, power and honour, is the reaction of that person going to be, 'Goodness me, this is my world'?

From the poor to the quite separate group, the sinners. The evangelists in their various ways saw the sinners as surrogates for the gentiles, and to a degree – a limited degree – they were right. For the sinners were those who opted out of being Jews in any significant sense. But what was determinative in the setting of the mission of Jesus is that they were themselves, deviant Jews, and not surrogates for anyone else, gentiles. Renegade Jews at the start, they are renewed Jews at the finish – and between start and finish there stands the grace-extending figure of Jesus. What made their reception by Jesus an effective exhibition and sign of the gospel was their individual and personal repentance, which Jesus took seriously at the same time as others took offence, and his warmly inclusive welcome to celebratory meals, whether hosted by them (Luke 19:1–10) or by himself (Mark 2:15–17). In such meals was found the essence of his purpose, and the experience of a healing which extended beyond the sphere of medicine: 'Those who are well have no need of a doctor, but those who are sick; I have come to call not the righteous but sinners.'

Nothing that we have found spelt out in the resurrection narratives of the Gospels drops the slightest hint that the principle embedded in Jesus' fellowship meals has been modified. And if the meals were made the sign of the kingdom, two things seem to follow. The first is that Paul was right – on this, as on quite a lot else! For him, the meal was to be expressive of the new post-resurrection reality, a community of those who acknowledged the universal lordship of Jesus, and whose ethnic background, however much sanctified by salvation history, was irrelevant within the community of faith. The divisive effect of the food laws? Prohibited! The old exclusive equation between the Jewish people, identified in part by those food laws, and the people of God? Abandoned! The message of the post-resurrection Gospel conveyed through the medium of the meal? Yes, and yes again! Paul was right, for he found in the risen Christ the new corporate body where 'neither Jew nor Greek' applies. And in the meal – it matters not whether the meal is eucharistic or non-eucharistic, for both are covered – the resurrection people find their true life.

But that points us to the contemporary corollary of the fellowship meals of Jesus which, according to the resurrection narratives of the Gospels, are in a line of continuity between the before and after of resurrection. That corollary must be that the meal, whether eucharistic or non-eucharistic – and again it matters not which, for both are covered – the meal is a non-negotiable manifestation of wholeness and oneness. Therefore the development of an ecclesiastical-political strategy which involves imposing conditional qualifications upon the unconditional, unqualified and ultimately unqualifiable fellowship of the gospel deserves a prophetic protest in the name of the gospel. Those whom God has included – whether as individuals or as communities – let no one exclude.

The two special cases of the poor and the sinners do not exhaust the theme of the historical Jesus as the prophet for *the whole of Israel*. What has been said so far points up the combination of continuity and discontinuity which the resurrection set in train. If it is correct that the definition of the people of God was changed, indeed had to be changed, then here is discontinuity, and here are important implications for the dialogue between Christians and Jews. The historical Jesus as a prophet for the whole of Israel can assuredly be recognised by all partners in that dialogue, but the Christians cannot be true to post-resurrection Christianity – unless, that is, they identify with the anti-Pauline position, which in practice they don't – if they make the historical Jesus their focus rather than *the historical Jesus who became the risen Lord*. Every time they echo the great Pauline phrase 'in Christ', which by virtue of their baptism it is meet and right that they should, they signal that the Christian community is the corporate person of the one who died *and was raised*. His resurrection is their resurrection, and they are therefore resurrection people. Put otherwise, they are saying – as they must – that, once the implications of the resurrection are teased out, Christianity is not the same as Christian Judaism.

Reference was made above to the style of any prophet, and therefore the style of *the* prophet Jesus, in working within a Mosaic framework, but voicing demands rather than laws. An example of how this works needs to be included in order to give a rounded wholeness to our reflections, and as good an example as any is the treatment of divorce by the historical Jesus. This treatment is, of course, particularly sensitive and liable to be interpreted *either* as an abrogation of the Mosaic law *or* an indication of its provisionality, and the handling of it by the Christian Churches – who most of the time seem to try and make a virtue out of ignoring the tradition-historical facts of life – amply attests an unfortunate tendency to apply what Jesus says as if it were a law.

The debate tradition, whose earliest form is found in Mark 10:2–9 – and not, repeat not, in Matthew 19:3–9 – corresponds formally to the five-point pattern of rabbinic discussion of a topic which is disputed, or a topic concerning which two texts appear to clash: (i) the controversial topic is introduced; (ii) a passage of scripture is cited which might settle the matter; (iii) the relevance of that passage is restricted by its being placed in a very specific setting; (iv) a second passage is cited which will indeed settle the matter; (v) a conclusion is declared. The Gospel tradition fits that pattern exactly! Jesus' argumentation and his conclusion, 'What God has joined together, let no one separate', is therefore an affirmation of Moses and also a confirmation of the *dissolubility* of a marriage, while at the same time the voicing of a demand – emphatically not a law! – for commitment to the foundational and original intention of God. Deuteronomy 24:1–4 remains in place, divorce is allowable and achievable, but Genesis 1:27, 2:24 define the primary and foundational will of God when 'hardness of heart' does not damage human life. A prophet long before Jesus had similarly declared the mind of God, 'I hate divorce, says the Lord, the God of Israel' (Malachi 2:16), but the thought of abrogating Moses would not have occurred to him, any more than it would have occurred to Jesus of Nazareth.

Alongside the debate tradition must be set the multiply attested remarriage saying (Matthew 5:32/Luke 16:18; Mark 10:11–12; 1 Corinthians 7:11), the original version of which was probably preserved by Q rather than by Mark, and by Luke 16:18 rather than by Matthew 5:32: 'Anyone who divorces his wife and marries another commits adultery, and whoever marries a woman divorced from her husband commits adultery.' This is prima facie not a Mosaic view, and it also seems to presuppose the *indissolubility* of a marriage, which is also not a Mosaic view, so the tension between the two traditions, Mark 10:9 and Luke 16:18, is plain. That tension cannot be eased in any way whatever by artificial harmonising, which would be necessary if the two sayings were to be viewed as laws. The tension could in principle be eased by rejecting the authenticity of one or both of the sayings, but the normal criteria of authenticity favour both. A better approach would therefore seem to be to have recourse to the notion of 'social function'. That means that, though logically incompatible, the two authentic traditions involve a varied strategy but a shared intention to underline the fundamental pro-marriage design of God for human well-being. That will suffice. It happens also not only to reflect the overall tenor of the mission of the prophetic Jesus, and to respect the hard and painful facts of human life, but it also points away from casuistry, the pretence that a marriage has not in fact existed in order that human beings should not dismantle it, or the legalistic position that divorce is allowable but remarriage is not.

So Jesus is not a lawyer – he is a prophet, who goes in for demands, expressions of the highest divine ideals, and in this case a demand which is grounded in the original design of the Creator for created humankind. It is a demand – a statement of what ideally *should* not, but in practice most certainly *can*, take place. As such, this prophetic demand of Jesus is simultaneously strict and sensitive. And while Christian Churches are adept at setting up systems, commissioning commissions, and ignoring the tradition-historical facts of life in respect of the Gospel material, they have more than a little difficulty, it seems, in breaking out of law-inspired straitjackets and legal fictions to witness to the sensitivity which, we dare to believe and affirm, was a mark of the historical Jesus. More than that, those who dare to read the historical Jesus divorce traditions from a post-resurrection perspective may add something else as well. Human experience – not least marital experience – sometimes includes relationship-type deaths. But resurrection people do, as a matter of fact, believe in resurrection. They specialise in fresh starts. It has to be said, with regret, that the Churches do not very often sound like communities of the resurrection when making judgements about marriage and divorce. Maybe here to learn to live with the prophetic Jesus is to learn to be judged for those judgements.

Finally, in our exploration of that continuity-cum-discontinuity situation which the resurrection introduces, we must recall that all the resurrection narratives in the Gospels give a high profile to women. The probable historicity of their discovery of an open and empty tomb gives them a place of honour in the Christian tradition which cannot be taken away from them. That being so, those same resurrection narratives contain their disappointments for women readers and for men who identify with many of the concerns of women. Do the patriarchal instincts of the evangelists reflect the position during the mission of the historical Jesus, or have things gone downhill since then?

It is extremely difficult to demonstrate that Jesus did anything about the prevailing view of the male/female status situation. (i) The presupposition of the earliest version of the tradition about anxiety (Matthew 6:25–33/Luke 12:22–31) is that some women, like the lilies, as well as some men, like the ravens, are not engaging in conventional life-sustaining work. They are told that they can safely depend on the active care of their heavenly father. The setting in life of this tradition would appear to be that of the itinerant mission of the disciples, a mission with which women are therefore implicitly associated. Yet the logic of that situation does not dictate that they were prophetic proclaimers alongside the men: Luke, after all, alerts us to a situation in which they can 'follow' and 'serve', but be serving the men as well as serving Jesus. (ii) Commitment to 'follow' may well be the presupposition of the peace/sword saying (Matthew 10:34–6/ Luke 12:51–3). It is noticeable that the saying in both its forms gives more attention to the female than to the male situation, and that the generational split takes account of marriage. So the married woman is called to alienation from both mother and mother-in-law, doubtless because of separation from the household. (iii) Other explicit sayings on the call to follow Jesus send a muted message on this issue. The Q saying deals only with severance from parents and children in one version (Matthew 10:37–8), so leaving the gender of the follower unspecific. In the other rather fuller version (Luke 14:26–7), those to be left behind include the household (οἰκία) and the wife, as well as siblings, so the gender of the follower is specifically male. In the related saying (Mark 10:29–30), those left behind do not explicitly include spouses of either gender, but the household (οἰκία) probably includes the wife, and the loss of fields probably hints at a male audience. (iv) If the twelve, whose origins in the pre-Easter period seem well assured, were a special sub-group of the wider company of followers, then whether we like it or not – and it pains me to say it – only males were selected. (v) The divorce material, which we have already considered carefully, maintains the status quo in respect of Deuteronomy 24:1–4 procedures and therefore in part the rights of a divorced woman. The remarriage saying (Luke 16:18) does extend the interpretation of adultery to make it an offence against a wife as well as a husband, but this is more a matter of voicing ultimate demands than of undermining society's norms. So Jesus' position in general is not obviously an attempt to change the status of women. Indeed, in general, the world of Jesus remains a world of men.

Where then is contemporary Christianity left, once the historical Jesus has been allowed to belong to his own world? Is our post-resurrection world to be a reproduction of his pre-resurrection world just because he was who he was? No, a thousand times no, for the resurrection was a catalyst for theological and religious change. The case for women's status *not* being determined by the pre-resurrection world and the pre-resurrection Jesus, the case for women's function *not* being limited to what was allowed in the pre-resurrection world by the pre-resurrection Jesus, the case for *drastic change* is a case which is grounded not in the historical Jesus but in the resurrection of Jesus – and not in what three of the four evangelists have to say about the resurrection but in what was said about the resurrection by their great predecessor, Paul. For Paul, the historical Jesus had become the Lord and, even more crucially, the corporate Christ. The corporate Christ was for him the death-and-resurrection Christ. In that death-*and-resurrection* Christ there has come into being a new world in which the old divisive and discriminatory distinctions are simply out of place – gone – irrelevant! As the pre-Pauline baptismal tradition put it:

As many of you as were baptised into Christ have clothed yourselves with Christ.
There is no longer Jew nor Greek;
There is no longer slave nor free;
There is no longer 'male and female';
For all of you are one in Christ Jesus.

The logic of that, from which contemporary Christianity dare not flinch if it is to be worthy of the name of Christian, is that everything to do with status and function within the community must be determined by the defining essence of that community. The community cannot be the embodiment of the risen Christ, and then make a decision to act as the pre-resurrection community. It cannot belong to the new, and exercise a preference for the old. It must be itself. So, for example, if a Christian Church has got as far as ordaining women, it is doing well. If it has got as far as ordaining women, but holds back from consecrating them as bishops, it must do better. If it has not got as far as ordaining them at all, and even resists such a change in the name of unreformed patriarchy, it has a huge and unresolved credibility problem. Something needs to be done about it – and quickly!

The resurrection of Jesus is the ground of the Church's being. It is the ground of every Christian's hope. The present is not everything: there is a future, and the message of the Gospels and of Jesus is that in that future we will be safe. But the future is not everything either. The message of the traditions we have been exploring is that the person who was raised is not only to be seen but also to be shared. 'He has been raised' means that 'we have been raised'. The resurrection people are not just those who align themselves to what the dramatis personae in the Gospel traditions saw, they actually participate in the risen Christ, and in the new era, the future made present, which he embodies.

In February 1899, Thomas Hardy wrote an uncharacteristic poem entitled 'On a Fine Morning'.

> Whence comes Solace? – Not from seeing
> What is doing, suffering, being,
> Not from noting Life's conditions,
> Nor from heeding Time's monitions;
>> But in cleaving to the Dream,
>> And in gazing at the gleam
>> Whereby gray things golden seem.
>
> Thus do I this heyday, holding
> Shadows but as lights unfolding,
> As no specious show this moment
> With its iris-hued embowment;
>> But as nothing other than
>> Part of some benignant plan;
>> Proof that earth was made for man.

For resurrection people the heyday is every day. Every day they are cleaving to the dream – and trying to live it already. Every day they are gazing at the gleam – and trying to live it already. Every day is Easter Day!

PUBLICATIONS MENTIONED IN THE TEXT

Mark

Barton, S.C., *Discipleship and Family Ties in Mark and Matthew* (Cambridge: CUP, 1994)

Collins, A. Y., *The Beginning of the Gospel* (Minneapolis: Fortress, 1992).

Dwyer, T., *The Motif of Wonder in the Gospel of Mark*, JSNTSS 128 (Sheffield: SAP, 1996)

Hengel, M., *Studies in the Gospel of Mark* (London: SCM, 1985)

Lincoln, A., 'The Promise and the Failure: Mark 16:7, 8', reprinted in W.R. Telford (ed.), *The Interpretation of Mark*, 2nd edn (Edinburgh: T & T Clark, 1995), pp. 229–51

Nickelsburg, G.W.E., *Resurrection, Immortality, and Eternal Life in Intertestamental Judaism* (Cambridge, Mass.: Harvard University Press, 1972)

'The Genre and Function of the Markan Passion Narrative', *Harvard Theological Review* 73 (1980), 153–84

Robbins, V.K., 'The Reversed Contextualization of Psalm 22 in the Markan Crucifixion. A Socio-Rhetorical Analysis', in *The Four Gospels 1992*, Festschrift Franz Neirynck, ed. F. van Segbroeck *et al.* (Leuven: Leuven University Press, 1992), pp. 1161–83

Sassoon, S., *Siegfried's Journey 1916–1920* (London: Faber & Faber, 1945)

Segal, A., 'Life After Death: The Social Sources', in *The Resurrection*, ed. S. Davis, D. Kendall, G. O'Collins (Oxford: OUP, 1988), pp. 90–125

Telford, W.R., *The Theology of the Gospel of Mark* (Cambridge: CUP, 1999)

Theissen, G., 'The Great Eschatological Discourse and the Threat to the Jerusalem Temple in 40 C.E.', in *The Gospels in Context* (Edinburgh: T & T Clark, 1992), pp. 125–65

Tomson, P.J., 'The Names Israel and Jew in Ancient Judaism and in the New Testament', *Bijdragen, tijdschrift voor filosofie en theologie* 47 (1986), 120–40, 266–89

van Iersel, B., *Mark. A Reader-Response Commentary*, JSNTSS 164 (Sheffield: SAP, 1998)

Watson, F., 'The Social Function of Mark's Secrecy Motif', *Journal for the Study of the New Testament* 24 (1985), 49–69

Wrede, W., *The Messianic Secret* (Cambridge: James Clarke, 1971)

Matthew

Davies, W.D. & Allison, D.C., *The Gospel according to Saint Matthew, Volumes I-III* (Edinburgh: T & T Clark, 1988/1991/1997)

Deutsch, C., *Hidden Wisdom and the Easy Yoke. Wisdom, Torah and Discipleship in Matthew 11.25–30*, JSNTSS 18 (Sheffield; JSOT, 1987)

Hays, R.B., *The Moral Vision of the New Testament* (Edinburgh: T & T Clark, 1996)

Hubbard, B.J., *The Matthean Redaction of a Primitive Apostolic Commissioning. An Exegesis of Matthew 28:16–20*, SBLDS 19 (Missoula: Scholars' Press, 1974)

Hurtado, L.W., *One God, One Lord. Early Christian Devotion and Ancient Jewish Monotheism*, 2nd edn (London: SCM, 1998)

Luz, U., *Matthew 1–7* (Edinburgh: T & T Clark, 1990)
  The Theology of the Gospel of Matthew (Cambridge: CUP, 1995)

Martyn, J.L., 'Apocalyptic Antinomies', in *Theological Issues in the Letters of Paul* (Edinburgh: T & T Clark, 1997), pp. 111–23

Meeks, W.A., 'The Image of the Androgyne: Some Uses of a Symbol in Earliest Christianity', *History of Religions* 13 (1974), 165–208

Neirynck, F., 'Les Femmes au Tombeau: Etude de la redaction Mattheenne', *New Testament Studies* 15 (1968), 168–90

Overman, J.A., *Matthew's Gospel and Formative Judaism. The Social World of the Matthean Community* (Minneapolis: Augsburg Fortress, 1990)

Schaberg, J., *The Illegitimacy of Jesus* (Sheffield: SAP, 1995)

Segal, A.F., 'Matthew's Jewish Voice', in D. Balch (ed.), *Social History of the Matthean Community* (Minneapolis: Fortress, 1991), pp. 3–37

Sim, D.C., *The Gospel of Matthew and Christian Judaism* (Edinburgh: T & T Clark, 1998)

Soares Prabhu, G.M., *The Formula Quotations in the Infancy Narrative of Matthew*, Analecta Biblica 63 (Rome: Biblical Institute Press, 1976)

Stanton, G.N., *A Gospel for a New People* (Edinburgh: T & T Clark, 1992)

Verseput, D.J., 'The Role and Meaning of the "Son of God" Title in Matthew's Gospel', *New Testament Studies* 33 (1987), 532–56

Wanke, J., 'Kommentarworte. Kommentierungen von Herrenworten', *Biblische Zeitschrift* 24 (1980), 208–33

Wire, A.C., 'Gender Roles in a Scribal Community', in D. Balch (ed.), *Social History of the Matthean Community* (Minneapolis: Fortress, 1991), pp. 87–121

Luke

Brown, R.E., *The Birth of the Messiah*, 2nd edn (London: Chapman, 1993)

Catchpole, D.R., *The Quest For Q* (Edinburgh: T & T Clark, 1993) [1993a]
  'The Anointed One in Nazareth', in *From Jesus to John. Essays on Jesus and New Testament Christology in Honour of Marinus de Jonge*, JSNTSS 84 (Sheffield: Sheffield Academic Press, 1993), pp. 231–51 [1993b]

Dillon, R.J., *From Eye-Witnesses to Ministers of the Word: Tradition and Composition in Luke 24* (Rome: Biblical Institute, 1978)

Fuller, R.H., *The Formation of the Resurrection Narratives* (London: SPCK, 1972)

Green, J.B., *The Gospel of Luke*, NINTC (Grand Rapids, Michigan, 1997)

Resurrection People

Holgate, D., *Prodigality, Liberality and Meanness in the Parable of the Prodigal Son*, JSNTSS 187 (Sheffield: Sheffield Academic Press, 1999)

Johnson, L.T., *The Gospel of Luke*, Sacra Pagina 3 (Collegeville, MN: Liturgical Press, 1991)

Moore, C.A., *Tobit*, Anchor Bible 40A (New York: Doubleday, 1996)

Nolland, J., *Luke 18:35–24:5*, Word Biblical Commentary 35c (Dallas: Word Books, 1993)

Reiser, M., *Jesus and Judgment* (Minneapolis: Fortress, 1997)

Robinson, B.P., 'The Place of the Emmaus Story in Luke-Acts', *New Testament Studies* 30 (1984), 481–97

Sanders, J.N., *The Jews in Luke-Acts* (London: SCM, 1987)

Sanders, E.P., 'The Testament of Abraham', in J.H. Charlesworth (ed.), *The Old Testament Pseudepigrapha II* (London: Darton, Longman & Todd, 1983), pp. 871–902

Seim, T.K., *The Double Message. Patterns of Gender in Luke-Acts* (Edinburgh: T & T Clark, 1994)

Smith, D.E., 'Table Fellowship as a Literary Motif in the Gospel of Luke', *Journal of Biblical Literature* 106/4 (1987), 613–38

Tannehill, R.C., *The Narrative Unity of Luke-Acts I* (Philadelphia: Fortress, 1986)
   Luke, Abingdon New Testament Commentaries (Nashville: Abingdon, 1996)

Vielhauer, P., 'Das Benedictus des Zacharias (Lk 1:68–79)', reprinted in *Aufsätze zum Neuen Testament* (München: Kaiser Verlag, 1965), pp. 28–46

Wanke, J., *Die Emmauserzählung. Eine redaktionsgeschichtliche Untersuchung zu Lk 24,13–35* (Leipzig: St Benno-Verlag, 1973)

John

Ashton, J., *Understanding the Fourth Gospel* (Oxford: Clarendon, 1993)

Borgen, P., *Bread from Heaven*, NovTSup 10 (Leiden: Brill, 1963)

de Goedt, M., 'Un Schème de Révélation dans le Quatrième Evangile', *New Testament Studies* 8 (1962), pp. 142–50

Hardy, T., *Jude the Obscure*, The World's Classics (Oxford: Oxford University Press, 1987)

Käsemann, E., *The Testament of Jesus* (London: SCM, 1968)

Lindars, B., *The Gospel of John*, New Century Bible (London: Oliphants, 1972)

Martyn, J.L., *History and Theology in the Fourth Gospel*, rev. edn (Nashville: Abingdon, 1979)

Neirynck, F., 'John 4,46–54: Signs Source and/or Synoptic Gospels', *Ephemerides Theologicae Lovanienses* 60 (1984), 367–75, reprinted in *Evangelica II* (Leuven: Peeters, 1991), pp. 679–87 [1991a]
   'John 21', *New Testament Studies* 36 (1990), 321–36, reprinted in *Evangelica II* (Leuven: Peeters, 1991), pp. 601–16 [1991b]

Neyrey, J.H., *An Ideology of Revolt* (Philadelphia: Fortress, 1988)

Scroggs, R., 'The Earliest Christian Communities as Sectarian Movement', in *Social-Scientific Approaches to New Testament Interpretation*, ed. D.G. Horrell (Edinburgh: T & T Clark, 1999), pp. 69–91

Smith, D.E., 'Table Fellowship as a Literary Motif in the Gospel of Luke', *Journal of Biblical Literature* 106 (1987), 613–38

Tomson, P.J., 'The Names Israel and Jew in Ancient Judaism and in the New Testament', *Bijdragen, tijdshrift voor filosofie en theologie* 47 (1986), 120–40, 266–89

Watson, F., *Paul, Judaism and the Gentiles: a sociological approach*, SNTSMS 56 (Cambridge: Cambridge University Press, 1986)

Jesus

Bauckham, R., 'The Rich Man and Lazarus: the Parable and the Parallels', *New Testament Studies* 37 (1991), 225–46

Brown, R.E., *The Death of the Messiah II* (New York: Doubleday, 1994)

Campenhausen, H. von, *Der Ablauf der Osterereignisse and das leere Grab*, 3rd edn (Heidelberg: Universitätsverlag, 1966)

Davis, S.T., ' "Seeing" the Risen Jesus', in *The Resurrection*, ed. S.T. Davis, D. Kendall and G. O'Collins (Oxford: Oxford University Press, 1998), pp. 126–47

Evans, C.F., *Resurrection and the New Testament* (London: SCM, 1970)

Harvey, A.E., 'They discussed among themselves what this "rising from the dead" could mean (Mark 9.10)', in *Resurrection*, Essays in Honour of Leslie Houlden, ed. S. Barton and G. Stanton (London: SPCK, 1994), pp. 69–78

Lüdemann, G., *The Resurrection of Jesus* (London: SCM, 1994)

Nickelsburg, G.W.E., *Resurrection, Immortality, and Eternal Life in Intertestamental Judaism* (Cambridge, Mass.: Harvard University Press, 1972)

Perkins, P., *Resurrection* (London: Geoffrey Chapman, 1984)

Reiser, M., *Jesus and Judgment* (Minneapolis: Fortress, 1997)

Segal, A.F., 'Life After Death: The Social Sources', in *The Resurrection*, ed. S.T. Davis, D. Kendall, and G. O'Collins (Oxford: Oxford University Press, 1998), pp. 90–125

Swinburne, R., 'Evidence for the Resurrection', in *The Resurrection*, ed. S.T. Davis, D. Kendall, and G. O'Collins (Oxford: Oxford University Press, 1998), pp. 191–212

Wedderburn, A.J.M., *Beyond Resurrection* (London: SCM, 1999)

Witherington, B., *Women in the Ministry of Jesus*, SNTSMS 51 (Cambridge: CUP, 1984)

Resurrection People

INDEX OF MODERN AUTHORS